Jolts, Synchronicities, Dream Catchers, and Milagros

A Memoir
Into the Fire of Original Experience

Dennis Swiftdeer Paige

Dreaming Coyote Press—Conifer, CO
ISBN: 979-8-218-15842-2
Library of Congress Control Number: 2023904455
Title: *Jolts, Synchronicities, Dream Catchers, and Milagros: A Memoir. Into the Fire of Original Experience*
Author: Dennis Swiftdeer Paige
Digital distribution | 2023
Paperback | 2023

Dedication

Dedicated to the brave questers, listening to their own truths, following an original experience who are humbled and grateful for the love, wisdom, and humor discovered along their journey.

Acknowledgements

How does one measure the high point in writing the book? I suppose it was the moment I reflected upon all the people and memorable affinities with nature that helped bring this memoir to fruition. To my publisher New Book Authors Publishing for making this story come to wonderful life in print and photos. To Nick S. at ProofreadingPal for his affordable and no nonsense proficient professional editing. To noted ardent environmentalist/social activist Hazel Wolf who encouraged me to pursue an inspiring rabble rousing writing career for nature. To my brother Wayne, sisters Janis and Joyce for filling me in on relevant tidbits about my family history. To Dan Creely for writing the foreword with his deep regard for indigenous wisdom. And a special note of gratitude to my critically tough soul partner, Randee Lawrence, who constantly touched on ways to improve my writing and quality of photos while providing important tech support.

Table of Contents

Foreword

Grandmother Keewaydinoquay, an Anishinaabeg Elder of the Crane Clan, was a revered herbalist, teacher, and medicine woman. In 1998, she came to give the keynote presentation, after lunch, at our Teachers of Experiential and Adventure Methodology (TEAM) Conference at Northeastern Illinois University, in Chicago. Her theme was "Your Life's Purpose." You could have heard a pin drop when she was speaking. As she finished the 300 people in attendance gave her a standing ovation. There was a quality about Kee, when you were with her, where you felt she *lived a life of purpose and enjoyed leading others to discover their own purpose.*

Sunday morning after the TEAM Conference Kee and I were sitting quietly at my kitchen table. She reached into an old beaded leather bag she carried on her person, slowly pulled out an old, cracked, and yellowed complete canine tooth from an adult black bear, gently placed it on the table in front of me, and said, "This is my major medicine piece." She spoke deliberately and slowly to make sure I listened to the teaching. "This tooth is much like all situations in life. There is much more involved than what is merely exposed on the surface."

If Dennis Paige was born in Indiana, his last name was Jones, and he wore a weathered fedora you would have a graphic image of where his life adventures have carried him. On his journey into *becoming* he has lived the 3 P's …sharing his *Passions,* modeling the *Principles* he lives by, and working for a *Purpose* larger than himself… *a life of permanent Purpose.* As you read the experiences Dennis shares look below the surface.

His openness to "living in the moment" and "jumping into new things" is the essence of who Dennis is and continues to be. The catalyst may have been when his heart stopped for 10 seconds at six weeks old and for the first three years he was taciturn. His parents wondered if he would ever come out of his shell of quietness. But

Dennis made a remarkable turnaround. His mother said, "We could not shut him up." Since that incident he seemed programmed to energetically embrace every moment life has to offer and to share his *Good Medicine* while his heart is pumping.

Readers will find a bit of themselves in this book. Reliving your own experiences as a youth, reflecting on moments with your parents, seeking purpose in meaningful work, and feeling an umbilical cord like connection to spirit and moments that cannot be logically explained.

Dennis has been on *The Path With a Heart* his entire life and it has provided him with many opportunities and experiences: classroom teacher, naturalist, environmental educator, author on native plants, conservation practitioner, ecological landscaper, storyteller, and percussionist to name a few.

His *calling* to work in the Peace Corp, in 1970, was eye opening. In West Africa he met a 110-year-old tribal chief with 9 wives, 36 children and 200 grandchildren who drove a new Mercedes Benz. His work in a mission school shattered many of his ideals where he observed the principal, a man with a PhD in theology, implement a bamboo stick for corporal punishment by his nephew on a child. Dennis and all the teachers refused to participate or condone it except his subordinate nephew teacher. It left a permanent scar on his heart.

From 1975 – 1984 Dennis decided to work at the 10-acre Santa Fe Community School. It was a poor struggling alternative school in New Mexico but the leader Charlie Bentley had a bold, honest and gentle way to work with children. It was Charlie who inculcated into Dennis to have *faith in children* and helped heal that scar.

Dennis began his tenure by getting kicked in the chest by the school horse as an initiation into what would lie ahead. He also lived for 6 years in an adobe house on the school property he built with 1400 bricks he molded himself. When his white-collar working father with Chicago south side roots came out and watched him making the bricks he said, "You have a Master's Degree from Northwestern University, and here you are playing in the mud." The thought of getting his hands in soggy clay was excruciating.

Dennis continued to realize that for him nature was not a "place" but it was a *new found home*. It was confirmed and imprinted during his Audubon Expedition Institute through a rigorous traveling school bus program. The exclamation point came later after graduation in the backyard of a Berkeley, California home when he was awakened at sunrise by a loud shrill call at the foot of his sleeping bag. As he peaked his head out, the magical plumage of a peacock looking right at him was in full regalia.

Music has always been an integral part of his life. Playing his native flutes could always ground people to the earth, his rhythms on percussion instruments could energize an entire gathering, or help children from war torn countries at a Sufi Camp, in Virginia, feel welcome. At one outdoor "calling the rain" drumming assembly he and the children together welcomed a 5 min shower where the area had been drought ridden for 12 years. The adults were astonished while the performing children laughed, chanted, and drummed ever so fervently.

I recall a Potawatomi Elder, Nowaten Dale Thomas, once shared that people search their entire lives to find spirit. What they do not realize is, you cannot find spirit, spirit finds you, and then you need to listen.

In 1992 that invisible umbilical pulled Dennis into the Native traditions. His sacred mystical journey escalated when he met Dr. Jim Gillihan (1935 – 2002) and he participated in a Lakota Spring Equinox Ceremony. Over the next 12 years Dennis would participate in many ceremonies and learn the ancient traditions of the Lakota people.

Jim Gillihan would become one of his native teachers. Jim worked with the Smithsonian Museum, and was also awarded the highest civilian honor in four different states for his work by their governors. In addition, for 24 years Jim was the 4th Keeper of Sitting Bull's Chanupa (pipe). He was asked to accept that responsibility by Lakota Holy Man, Grandfather Frank Fool's Crow, and did so with total dedication and humility.

In 1995, their 12-year cycle of teachings and ceremonies culminated in Jim performing the wedding ceremony for Dennis and his wife. A stunning sky hole appeared during the service in the midst of an ominous thunder storm above the middle of the circle gathering where a small fire pit was placed, while two dancing butterflies followed by a couple of passing Canada geese flew over the fire. Jim said," It would all be fine until the ceremony was over." As they placed the Hopi rings on each other's fingers while Jim turned the pipe bowl over to show that no ashes remained in there, it began to rain nickel size hail.

Michael Brown, a writer for The David Letterman Show, seemed to capture Dennis 's essence and life experiences in a single quote. "Life is so rich when you step off the path and experience illogical adventures."

Dennis is the stone that was dropped in a still pond. He has educated, and inspired thousands upon thousands of children, teens, and adults at the Spring Valley Nature Center, other nature centers, schools, conferences, summer camps, Scout gatherings, libraries, theaters, and places of worship, His adventures are many and his stories are endless. Andy Andrews in his book *The Butterfly Effect* shares "That with a little perspective you can live a life of permanent purpose. Where every move we make and every action we take, matters not just for us but for all of us *...and for All time*." Dennis Swiftdeer Paige has lived a life of permanent purpose. His *Ripple Effect* has touched the world. Mitakuye' Oyasin.

Dan Creely Jr. Professor Emeritus,
Co-founder, Teachers of Experiential and Adventure Methodology,
Northeastern Illinois University

Preface

People say that what we're all seeking is a meaning for life. I don't think that's what we're really seeking. I think that what we're seeking is an experience of being alive, so that our life experiences on the purely physical plane will have resonances within our own innermost being and reality, so that we actually feel the rapture of being alive.
—Joseph Campbell

One heart each of us carries in our life journey. One heart is all we receive from the time we are born to the time we cross over into the great mystery. I was born in Chicago on April 2, 1948. My mother held back purposely to have me because she didn't want her son born on April Fool's Day. I was named after a well-known actor-singer Dennis Morgan in the 1940s whose name became practically unknown in the 1950s. My parents preferred naming their children after famous American movie stars of the 1940s since my Mom in particular toyed around with the possibility of being a night club singer. Unfortunately, when the 1950s arrived the most popular character with the name of Dennis to capture the hearts and minds of children was a comic strip child with an insatiable curiosity continually getting him into trouble. His name was Dennis the Menace. I literally acquired an unfair reputation during the first few years of my life receiving a stigma associated with this overly energetic child who caused daily havoc to his parents. But admittedly, I began to believe I was Dennis the Menace reincarnate after all the ridiculing from possessing that first cursed name.

When I was six weeks old, my heart stopped beating for 10 seconds as a result of surgical complications from a clogged stomach valve (pyloric stenosis). I wound up receiving 16 stitches vertically over my diminutive belly, which became a permanent scar. The threat of death came early but so did my affirmation for life.

My parents nonetheless were grateful to our physician for keeping me from becoming a permanent flatliner, despite having a notorious reputation for scarring up his patients and injecting much pain in the process. We would pay periodic visits at his cottage home off the shores of Lake Geneva, Wisconsin, to thank him for saving my life. For the first few years, my parents worried about me barely speaking, but they allowed mother nature to work out her internal chemistry on my perplexing, quiet condition. After about three years, in the words of my mom, "you couldn't shut him up." Suddenly, I acquired the reputation of being a cute, curly haired Dennis the Menace and was given the nurturing awareness at an early age to not take life lightly but to energetically embrace every moment while my heart was still pumping those life-affirming juices.

I am a naturalist, ecological landscaper, earth-friendly storyteller, conservation practitioner, environmental educator, nature photographer, eclectically driven percussionist, author of a book on eco-gardening, divorcee survivor twice under irreconcilable differences, an uncle, godfather, brother, husband, and step grandfather, and I'm living for the rest of my life with my loving, adventurous compatible soulmate in the montane beauty of Colorado. I hope to some I am a friend.

I also bird, hike, and run up mountains. I connect with the great outdoors and humanity. I'm a seeker and an observer in awe of the micro and macro side of the universe. I'm a lover. My being finds its solace and deep psychology in wild natural places. I resist the easy path and claim the implausible, indecipherable, irreverent, and unconventional. I can be a genuine pain in the ass. I'm youthlike, a lucid dreamer, a critical thinker, garrulous at times, and enigmatic, and I regard myself a temperamental empath. Now a very grateful and healthy retired septuagenarian, I wish to share some good medicine for you to keep close to your sacred heart and mind. Often considered untranslatable, the ancient Japanese phrase *mono no aware* refers to the bittersweet realization of the ephemeral nature of all things. It is the awareness that everything in nature is short lived. The fleetingness of childhood and youth, various rites of passage, the pathos of painful experiences, the joys of catching momentary wondrous glimpses of nature, romantic flings, the changing of the seasons, close friends and families who have moved away from our lives, new relationships built on those very same familiar losses, passing fears experienced firsthand, the coming and going of love, the dream catchers who inspire our chosen quests to follow our heart's journey, the basic cycles of life and death.

Is there a purpose, a plan, or a reason for everything that happens? Such consequential forces in retrospect have generated physical and emotional jolts, leaving deep transformative imprints in my journey, encountering a confluence of profound serendipitous synchronicities that have awakened a sense of being beyond this human world, deeply indebted to the mentors and inspirational figures who caught my desire to be who I am and what I dream to become. And I am grateful to have captured momentary miracles that ask the following question: are there spiritual forces playing with our lives to help us become better human beings?

These personal, compelling, accumulative influences explored in this book, impermanent in their dynamics, could lead to permanent imprints of becoming something much deeper than what we were before we encountered these growing pains and joys of living. Call it the soulful molting of my being. We are all the unreliable narrators of each other's stories and are not defined only by what we see but also by what we may never see.

Ultimately, the truth lies in the beauty of living in the moment, knowing how important it is to revere this sacred journey of nurturing impermanence. May you all catch the paradoxical cosmic joke of jumping into this temporary experiential sea of vision and mystery, as shared through these actual personal stories presented, which have molded in me a profound curiosity for life and death while living on the edge between light and darkness and exploring extraordinary experiences as an ordinary earth traveler.

Every secret has a weight to it, and you can only carry it so long. This is my gift for all of you reading this life quest, searching to find transcendent moments worth remembering and becoming. My memoirs are divided into an interwoven personal experiential tapestry of four distinctly profound, influential categories with each category described in chronological order: Jolts: blindsiding challenges that have greatly shaken my view of life; Synchronicities: peak experiences and serendipitous encounters that have remarkably placed me in the right place at the right time, propelling me toward the direction of my destiny; Dream Catchers: inspirational people and nature revelations instilling compelling lessons of eternal wisdom; and Milagros: miracles guiding me toward a deeper spiritual and more mystical awakening with the universe.

Part I:
Jolts

(Blindsided mental, emotional, and physical challenges that have
profoundly altered my view of life)

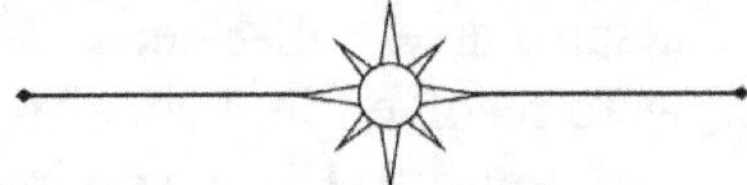

Chapter One
Carving a Path of Original Experience

The great man is he who does not lose his child-like heart
– Chinese Sage Mencius, 4th century

When my family moved from Chicago to the working-class industrial suburban town of Maywood, Illinois, during the mid-1950s, I had more opportunity to fulfill my free-ranging boyhood aspirations in the great outdoors. My parents would let me roam the neighborhoods, the open fields pre-dating commercial development, and local wetlands, all part of my expansive playground. I enjoyed lying in the wild wavy grasses, drawn to the infinite mysteries of how nature moved, watching clouds float over on a slow, late summer day, stalking ring-tailed pheasants to get a closer look at them, chasing cottontails, blowing fluffy dandelion seeds in the air to see them rise into the sky, or snatching crawdads with my hands in marshy channels and open park ponds.

With my older brother four years ahead of me, we would explore forbidden places while my Dad was working and my Mom was tending to household chores. When I was six years old, we would hike over to the Indiana Harbor Belt Line railroad tracks, and, as the trains would pass slowly through the town, we would jump onto the boxcar ladders and climb up to the top of the world, seeing views to captivate our day, then jump off under the extended Roosevelt Rd. Bridge, where we would hang out with drifting hobos. That didn't last very long because one day my dad caught my brother and I and whipped us good with his belt. I had to find some other way to survive in my new, less dangerous "playgrounds under the open free sun."

One day, I was walking in front of my home when an unfamiliar herd of festering kid bullies started picking on me. I didn't know their names. I was the new kid on the block and was being tested by the neighborhood pack. A fight seemed imminent, but who the randomly chosen challenger could be would ultimately determine the outcome of newly gained friendships and self-esteem as a result of these fisticuffs. All worries were resolved in a ritual formal bout between an equally aged kid and myself. His name was Mickey Freund (pseudonym). We decided to punch it out later on a weekday officially in the backyard a couple doors down from my home, with neighborhood kids attending while most of the parents were away from home working. The sides were arranged so each opponent was provided with an advisory training program in advance. For three days, my brother and his next-door neighbor friend coached me on how to box while Mickey had a dozen thrill seeking kids from both genders feeding him punching tips on how to put me away where it hurt. Tired of being harassed, verbally teased, and physically bullied by home-grown unsupervised rascals, I was ready to take on Mickey with all the fierce, inventive determination I could muster.

All the kids who attended this scheduled fight on a scorching, sultry August afternoon in 1954 were on the side of my opponent. Just my brother and his friend John Nichols sided with me. Stools were set on the backyard lawn to accommodate the fighters. I was scared, looking at all these new faces that were cheering against me, wanting to see this new kid on the block get initiated into this inauspicious, pecking order peer world. Without an adult to ref the match, the "fight of the summer"—and perhaps my life—commenced. Having no experience wearing boxing gloves I slipped them on and wondered if my punches would have any impact on this unfamiliar challenger everybody was rooting for. The first round proved to be a clear standoff of pugnacious equals, with verbal exchanges and missing jabs flying by under untapped strength and coordination. The second round proved different. Forgetting everything my brother and his friend trained me to anticipate, I planned out a way to confront this rite of passage into the neighborhood. I imagined three buttons vertically along the middle of my chest to push, each one weighing the temperament of my performance. In Freudian terms, these buttons were physical manifestations of my superego. In round two, the gallery of fans for Mickey began to cheer loudly while he started to punch me harder. I pushed my second middle button, defending myself from an onslaught of rapid-fire punches. They hurt. We were fighting with kid boxing gloves. I quickly lost my confidence. At the end of the round, my brother told me I had to get out there and punch him. I knew then I had to push my third button, which I labeled "the wild man" button. Under a complete visceral effort, I continuously swung my adrenalin-fed arms in the position of grenade-thrusting arches, eventually causing Mickey's nose to profusely bleed and eyes to burst into self-effacing tears. As blood rushed down over his mouth down his chin, the fight was over. I had earned a TKO. The kids were stunned. My brother and his friend were speechless and laughing with amazement. I knew then that I had it in me to fight and defend my status in the neighborhood as the new kid in the block who earned respect. Days went by, and I would later meet up with Mickey and his friend Jeff Welch, who were hiding in a construction pit. One of them called me over. When I got there, Jeff was holding a garter snake in his hand and said, "how would you like to be friends with us?"

I said "Sure!"

"Okay, then you can be friends with us if you can put this snake in your mouth."

It was a clear act of "I dare you," where I could attain immediate friendship. However, I innocently trusted nature, and so, being outdoors so much, at the age of six years old, I actually allowed a garter snake's tongue to enter the back of my mouth while holding this curious, cooperative, slithering reptile. They were both aghast and quite impressed. I achieved instant friendship with a couple of boys my age, one of which lasted for 10 years. As friends, Mickey and I were really tight. My favorite example of this was we both had a crush on a girl in our class named Sarin Miller. When we met one day at the corner of our block by my home, the moment had arrived. She liked both of us, but only one could give a kiss to her by winning a running race from the corner to the fire hydrant and back, which was about 30 yards, round trip. Mickey and I told her we needed to talk among ourselves to see if we could agree with such a sweet, exciting offer. What we were plotting turned out to be brilliant at our age of seven years. We whispered to each other that our race would be a tie. That way we would all be happy. We lined up, acting as if we were going to beat our opponent, and then Sarin yelled, "Ok, are you ready? On your mark, get set, GO!" We ran together, dramatically bumping into each other as if we were showing how much we wanted to win. I fell down, but Mickey slowed down a little for me to get back up and rush to the finishing line in a tie with him. Sarin was shocked. What would she do to handle this delicate situation? We all laughed and then Sarin said, "Since it was a tie, you can kiss me on each side of my cheeks." We did, and our little lives were never the same.

Mickey and I did everything together. We produced a handmade marionette puppet show of the "Three Little Pigs and the Big Bad Wolf," with classical Wagner music on a phonograph in his packed house basement, serving popcorn and lemonade. We actually went door to door selling tickets printed from a mimeograph machine and constructed a balcony supported by a minimal amount of stone blocks that collapsed during the show due to an overweight next-door neighbor, Mrs. Wertz, which completely knocked the house out with an uproarious collective laughter. We spent an entire summer constructing a sailboat to float down the mighty sluggish Salt Creek when we were 10 years old, only to have it sink immediately as soon as we pushed it into the water—even after Mickey's mom towed it about 8 miles all the way from Maywood to the nearby town of Riverside. We played in Mickey's basement with a Gilbert Chemistry Set, applying nonlethal mixes to stir our sense of smell in testy unsupervised experiments. That inspired me to produce a chemical rotten egg order permeating inside my home which infuriated my Dad. His father was an avid HO model train hobbyist who transformed half of his basement, including under the stairs, into a magnificent homemade landscape of little villages, train stations, mountains with petite trees, and a natural, dream-like rolling terrain.

We were inseparable in our Cub Scout Pack 122, especially when we attended Camp Shin Go Beek in Waupaca, Wisconsin, for a few summers, with Mickey eventually earning an Eagle Scout badge in the Boy Scouts, despite the fact he was slapped on the back of his head for acting rude and dismissed from an Order of the Arrow ceremony. The purpose of the Order of the Arrow was to recognize those Scout campers who best exemplify the scout oath and law in their daily lives, to develop and maintain camping traditions and spirit, to promote scout camping, and to crystallize the scout habit of helpfulness in a life of leadership in cheerful service to others. We were laughing at a dressed-up White guy in Indian regalia performing a ritual of strongly patting scouts on the shoulder, who were lined up on the beach during sunset, and singled out for this distinguished recognition. As mischievous buddies, we did like to get into trouble at the summer camp. One unsupervised experience almost cost me my life.

Before the crack of dawn, while the rest of the Cub packs were sleeping, Mickey, another scout, and myself snuck into a closed ropes course with a challenging zip line. I was pudgy back in 1958 but determined to zip down this high line with early morning zest and defiance in believing that nothing would happen without proper supervision. Looking down about 20 feet, I was nudged by my scout buddies and held on to the pulley without any straps to keep me from falling. Immediately, the pulley jerked, and I lost my grip, free falling to the ground only a hand's length from an exposed six-inch stake. First my feet fell on the ground, followed by my knees, then head. My chest felt completely caved in. I couldn't breathe. Gasping for air, I struggled to say these unforgettable words while my two buddies ran down from the platform to catch my farewell address. "I can't breathe. I can't breathe. Goodbye, guys, I'm going to heaven."

Fortunately, they laid me flat down on the ground and told me to start breathing. My chest felt as if my lungs had completely surrendered. Nonetheless, I did and recovered only to spend the rest of that week in bed in our assigned log cabin, feeling as if every muscle in my body had been stretched to the max. Remarkably, no bones were broken apparently due to a healthy fat reserve cushioning my fall. I didn't get into trouble, but I missed all of the recreational activities like swimming, archery, hiking, and just running around. Getting hurt like that was a lesson in and of itself. I had earned attending these camps by selling magazines to ultimately wind-up convalescing on top of my cabin bunk bed. But I was grateful for Mickey and my other friend, rescuing me from my precarious plunge.

A sharpshooter I was not. While attempting to earn a merit badge in marksmanship, Mickey found six holes on his target sheet and wondered how that could be, since he only fired five shots from his rifle. Unfortunately, I was shooting next to him and actually shot that extra hole in his sheet, unintentionally disqualifying Mickey's entry. He did reapply after explaining the botched-up myopic mess I created and received a merit badge the second time around. Mickey and I would ride our single speed bicycles to fishing spots several miles away from home, sometimes traveling 30 miles round trip at the age of 11. One time, I rode my weather-beaten bike 80 miles round trip from Maywood to Romeoville with Mickey to a cold, no-fishing swimming quarry lake teeming with enormous blue gills, sunfish, along with behemoth largemouth and smallmouth bass. On another occasion, we rode our bikes to the Brookfield Zoo, only to have them stolen for a joy ride and thrown into the muddy Salt Creek. We eventually found them half submerged in the algal muck and mire, where we were allowed to wash them off in the zoo. We continually fed off each other for increasing our daring escapades close to home. Just a few blocks from home we dragged our sleds on moonless nights by a highway bridge and confronted the most treacherous dense thicket of multi-flora roses to speed through face first down this icy hill called "dead man's alley" with the ultimate ride ending only inches from the edge of a highway exit. Sometimes we would be entangled in the heart of these wretched thorny branches and have to pull ourselves out of theses bloody predicaments. In contrast during the warmer seasons we would collect wax coated card board boxes and use them for swiftly sliding down steep grassy slopes off a highway bridge.

We pulled a daring creepy challenge during our junior high school mischievous years of entering a local cemetery on Halloween, waiting to touch a gravestone at midnight and then running like the dickens home. We never quite made that time objective, missing by only a few minutes, antsy to get this self-scaring escapade done. While running home, we were attacked by familiar bullies. Mickey was hit on his shoulder with an egg, splattering the yolk all over the back of his buffed brown suede coat. The stain was permanent.

On another Halloween night as mischievous pre-teens Mickey and I created a dummy hung with a noose under a railroad bridge by the highway to watch drivers go by and be shaken by the terrifying sight. It was fun to watch these expressions on their faces until a police car arrived and beamed a light across the area to spot any festive pranksters. Not finding us, we along with two other friends, one of whom was quite chubby, made a mad dash across a main road and hopped over my school yard six foot chain link fence.

Unfortunately, I was left with the corpulent girl who could not make it over the fence by herself. With all the pre-adolescent strength as a short pudgy kid, I pushed her over and she landed on her head cushioned with her hands and long thick hair to ease the impact. We scattered our separate ways that panicky night making it home safe and sound. Our parents never knew what happened during this prankish nocturnal escapade. If there was a world beyond the confines of my town, it was as distant and as irrelevant as the planet Jupiter.

Entering high school, Mickey advanced in his academics, excelled in his grades, and attended night college courses in science—while I was grappling with high school college prep courses. Eventually, our friendship ended when he moved to another town too far for me to visit.

Jump 55 years later—retired, with plenty of time to look into my past, I decided to track down Mickey Freund on the internet. I located him through an online research criminal check site in a small southern California desert town. The results were mostly profoundly sad. First off, it was so gratifying to talk to him on the phone after several decades of losing touch. I mentioned that he was my first buddy in Maywood as a result of a fight we had, with all the kids in the neighborhood cheering for him. I was about to describe how the fight ended when an astounding recall happened. Mickey interrupted me and said, "When you hit me in the nose."

Oh, my goodness, he remembered that moment! Thousands upon thousands of life experiences and millions of moments had passed between us, separate from our personal journeys, and he remarkably remembered that punch in the schnoz. I thought our conversation would reconnect us as friends, but as I began to find out more about Mickey's life, I became disheartened, as a cloud of continuous tragedy enveloped his journey. His voice had a consistent whispering, somber tone. I found out Mickey attended the Naval Academy for two years then dropped out and attended the University of Illinois to earn a divinity degree. He worked as a chaplain serving in the Navy for a few decades. He also served in the 1991 Persian Gulf War, witnessing many suicidal soldiers coming back with PTSD, and he retired from the service with a rank of lieutenant commander. Married with two children, he eventually became a chaplain in a small church community close to the Mojave Desert, where a lot of marines are based. I felt a somber tone coming from his voice, and so I changed the direction and asked how his siblings were doing, and that was a mistake.

"Both are gone," he said. "Dave (pseudonym) died of colon cancer in his forties and Bonnie (pseudonym) was killed in a car accident about 20 years ago."

All that air I wanted to fill with our past lives, the way we were growing up as innocent, adventurous, inseparable *amigos* learning to embrace the joys of experiencing life in a relatively safe community, had emptied out. We had very little to say to each other after he shared an update on how hard his life had been. As a retired chaplain raised as a devoted Lutheran since childhood, living a life while diminishing his past, he was in a hurry to get out the door to someplace with his wife, so we wished each other well and ended our talk, knowing that our time spent growing up was only a dormant collection of dust on an old forgotten book of memories. It was a jolt of life that I must acknowledge now. We had followed our destinies, becoming strangers to each other. Personal losses with his family combined with a religious mission to comfort the wounded warriors along with his desert community congregation gave him no reason to remember the way we were as best friends for a decade. Perhaps recalling who we were as friends was too painful to remember, when his brother, sister, mom, dad and collie companion were all alive as a wonderful family unit, and we were allowed to trustingly roam the greater neighborhood as fervid free-ranging kids. At least I had my two sisters and brother still around during the later years of my life. But he did raise a family to fill the pain of losing his parents and siblings serving his country well. Remembering how close we were as inseparable childhood friends during our generation that now seems incomparably distant and so innocent, I can only wonder at how unprepared we were as suburban kids for the loss of innocence that took place in America with the series of hammer blows beginning with the assassination of President Kennedy followed by the struggling civil rights movement, the divisive and turbulent Vietnam War, disruptive anti-war protests, other heart-breaking political assassinations not to mention catastrophic urban riots breaking out across the country.

We were both baptized into two worlds of which ask for our souls. As infants, water was poured and sprinkled on our foreheads from two different Christian sects to enroll us into a world of faith and mystery beyond our five senses. This world asks us to honor a soul created by God and placed in a temporary sanctuary on this earth. The future of that soul beyond death depends on how this Earthly body performs its sacred duties. Our birth given rights to follow our faiths were different but still Christian. Mine from the Russian Orthodox church, his from a Lutheran church. I moved away from following a salvation route, he embraced it. I chose to question organized religions. He never gave up his birth given faith and continued to proselytize under an ordained ministry through his deep belief in Jesus Christ as our Savior. We as adults both made our choices in life with transformative jolts of different pains and chosen paths, but I'll always remember the way we were, growing up with much freedom to explore on our own without parental supervision to intervene with our play and cherish those times dearly. Our separate journeys molted us away from each other, leaving a sad aftermath that this long-term childhood free ranging friendship had faded into dusty memories the way we use to be for Mickey but not me. He was my best friend in childhood but life threw many curve balls to distance ourselves from ever re-uniting as friends again. Yet, I still remember our stories and it hurts to know he wishes to forget those amazing innocent adventurous deep buddy times. But I am so grateful to have ventured into so many rich experiences with him as timeless treasures of the heart.

Chapter Two
Kidnapped by Local Bullies

*I have thick skin; I think the fact that I was severely bullied in my
childhood helped me build strength and believe in my artistic vision.
I deal with rejection very well. I have a lifelong vision and an
unbreakable spirit.*
– Nuno Roque

On a lazy, sultry summer afternoon, I was playing by myself in an empty baseball field at Pioneer Park in Broadview, Illinois, a mile from home. I was just running the bases and pretending to be some heroic base-running speedster, rounding the bases to score the winning run at home. Three boys a year older than me who had a reputation for picking on younger kids of their gender approached me and asked what I was doing. I knew all of them. They all lived in my neighborhood. I didn't have a chance to finish my answer when they immediately grabbed my arms, pressed them behind my back, and forced me to walk with them under a railroad bridge along a thick shrubby woodland creek to an abandoned farmhouse surrounded by swamp and wretched bottomland odors from industrial toxic discharges.

Nobody saw this kidnapping unfold, even though I screamed for help. Beyond the railroad tracks, there wasn't a single occupied residential dwelling as far as the eye could see. I was only eight years old and totally terrified, heading to a place that seemed so far away from home. Telling me to be quiet or face more pain, twisting my arms behind my back, the boys pushed me into this dilapidated abandoned home without stairs. I noticed there was no door. It was dark, barren, with a lot of broken debris, shattered windows, and a shaky stairway going up to the attic where they would try to scare me into performing acts of youthful, sadistic fun.

One of the bullies said, holding a lit cigarette in his hand, "Do you smoke?"

"No," I replied, staring up at him, pressuring me to smoke.

"How about puffing on this one," he demanded.

I refused while he tried to push the lit stick into my mouth. As a way of forcing me to concede, I was dragged to a broken window with sharp glass fragments on the floor, looking directly into a wasp nest. They grabbed my head and pushed it a few inches from this gripping, active community of stingers. I agreed to be submitted to their wishes and given the cigarette to inhale my first puff ever of a toxic, unfiltered cigarette as a healthy lung 3rd grader. Like a little gifted child actor, I dramatically pretended to have serious coughing spasms from the drag and insisted I needed fresh air to catch my breath. Seeing my reaction, the bully trio retreated from their games, allowing me to head to the open entrance doorway from where we entered. I stood there, taking a few fear-driven breaths of recovery, then I instinctively leaped off from that stairless gateway to hell and ran like I was the fastest base runner to ever play the game. After racing beyond sight of that creepy dilapidated house, I looked back and saw one of the bullies just standing in the open field, surrendering the challenge of catching up with me. Perhaps they had too much smoke in their youthful carbon-congested lungs to keep up. As I escaped these territorial bullies, bored on a hot summer day and willing to torture me into some form of afternoon delight, I realized I ultimately had the run of my life. My day was unforgettably complete. I made the winning run, safe at home.

Chapter Three
Swimming on the Edge

The ocean is unstable and threatening as the earth is not;
it spawns new life daily, swallows up lives.
-Adrienne Rich

As I am writing while the snow is gently coming down in the mountains around my retirement home, I feel safe and far removed from the ocean. Ever since my first visit to the grand vacation balmy shores off Miami Beach with my brother and Dad at five years old, I was introduced to potentially meeting my fate at an early age. With just a dinky souvenir inner tube to keep me afloat, waves as high as my little body would boost me up to see the vast endless space of restless water, I was petrified and ecstatic at the same time.

Finally, one energy charged wave undercut my inner tube, flipping me over, submerging me upside-down in a rough world of turbulent give and take. I couldn't escape from my inflated donut, tightly fitted around my waist. I tried to push my myself up but couldn't. I was losing my breath. A passing barracuda caught my cloudy sight as I struggled to flip over. I still remember those rough turbid waves pounding against me, ruining my chances of reaching the surface. Then I felt a great force of power grab my legs and lift me up out of the abyss. My dad, who had been basking on the beach distant from the beachcombers, saw my legs projecting off and on between the high waves. Only a few yards away, he pulled me up, with the inner tube embedded around my waist, and carried me to safety, where I fully recovered thanks to my Pop, who was my only rescuing link between life and death.

That traumatic encounter with the sea was just a prelude for what would be a true test of endurance and courage to solidify my deep respectful fear of the oceans. As Peace Corps volunteers, my traveling partner Bill Fasulo and I decided to take a short trip along the West African coast. We found our way to an incredibly pristine beach outside of Abidjan, Ivory Coast. The oceanic waters of the Atlantic tend to be dangerous, with extremely treacherous surf. Riptides and heavy undertow make even waist wading risky. On a gusty sultry day in early 1972 under a strong equatorial sun, I decided to enter the ominous realm. A little over my shoulders, I playfully jumped while the modest waves spilled over my head. As I began to release my feet from the bottom, I started to swim around while Bill was basking in the intensely bright bliss, napping. Suddenly, as the water from the beach pushed me back out to sea, I felt a tremendous tug pulling me away from where he was peacefully relaxing. I had never experienced a riptide before and panicked. Instead of correctly swimming out to where this powerful tide was taking me to eventually swim parallel along the shore to return back to the beach, I shouted for Bill's help, only to be drowned out by repetitive pounding waves, soothing his comfort into a deeper sun-baked rest. I swam straight into the current, using every muscle I had to endure this great force of reckoning. Only about 50 feet away from shore, I made it back to the pure white sandy beach on my hands and knees, gasping for air. It felt as if I had just completed a marathon swim across the English Channel.

As I plopped down, dripping all that salty water on Bill, he woke up disturbed and exclaimed, "Hey, man, why did you do that?"

I could have been a dead body floating around for some scavenging shark to feast on, but Bill would never know. Indeed, I probably should not have faced this riptide head on, but such a dispassionate decision to understand without any direct experience was not in the picture. I defied the laws of nature and assumed this terrifying encounter with the ocean's rhythmic patterns of indifference would never happen again.

I was gravely mistaken.

Teaching in an alternative, progressive, free school in Santa Fe, New Mexico, the staff and students decided to take a break together to the pearly white sandy beaches of Panama City, Florida. Ranging from 8 to about 17 years of age, we were an innovative community school of multi-aged, non-graded students, learning how to be independent yet connected to learning together. In the late spring of 1981, Jack the Riptide was calling me again. Too early in the swimming season, the beaches were closed. No lifeguards were sitting on their towers, ensuring the safety of the swimmers. It was just us on a wide-open pristine- shoreline, not a single beachcombing soul to be seen except our tightly knit school group. With the cool air and water temperatures matching each other, we all jumped in the clear, off-season, turquoise waters, frolicking in the wavy ebbs and flows. Off in the distance, you would only see the children playing up to their waist a couple hundred feet away from shore. Then, like a terrifying scene from *Jaws*, I could see children being pulled out to sea, as if a great white shark was grabbing their legs. Mike, who was 17 years old and a very good swimmer, swam out to rescue the principal's 10-year-old son, Wyatt, while I could see nine-year-old Oren Appleby, state champ juggler, whose uncle was the famous Irish virtuoso flute player, James Galway, pulled out to sea too. I signaled to Mike to go after Wyatt while I headed out to rescue Oren. Catching up with him, I told him to hop on me, then together we endured a grueling piggyback ride back to shore. Once again, I defied the laws of nature and pushed myself to the limit, stroking into the powerful Jack the Riptide. The waters were tranquil as I put my feet back down on the soft sandy bottom while Oren still held on to me, safe but shaken.

Both Wyatt and Oren came back with harrowing stories to tell. Oren and I decided to climb up that empty lifeguard tower and stare outward to this vast, ominous oceanic mystery. We said not a word but knew what this moment meant. All we could hear were the gulls and ancient rhythmic timeless waves. We were alive and so grateful. Growing up in the prairie flatlands of Illinois not too far away from Lake Michigan, where riptides do happen, I can now feel a beautiful peace of mind living in the higher elevations where mountain grandeur abounds. Knowing the Pacific Ocean's stormy moisture moves across the Western states into the Rockies is a comfortable distance I can feel connected to yet safely far away from. I can feel the riptides waiting to catch me if I ever return to defy the laws of nature again from Jack the Riptide.

Nestled in the dense coniferous montane region of Colorado, I know there was a geologic time when the waves of the open sea once rolled while tides ebbed and flowed, unhindered by rock or shoal. Underneath my home lies a marine memory of a sea once present before humans ever swam, and it feels so reassuring to know those primeval riptides will not be knocking at my door.

Chapter Four
Captive Moments in Terror while Hitchhiking

You can't just ask strangers to drive you up and down the country. This is the twenty-first century. Strangers are more dangerous than ever; we've never been more dangerous.
–Ali Smith

Back in the late 60s and 70s, hitching a ride to your temporary destination was common. Most of my travels across the country by thumb were positive and rather innocuous. I met many interesting people with personal stories to share. But there were a couple rides that certainly brought a halt to the Americana feeling of tapping into a generous national heartland community.

Leaving my hog-smelling college campus of Northern Illinois University in Dekalb for the weekend in the early fall of 1969, I was dropped off at the intersection of Route 38 and Plank Road. I began to walk away from the farm town of Sycamore, singing James Taylor's "Country Road," when a man in a souped-up red Trans Am pulled off to the side and asked if I needed a ride.

I said, "Yes."

"Where are you headed?"

"Schaumburg."

"Hop in. I'll take you there."

I felt relieved that I didn't have to worry about hiking in a harvested cornfield highway for miles and miles, remembering a most memorable chilling cornfield scene in Alfred Hitchcock's *North by Northwest* cinema classic, when the nefarious attacker flies a crop duster, attempting to shoot the oblivious protagonist Cary Grant down.

This time my thumb was not needed. Sitting in the front seat, I saw the driver had a scary weathered face, reminding me of the infamous mass murderer in Chicago, who systematically raped one and tortured and murdered eight student nurses in the summer of 1966 at his home, all within a 24-hour period. This brutal psychopath was Richard Speck, and he looked just like him, with pockmarks on both sides of his face, healthy blondish hair combed back like Speck, muddy work boots, and suspicious signs that he may be a very violent man.

"So what do you for a living?" I asked.

"I'm a contractor for a construction company."

"Where do you live?"

"Chicago."

"Do you commute every day? That seems like a pretty long day for you."

"About a hundred miles round trip every day."

During a pause in the conversation, I noticed on the windshield no required Chicago city vehicle sticker, but I kept that observation to myself. An unspoken tension began to mount. As we were both quiet, he began to accelerate on Plank Rd. to 70, 80, 90 mph. He started to look straight ahead, with the most haunting face I will never forget, going deep in his thoughts and bursting out a harrowing confession with a creepy smile.

"I once killed an older woman crossing the road going too fast."

He didn't let his heavy, steel-capped boot off the peddle but pressed harder on it, hitting 100, then 110, until we literally left the ground and jumped over the railroad tracks landing several feet on the other side. I was about to have a panic attack but kept my cool and just looked straight ahead, with my right hand firmly gripping the inside door release handle. Totally trapped, caught in a car with a potential murderer looking like a mass murderer, we drove about another 15 miles in complete silence before I told him to drop me off at the intersection of Plank Rd. and U.S. 20. He insisted he could drive me all the way to Schaumburg, about another 12 miles, but I was so scared that I took my last dollar out of my wallet and told him to keep it. He accepted.

When I opened the door on a busy rush hour Friday afternoon, the cars and semi-trucks were zooming loudly by, and I felt so liberated closing that door of fear and saying thank you for the ride. I walked to a local gas station and made a call to have my parents pick me up. Thankfully, my parents came to the rescue, picking me up and treating me to a local meal near home.

Another hair-raising episode on the road happened in the late spring of 1977. I'd been thumbing for a ride off of Interstate 88. I crossed the Fox River and waved to a fellow hitchhiker on the opposite side of the highway to wish him well. Looking forward to coming home after a grueling 36 hours of open road, traveling from Santa Fe, New Mexico, I used just my thumb as a ticket to ride. A gentleman in a Ford Mustang pulled off the road just ahead of me and asked if I wanted a ride. I jumped in immediately.

"Where are you headed?"

"Schaumburg."

"How about you?" I asked.

"Chicago."

"Where are you coming from?"

"Santa Fe, New Mexico."

"What do you do there?"

"I'm a teacher at a little alternative school? How about you?"

"I'm a retired Air Force lieutenant."

The man looked to be in his mid-forties, and I was in my late 20s. I really didn't have much to say to him after he announced he was a career military man, as I was a nonviolent peacenik. We were quiet for a few minutes, and then he dropped a sexual bomb on me. "Can you take your pants off and let me play with you? I'll drive you all the way home to Schaumburg." I couldn't believe this unprecedented proposition and didn't know how to answer such an outrageous offer, knowing this man could be a predatory killer if I refused. But I did have a quick-thinking disingenuous answer to redirect his interest.

"Man, I've been hitchhiking for more than 36 straight hours, I don't think you can expect much of a rise from me."

"Okay, did you see any guys down the road when you were hitching for a ride?"

Just to keep him from pursuing his extremely uncomfortable desire, I said, "Yes about 5 miles back toward the Fox River, there was a young guy on Interstate 88 heading east who you might check out."

I assumed by the time this horny military guy got to the place where he was, the lone hitchhiker would probably have been picked up and was heading safely to his destination. He kindly exited onto Route 59 in Plainfield and dropped me off while he headed west away from Chicago to pursue his new sexual target. I must say he was a considerate sexual predator, but a predator nonetheless. I made it home in the back of an empty circus truck, stacked with hay, where elephants are transported. Entering the door with my backpack, my parents could tell by the way I looked and smelled that I had a knackering rough ride. When I shared my stories of my adventures, especially with this Air Force predator, they laughed and said, "Well you're safe and sound now, son. Just relax and get some rest." Knowing how close I was to home before encountering these two lurking, alienated individuals certainly made me think about the dangerous, lonely people driving on these Illinois highways looking for their next prey.

Chapter Five
Calling Dr. Wolf

Within the realms of what goes around resides the magnitude and
severity of what comes around.
– Sandeep N. Tripathi

After I finished graduating from Northern Illinois University in the spring of 1970 with a BS in Secondary Education, I had hoped to be hired by my high school, where I student-taught as a social studies teacher. It didn't happen. So I decided to drive full time during the summer for a local taxi service and then work during the fall as a substitute teacher until I locked in a full-time teaching position. I must admit that, while driving people to their destination, I really got to know them in a short amount of time. But the one experience that sticks in my mind the most was a dispatch to pick up a most insistent neurosurgeon named Dr. Wolf.

I picked him up at his home in Elk Grove Village, where his wife had kicked him out of the house, leaving him only his workout clothes and shoes in a gym bag to channel the major changes facing him. Apparently, he had been seeing another woman much younger than him and decided to jump the marital ship on behalf of this beautiful lady. He directed me to drive to the Barrington Hills Country Club House, a luxurious place to hang out and relax. We sat down together while my taxi meter was ticking the whole time. Dr. Wolf constantly shifted in his conversation from the separation of his wife to his new passionate love. At one point, he stopped, grabbed a napkin, and wrote a short poem describing how irrepressibly in love he was with this infatuated woman outside of his marriage. I just listened and began to feel very uncomfortable about his personal disclosures. He tried to buy me lunch, but I only accepted a cup of coffee. Afterwards, he said he needed to work out at the Chicago Health Club in downtown

Chicago by the lake close to the Oak Street Beach. That was approximately 40 miles away from the golf club. He was quiet and somewhat subdued most of the way, and I thoroughly appreciated that. As we approached the health club, I noticed it was a one-way street and told the doctor I needed to go around the other side to enter.

He exploded by saying "No, turn in here!"

I told him I would get a traffic ticket for sure if I went against a one-way street. And these words he uttered stuck with me even to this day. "Don't worry, kid, go ahead and turn. I'm a doctor and will tell the officer this is an emergency."

I conceded. Fortunately, there was no traffic at the moment, but a traffic officer still caught my illegal move. He pulled me off to the side about a hundred feet or so from the health club. The moment of truth had arrived.

"Looks like I'm going to need your help on this one, doc."

Dr. Wolf didn't look at me directly, only handing me his taxi fare with a measly tip and said, "I'll take care of you later, kid." He ran with his gym bag into this high-priced health club to work out his emotional imbalances. I received my third ticket in a year, and, after the officer left me alone to drive back to my home base in Schaumburg, I cried out in anger and despair, knowing how this contemptable man had bailed out on a promise. I called my dad on the phone in tears, describing my predicament, and he said, "Don't worry, son. I'll take of it."

What he meant was he would contact a friend of his, an Illinois Representative, a very influential Chicago Democratic politician from the 5th district, who also provided a legislative scholarship for me. My dad knew how to work out problems the *Chicago way*. As a result of this connection, I never received that third ticket, which could have suspended my license for a year.

A few months passed into the dead of winter, and my dad was driving to work early that morning to Chicago from Schaumburg in a fierce blizzard and noticed two stranded men by their car, stuck in the snow, wanting a ride to work. My dad, who rarely picks up strangers, decided to help them out. Once they got in the car, they expressed thanks to my dad for picking them up. As they warmed up, a conversation unfolded. "So where do you need to go?" my dad asked.

"Alexian Bros. Hospital," one of the men said.

"What do you do there?"

"I'm a neurosurgeon."

"Really? That must pay pretty well."

"Very well indeed."

Through the course of their casual chat, everyone introduced themselves.

"My name is Dr. Wolf."

"Dr. Wolf? *The* Dr. Wolf? The one who left my boy hanging to receive a ticket going the wrong way because you promised him you would take care of it? He was your taxi driver. Where the hell do you come off leaving my son hanging like that?"

Dr. Wolf didn't say a word. All he could do was submissively listen to the verbal blows, knowing he had no choice, with a fierce winter storm to greet him if he gave my dad a hard time.

As spring jumped ahead, I decided to postpone pursuing teaching full time in public school and decided to join the Peace Corps as an alternative to serving my country without going to Vietnam to fight in an unjust war. By June 1971, I traveled to Liberia in the hinterland, learning Kpelle, the main local tribal language, teaching social studies, English as a Second Language, and math, as well as coaching soccer at a Presbyterian Mission School. It felt wonderfully liberating to leap into a communal culture far away from the hustle and bustle of suburban boredom of driving arrogant bad karma people like Dr. Wolf around to cater to their narcissistic needs, flaunting their status, power, and the all-American dollar as a polished high-professional sleazeball.

Chapter Six
A Peace Corps Vacation Made in Hell

It was a voyage into the absurd.
– Iris Murdoch, *The Black Prince*

Bill Fasulo and I were traveling Peace Corps buddies serving in Liberia. We traveled throughout West Africa, driving through back bush country, where people had never seen a White person before, a coastal area covering Ghana, Ivory Coast, and Liberia. However, one trip will be forever remembered as the most unanticipated harrowing experience ever. During the dry season in January 1972, we embarked as stowaways on a Liberian passenger cruise from Monrovia to the port of Takoradi, Ghana. The German captain of our ship knew we were PC volunteers, and, despite a full capacity, he granted us permission to stowaway for a small price for two days and a night till we docked at our destination. We didn't want to blow our cover but decided to mingle with the legitimate passengers throughout the open deck, viewing playfully curious leaping dolphins following the ship on an open calm sea. Our sleeping quarters was on a backroom kitchen floor, where we developed a serious case of sea sickness, so we decided to wander the night scene incognito. We avoided conversing with people, except for a British Black gentleman who looked like the *Shaft* fame soul singer Isaac Hayes. He wore a stunning gold chain over his dashiki, and he would take us to his room, where we drank the night away with heavy liquor and plenty of stories to share.

The next day, recovering from seasickness and being hungover, we docked in Takoradi and were shocked to see our drinking acquaintance detained by the authorities at the gate of entry, charged as a stowaway from London. He was standing, tired and dejected, with his head down, arms handcuffed behind his back, still wearing the same clothes he had when we met him.

We felt we would be next.

We had our passports ready but no stamps on them indicating we had legally entered our Liberian passenger ship. The authorities seemed so occupied with this detainee that we walked right by them and into another post at the exit. The official stamped our books, and, realizing we were Peace Corps, told us to be careful, as there had been a *coup d'état*. Colonel Ignatius Kutu Acheampong had become the next leader in a bloodless military takeover of Ghana. There were tanks and jeeps and soldiers stationed everywhere, ready for battle, a complete war zone, and we were walking down a main street completely free from authorities checking our passports. But that sense of security and great relief did not last long. As a couple of White foreigners crossing a main street, we were approached by a belligerent Ghanaian officer in a jeep.

"Get in!" he commanded.

"What? We're Peace Corps," I fearfully replied.

"I said get in!" he bellowed.

I could smell he'd been drinking, but we reluctantly agreed, and he drove us to a temporary military compound, where we sat completely silent amid a cigar smoke-filled closed tent in broad daylight. It was dark inside, except for a couple of lanterns casting a strong light toward the meeting table. As I sat and looked at these officers, planning out strategic assignments, I began to have flashbacks of my sleepy little rural suburban home town of Schaumburg, Illinois, being with my family, and I started to smile about how surreal our situation felt. I smiled into space, wondering how did I ever get to this place in my life. The officer in command took that as a serious smirk, thinking I was defying his prowess to keep us in check.

He pulled a pistol out of his holster and pointed it a few inches from my nose. "You wipe that smile off your face, or I'll blow your goddamn head off." I bit hard on my upper lip to keep me from smiling.

With tension building around the city, his breath smelling like a distillery, and his emotions about to burst with pent-up anger, I could tell we were in trouble. He then looked at me and said, "Both of you come with me."

We thought we were going to be executed in some remote secret location on the outskirts of town, but we cooperated, thinking we had no choice. He ordered us to get back in the jeep, and we drove through running crowds and traffic jams, surrounded by chaos and fear. When we reached a checkpoint, the officer took his cigar out of his mouth and told the guard to "open the goddamn gate and let us through." All Bill and I could do was stay still, as his vituperative tongue was scaring the hell out of us.

The guardsman did not resist and lifted the gate for us to pass through, heading to the outskirts of Takoradi on the edge of a rainforest. Could he be taking us to a place of execution, dumping us in a designated ditch, buried and forgotten as another Amnesty International murder case? It was pitch dark, and we began to drive up a maintained dirt road, leading to a community compound.

The lights in the building were radiating with hope. It was there that our lives were liberated from this dangerous, highly volatile officer and the madness of what we had endured. All the Peace Corps volunteers in the area were rounded up and brought to this protected American embassy indefinitely.

When we jumped out of the jeep, the officer with a loose cannon temperament yelled, "You're safe now."

It was the most terrifying and strangely gratifying vacation I ever experienced.

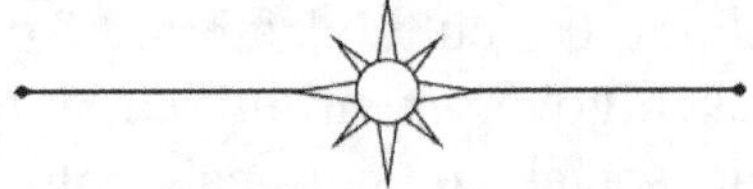

Chapter Seven
When Ideals Are Shattered

To be a good human being is to have a kind of openness to the world, the ability to trust uncertain things beyond your own control that can lead you to be shattered.
– Martha Nussbaum

Within the equatorial hinterland of West Africa adjacent to a Firestone Plantation, I served as a Peace Corps volunteer in the early 1970s. My assignment centered in a quaint traditional hamlet appropriately called Gobata, since the governing founder of the village was allegedly a 110-year-old tribal chief affectionately nicknamed "Old Man Goba." Having acquired nine wives consisting of 39 children, two hundred grandchildren, and a relatively new Mercedes Benz, he certainly earned that noble title.

The chief took pride in his prized possessions. Incredibly fit for someone who could be in their 70s with all of his royal teeth in superb, pearly white condition, he seemed to defy the laws of nature, having a firm grip on the secrets to longevity. The village was a patriarchal clan. I was never mistreated there and felt a genuine tenderness and warmth that reaffirmed my hope in pursuing a simpler, more humane life.

I was the only white-skinned non-Liberian resident in Gobata among a multi-tribal population of 270 villagers, and we felt a good-hearted convivial regard for each other, although some people were amused by my skin color and my attempts to speak their language. The curious hands of the breast-fed children were warm, trusting extensions of curiosity, kindness, and spontaneity. When I arrived amid a large village turnout, I sensed myself on display before a collective public tribunal. As my stay intensified, I discovered the once-thriving communal way of life waning due to three ominous influences: (1) a government road cut through the center of the village, leading to a national guard compound; (2) a mission school was established, undermining the cultural fabric of tribal traditions; and (3) a corrupt US-backed government thrived, aiming to develop and maintain an economic, social, and political evolution for the few.

Every weekend, rumbling military trucks would erode the peaceful flow of living in this quiet, somewhat intact village by emitting clouds of dusty red earth around these time-honored huts and tin-roofed homes. Roaring vehicles frequently zipped through the traditional agrarian community, making simple conversation outdoors along the road almost impossible. In short, the town was becoming a split personality. Western culture had arrived, speeding up life while undermining the very essence of indigenous identity and respect. I discovered a crushing realization that the very government that invited the Peace Corps "to help their country help themselves," actually produced an adversarial effect upon the people of the hinterland. Hunger, infant mortality, economic disparity and deadly bacterial diseases were widespread.

That summer when I arrived, the heartily embraced "father of modern Liberia" William Tubman died after serving as president for 27 years, leaving a serious gap of leadership and a major power struggle to replace such a stable and honorable man, who just wanted to bring the indigenous people and Americo-Liberians together as a nation. Although Tubman made the best of his presidency under a benevolent authoritarian government, once gone, his one-party-rule powers demonstrated an acute insensitivity to the country's indigenous people, providing grossly ineffective measures for the health and care of Liberian citizens. The leaders, under a close-knit hegemony of families of that allegedly proclaimed "independent" country, were too preoccupied in preserving and evolving their own Americo-Liberian privilege. President Nixon was proclaiming a national and international cry for "law and order," and the new President William Tolbert was determined to crack down on criminals by introducing numerous public hangings throughout the country to receive foreign aid, one of which I unfortunately witnessed only three blocks from the Peace Corps headquarters in Monrovia. Tolbert's hope for cracking down on serious troublemakers was to receive major funding from the Nixon administration, and he succeeded by receiving major support for national security.

Serving in the Peace Corps in a small hamlet in Liberia I taught in a Presbyterian parochial school becoming the only non-African among staff and students. Teachers in this fading photo from left to right were from Ghana, Liberia, Sierra Leone, Mali, and Togo. Unknown photographer, *1971*.

Throughout the school year, I taught in a boarding mission school, high on a hill overlooking the village, and endeavored to facilitate a candid exchange of politics, life, and religion to the secondary education students. Such an open dialogue was seldom apparent in the school yard, and it was evident to me that the iron hand of oppression could not be penetrated, because an erudite principal, whose academic and political credentials were stellar, had an utterly incumbent obsession to convert the so-called "backward tribal natives"—even though they were world-renowned for folklore storytelling and herbal medicine—into disciplined African Christianized White Anglo Saxon Protestants (WASPS). His methodology at Todee Presbyterian Mission School was ingenuous: teach the student body to hate their own social and economic conditions and cultural upbringing while forcing upon them subservience to unquestioned authority. This would make them learn to become respectful, loyal, national, acculturated citizens of their country. But first it was also necessary to eliminate their beliefs, modes of traditional dress (the school had a uniformed Catholic style dress code for both genders), and thought. His means of persuasion included fear tactics, such as flogging accused liars within a public assembly, or swatting a disruptive,

29

disinterested student on the bare knuckles with a bamboo stick in the middle of a classroom lesson.

I was involved with one incident where a student had spread rumors that the principal's daughter received acceptance into a college not because of her academic ability but because she was the principal's daughter. Such an accusation brought the student to the office to retract that rumor. The 8th-grade student would not renounce his claim that this was true. Consequently, the principal gave him an ultimatum. Either he publicly announced to everyone in the school courtyard that what he said about his daughter was false and face corporal punishment, or all of his academic records would be stripped away from the school since he was in first grade.

The boy refused and asked if his brother could replace him for the public flogging in the school courtyard. The principal adamantly said no. Eventually, he agreed to take punishment and retract his comment about his daughter. That afternoon I was to witness a punishment that pushed me over the top and ended my desire to teach there. All the faculty were lined up with the entire student body of 250 students from first grade through high school, all assembled to witness this appalling sentence. Students literally had no rights to appeal to such a coercive procedure. The reverend had a worldly, almost imperial background, holding doctorate degrees in theology from the University of Heidelberg (Germany) and political science at Cambridge University (England), with a distinguished diplomatic career in Ghana as a United Nations delegate. He even had collective works on nonviolence from both Martin Luther King, Jr. and Gandhi on his distinguished book shelf. And yet this well learned principal of Ashanti origin instrumented extreme fundamental punitive means to reinforce his academic expectations through brutality and fear. After unsuccessfully plotting with his cabal to assassinate the renowned socialist Ghanaian leader Kwame Nkrumah, the reverend sought political asylum in Liberia, choosing the little hamlet of Gobata as his missionary objective. The villagers despised him because of his unbridled conversionary arrogance and aloofness with the indigenous community. But he was still in their eyes "a gentleman and a scholar" to be feared.

The principal made it quite evident that he would not tolerate false rumors to undermine his family's reputation. The boy eventually did apologize in public before a large crowd of his student peers and staff, waiting for his punishment. The principal handed the bamboo stick to each teacher standing before the dead silent assembly. One after another, they refused to flog the student. The stick was offered to me. I refused. The next in line was a nephew of the principal, and he accepted. The accused boy took his shirt off. Two high school freshmen held the boy's arms while the teacher, a nephew to the principal, flogged him 13 times over his bare back. With several open gashes bleeding down his back, he was assisted back into the classroom to recover while the student body returned to their normal routine. How could such a well-educated man use such a barbaric method for getting the students to learn from their mistake? Maybe what the boy said could have been true too. I grew to loathe the principal's treatment of people in the indigenous community.

One day, I confronted the Rev. about how he treated the people in the village, especially the children, as "unruly, illiterate, and primitive."

His answer was simple. "Mr. Paige, this is not Vietnam," which I assumed to mean protesting against his arrogant punitive ways of disciplining the students would only be in vain.

After one school year of serving in the Peace Corps as a soccer coach, a social-studies, English as a second language and math teacher, I could no longer endure the governmental indifference to struggling villages, the conversionary arrogance of the mission's school administration, and the slow death to an ancient way of life in the village of Gobata. I left, with a strong desire to never partake in any educational system that allows students to be brutally treated that way. Education is a learning process of building confidence in what we can become, not what those in power coercively demand us to be.

I left Gobata mentally exhausted, sad, alienated, and feeling somewhat exploited, with my idealism shattered. I left most of my personal belongings to be shared among the villagers as a memory of my stay. Economic privilege had afforded me the freedom to live in an oppressed situation or to escape from it. The communal people of Gobata, except for a Lebanese storekeeper and Old Man Goba and his diamond mine-owning family, did not have that escape valve.

Accepting that privileged status, I returned home as an active, guilt-ridden, anti-war protester and civil rights activist, campaigning against cultural and economic imperialism, racism, and the inhumanity of policies that destroy other countries while undermining the moral conscience of ours. Years passed and, in 1980, all hell busted loose with the assassination of Liberia's True Whig Party President William Tolbert, under a popular rebellious coup lead by Samuel Doe, who became the first Liberian President of non-Americo-Liberian descent. Doe established a military regime called the People's Representative and enjoyed support from Liberian ethnic groups who were denied power since the founding of the country in 1847. Over time, Doe made every effort to tip the power in his direction, which led to more bloody conflicts and inter-tribal wars. It was a total, bloody horrific mess. It didn't have to be that way.

Today, after decades of civil war, Liberia has a multiparty system, with numerous political parties, in which no one party has a chance of gaining power alone, and the parties must work with each other to form coalition governments. In 2006 Ellen Johnson Sirleaf became the first woman President of Liberia and the first woman to serve an African country Why our US government didn't see the True Whig's Party betrayal and inability to diversify and respect the variety of tribal traditions as a political means of unifying Liberian citizens in the democratic process, strengthening the character of the nation, is a mystery. I certainly felt that tension while I was there, and it deeply catapulted my concerns for getting involved in worldly matters locally.

Chapter Eight
Black Like Jesus

Sons have always a rebellious wish to be disillusioned by that which charmed their fathers.
– Aldous Huxley

I knew from my high school experience with people of different colors that my dad was a racist plain and simple. The language he used to make him feel as if he was better than them was terribly upsetting. When we moved from Maywood to the rural suburb of Schaumburg as an act of white flight, I learned firsthand that my dad wanted nothing to do with African Americans living next door to us. The realtor at the Timbercrest Model Homes Office, where we planned to move, assured my father in the late winter of 1966 that no Blacks were present in the subdivision and that no developments were accepted to build federal housing projects. Present in the meeting room, I overheard further assurances that Blacks would be discouraged from entering the community through a capricious application of jacking up the prices of the homes in the event of a possible purchase. To the three-piece-suit realtor and my dad, such a precarious investment to attract unfavorable groups of people into this residential subdivision would lower the property values—and thus my father's social and economic esteem. Through the course of this insidious discussion, I discovered that my dad simply wanted to protect his interests, increase his profits, accept the hidden discriminatory practices in the community, remain somewhat inactive in neighborhood affairs, and ultimately sell the home when the time was right, praying that no aberrant group of people who descend from different, darker complexions enter the neighborhood at the time of sale.

Living in a home where these blatant prejudices tore into my love for my family eventually propelled me on a quest away from Schaumburg. I joined the Peace Corps and served in a predominantly multi-tribal dark-skinned village where there was only one White person living in the hamlet out of a population of about 275. I purposely chose a country where I could force myself to adapt to teaching and living where people looked much different than me. I was truly embraced by the villagers and affectionately called "Flomo" in Kpelle meaning *wise fool,* because I tried to speak their language and always seemed to make them smile. Having returned from my crushing yet life-changing Peace Corps venture, I campaigned door to door vociferously for the proud liberal George McGovern in my hometown suburb of Schaumburg, but I only became increasingly disillusioned over the predominance of lily-white bigoted Nixon supporters favoring our involvement in the Vietnam War, indifferent to the Watergate scandal brewing while ignoring blatant abuses of power at the highest level of government.

With the seeds of culture shock gnawing away in my gut, my heart grew more intensely withdrawn and restless. Several heated family confrontations unfolded. I had left a familiar, racially homogenous suburban subculture for a year, absorbing the multi-tribal conditions of hunger, marriage offers, tropical diseases, and spontaneous hand-shaking-snapping-finger greetings, returning as a genuine product of *normlessness.* One illuminating example was illustriously apparent during my first Christmas home since parting from West Africa. Each year, I heartily seasoned my family's house with an enchanting assortment of electrifying holiday decorations; however, this particular year, a time bomb of unresolved emotions waited to explode. It was, and probably forever will be, the most memorable confrontation of compromise with my father. Historically, the whitewashing of Jesus contributed to Christians being some of the worst perpetrators of anti-Semitism, as well as eager participants in physical and cultural genocide against indigenous peoples and African Americans. And this continues to manifest to several degrees in the "othering" of non-Whites.

Because the Timbercrest community was predominantly White middle-income homeowners, the citizens took pride in cultivating a Coppertone tan on the beaches, and since I had grown more cognizant of color barriers in America, I was self-righteously determined to portray our "Jesus in the Manger" outdoor adornment as a Black African-rooted baby. I simply painted him ebony. When my father discovered this clandestine plot to overthrow the myths of Jesus's imagery, he became choleric.

"Denny, what are you trying to do?"

"I'm painting Jesus this year a different color. From certain articles I've read, some scholars claim he had Black roots from Africa. In other words, Black African culture might be the true foundation of Christianity," I nervously announced.

"Oh no. Take the paint off. What will the neighbors say? After all, we have to live with them."

"Dad, we don't even know our neighbors. What difference does it make? The only time we ever see them is when we're cutting the lawn or when they've bought something we'd like to have ourselves."

"Son, I don't care. Look, your mother and I have to live here, and I'll not stand for this! Do you think people around here will treat this display kindly? I don't want to pay for any damaged windows. You understand?"

"Alright, then would you accept Jesus if I painted him brown?"

"That's okay. Jesus Christ, son, what else do you want from me?" he wearily asked.

"Thanks, Dad," I said while affectionately hugging him.

And so, the Nativity scene presented a special child, one who was brown that year and for the years to come. No windows were vandalized. No outdoor decorations were stolen or defaced. The neighbors generally accepted the change of face or ignored it altogether. As a result of our private brouhaha in the basement, my father and I grew closer to each other. He had realized my conflict between pursuing a life to help the dispossessed and reflecting my family's aspirations of seeing me climb up the economic ladder of social worth. At the same time, I realized his conflict between so-called status seeking conventional behavior and his love for his son. We were respecting each other, and the quality of our bond sharpened.

With one joyously altruistic visit to the depressed Skid Row along West Madison Street in Chicago, my dad donated his hardly worn dress shirts, slacks, and sport coats to impoverished wanderers. A suspicious police officer could not imagine that such a gesture of charity could be performed by an affluent citizen. In fact, the officer interrogated my father, but, to his true consternation, he discovered that this charitable suburbanite was for real. Personally, handing his clothes out to each downtrodden vagrant was his way of expressing a direct act of benevolence. The Chicago cop had never witnessed such an open, hand-to-hand, big heartedness in that forgotten land, where alleged derelicts drank and doped their lives away. Now they could wear fancy clothes while getting plastered or drugged out. Each lucky recipient, according to my dad, raved over his formal offerings, whether the sizes extended beyond the edges of the wrist or not. At least for a day, their hard times were suspended, and they could feel like respectable somebodies.

A few weeks later, my father decided to pick up a gentleman off an expressway ramp who had a flat tire and needed to get to a service station for help. He turned out to be a rabbi. But my dad was stopped by an officer for picking up hitchhikers off an expressway exit and tagged for a ticket. He lost his good Samaritan run for charitable actions after that incident, helping strangers less. I kept wondering whether, if each "Have" person touched another downtrodden "Have Not" person firsthand, face-to-face each year or perhaps on a monthly basis with a donation of clothes, food, and gift cards to nonalcoholic cafes, could we realize the rippling effects such a personal, heartfelt contribution can have in generating a greater connection with our fellow human beings? Looking into someone's eyes and touching a person ridden with suffering does much to cleanse the soul toward a better place in one's journey. I believe my experience in an integrated high school opened new doors for creating valuable inter-racial and cross-cultural relationships, helping me become more comfortable interacting with diverse people. My father never had such an educational upbringing and continually struggled with his racist attitude and desire to conform to and benefit from *white privilege.* However, I know my influence upon his life nudged him toward a greater self, albeit minimal in its outcome.

Chapter Nine
A Few Brushes with Death for a Dream Quest

Life's challenges are not supposed to paralyze you, they're supposed
to help you discover who you are.
— Bernice Johnson Reagon

The drive to visit the independent, nonpublic Santa Fe Community School was a crazy quilt pattern journey of survival and endurance. His name was Steven Freud, and he was looking for an extra driver to go West. I found his request on a bulletin board listed at the student center at Northwestern University. I accepted his offer, and, in early May 1975, I traveled over 1,300 miles with this musically gifted skittish eccentric in his spiffy 1974 Mercedes Benz. Steve proclaimed himself to be the great grandson to Sigmund Freud. He was enroute to Anaheim to attend the Walt Disney School for the Creative Arts and Sciences. He hoped to major in music. While on the road, Steve sometimes played his flute with a derby hat tipped slightly toward his nose. This may not seem so unusual except for the outrageous fact that he did this melodious routine while driving his plush car.

For some maddening defiant reason, I accompanied him, with my bongo playing on the dashboard. On long open highways, we performed blissfully. Steve effortlessly instrumented a dueling harmony of control, embracing the steering wheel with his knees while fingering the holes of his recorder. Through the course of this cocky, death-defying experiment in joy and celebration of the moment, a trusting relationship developed between Steve and me. Eventually, he allowed me to take over the wheel. However, our brief, growing friendship came to a shattering, almost apocalyptic conclusion. While traveling on the speedy freeway Interstate 80, halfway through the state of Nebraska in the midst of an icy blizzard, we reached a heated difference of opinion regarding each other's musical tastes. Steve thought Leonard Bernstein was a grossly overrated American composer and felt Beethoven was the best composer ever to face the earth. I argued that Bernstein was a musical genius. As we bickered about this issue while I handled the steering wheel, an unexpected spinout on the semi-truck driven main highway created one of the scariest yet delightfully thrilling experiences imaginable. After losing traction and suddenly swerving uncontrollably, Steve lost his merriment, panicked, and desperately grabbed the steering wheel from me—only to precipitate two full exhilarating spinouts. Feeling as if we were about to enter a muddy fairway to heaven, the car nevertheless skidded innocuously into a sodden, saturated median depression.

Freud immediately developed alarming paranoic tendencies and flatly refused any further request to share the load steering the wheel. He wanted to assure himself there would not be any "Freudian slips" if he took the wheel. We rode the rest of the way quiet and rather detached from each other to Albuquerque, where I bussed it to Santa Fe. With increasing stress and fatigue creeping into my exhausted body as a result of the fallout between Freud and me, and with the anxious anticipation of arriving at my long-awaited destination, I was on the brink of pure exhaustion. I became chilly, sweaty, and nauseous. Quick flashes of my past rushed before me. Yet I still possessed this insatiable drive to arrive at the place of my dreams. I wondered how the noted Sigmund would interpret such an obsession with existence.

Building up enough energy to speak coherently, I asked the bus driver if he knew where the community school was. He assuredly replied that he did, and he could drop me off Cerrillos Road, directly in front of an impressive, earthly designed educational complex. Using almost every conceivable muscle to carry my duffle bag under an intense fever, I strenuously approached the receptionist's desk to the hospital section of the conjectured community school and quickly confronted a passing doctor. "Excuse me, doctor, but is this the community school?" I asked.

"Yes."

"I'm very sick. Can you help me?"

"I'm very sorry, but we only treat Native Americans," the doctor replied.

"You're kidding. Isn't this place the Santa Fe Community School?" I breathlessly asked while attempting to emit any remaining reserve of energy in the hopes of receiving prompt attention.

"No, I'm sorry. This is the Institute for American Indian Arts. A lot of people around here call this place the Indian Community School."

"That's just great. Please, can you at least take my temperature?" I dishearteningly asked.

"Sure."

The doctor slowly sank the thermometer under my pallid, dehydrated tongue. As he observed the expansion of the red mercury liquid, the doctor became alarmed. "It's a hundred and three. I suggest you go to the emergency room at St. Vincent's Hospital at once."

"I'll call a taxi right away," one of the staff shouted.

The taxi arrived, and I traipsed my way from the cab door to the emergency ward, totally oblivious as to how much I paid the driver. Seeing this nearly collapsed pale, languid, and weak man, a doctor escorted me from the emergency entrance doorway to an empty, clean bed. Upon examining my pathetic health, two doctors confirmed I was suffering from pure, dehydrated exhaustion and provided water for me to steadily sip. They both recommended a long, undisturbed sleep. I left the hospital that same day, searching for a place to crash. I purchased a prescribed bottle of tetracycline at a local drug store and proceeded to wobble to a quaint charming adobe lodge called La Posada Inn.

Just a few blocks away from the hospital, I incurred a relapse at the corner of a Mobil gas station driveway and careened against an advertising post on the ground for a few forgotten minutes. Visions of a Bataan Death March trekked across my head. When awakening I tried shaking off my tiredness and made a move toward the inn. After completing one forgettable block, I apprehensively realized I had left the bottle of medicinal capsules on the curb side where I was convalescing in public like a street derelict. With turtle-paced reluctance, I returned to the site only to discover that the little brown bag of medicine was gone. My struggling death march to the drugstore resulted in another 10-dollar purchase of a prescribed game changer. I was relentlessly driven to make it to the serene adobe confines. After receiving the key to my assigned guest room, I hurriedly stumbled to the door, entered the cozy adobe premises with hanging ristra peppers, closed the main curtain, collapsed into bed, and pursued sleep uninterruptedly for about 17 hours. A book of critical essays on the pros and cons of A.S. Neill's *Summerhill* nestled faithfully by my side. When I awoke, my heart and mind fully restored, I was prepared to face the intended community school.

I took a taxi that morning straight to the Santa Fe Community School on the southwestern outskirts of the city and was shocked to see the dust ridden impoverished conditions, with somewhat burnt-out residents struggling to make a low-income intentional community work. I walked alone and saw how the children and adults moved throughout this 10-acre radical experiment in alternative education. Tacitly walking toward one of the children, I noticed on the deck of his permanent mobile home a dirty-faced three-year-old boy with an enormous bandaged lump on his forehead. He looked like a perfect character fit to act with the Little Rascals. I asked what happened, and he enthusiastically declared with a lisp, "I got kicked by a *horth*."

His sister, about two years older than him, sensitively moved into my lap and exclaimed, "Oh look at the puppies play!"

As I gently stroked the cuddly, furry canines, I began inquiring into these kids' lives. All they seemed to care about was who I was. "My name's Dennis. What's yours?"

The boy loudly and proudly replied, "Wyatt!"

The sweet, smiling, freckled, five-year-old, pale-faced girl who looked like she could easily qualify for a Norman Rockwell *Americana* painting, replied, "Kim Nagel. We're brother and sister."

Meanwhile, their mother was watering a carefully nurtured garden, wondering if this visitor who she knew was a possible teacher at the school would stay or split. My heart was touched by these sensitive, unintimidated, good-natured children wandering in a sea of playful poverty. My decision was to seriously consider returning to this paradoxical "community as a classroom" place not because of what it was but because of what it could be. However, I had one more job interview to check out before finalizing my commitment to work where the low-income children were respected, loved, and guided toward becoming honest free-spirited yet responsible people on the planet.

Brush Ranch Boarding School consisted of middle to high-school students and a young staff set within the serene forested mountains of the Pecos Wilderness. This pricey private school was very remote, yet the ranch seemed to be a hustling, stimulating educational environment for outdoor education. I met the headmaster of the school, and we drove to his very pleasant cottage home on the campus, where he told me he had a background in educational administration and psychology. In fact, he said he was a psychologist. We drove back to the campus in his open jeep, and he dropped me off to wander the grounds and talk firsthand to the students. I had an engaging conversation with a couple of the early high school students boarding there. They despised the principal and hated living there. Apparently, their parents forced them to attend this school. I was not impressed by what they had to say about how they were being treated.

As I walked back to the courtyard, the principal waved me over to view a photo op with some of the students who would be moving on with their learning. I watched the headmaster arrange the students to get everyone in the photo. One student preferred not to be in the picture. He felt pressured and was verbally adamant about being photographed. The headmaster must have had a bad day because he slapped that defiant young teen in the face and told him to get in his office until he got there. I watched him storm into the main building. The students present were somewhat startled, but I kept my cool and watched this panned group photo happen for posterity.

When it was done, the principal and I began walking back to his office when one of the nurses frenetically approached us, shaking with much trepidation, "He has a gun, and he's threatening to shoot your wife."

Apparently, the principal had a handgun in his desk drawer, and the slapped kid discovered it while waiting for him to receive an acrimonious lecture of wrongdoing. His wife happened to be in the room at the time and was held hostage. Thank goodness the headmaster was a psychologist, for, through the art of his manipulative craft to change minds, the teen handed over the gun. By the end of the school day, he was expelled and promptly driven to the airport within two hours to fly back to his hometown of Kansas City.

After witnessing two extremely contrasting job-hunting experiences, I returned to the Santa Fe Community School, knowing no guns were allowed on the property and people had to come together on a non-coercive consensus basis—both children and adults. I was ready for the challenge. I was soon provided with a free ticket to work in any open-hearted way I chose with the children, without pay, but with free boarding under a vow of poverty.

Chapter Ten
An Ornery Horse Teaches Me a Lesson

*The horse is a mirror to your soul and sometimes you might not like
what you see in the mirror.*
– Buck Brannaman

I lived and taught on the outskirts of Santa Fe in the mid-1970s on wind driven open-range land fit for riding horses. The little alternative community school had a corral with a variety of horses and a wonderful Shetland pony named Smokey for the children to ride. However, there was one in particular, a pinto named Tennessee, who was trouble. Several people living in the community warned me about forming any kind of trusting relationship with Tennessee. Owned by one of the older teen students, Lee Nagel, the consensus between the students and staff was that Tennessee had the notorious reputation as the most dangerous horse to ride among the other horses stationed there on the school land.

And for good reason. She aroused fears in many quarters because of her incredible ability to jolt the rider with lightning velocity when least expecting it. Tennessee had survived many earlier incidents of children throwing stones and spooking her. Now she was avenging the psychological and physical blows of abuse. Like a Moby Dick equine, this tense, muscular pinto created a casualty list to horrify any bronco buster, including a removed spleen from a six-year-old boy, a partially bitten off ear from an eight-year girl, kicks to the forehead, and countless other bruising electrifying jolts. They all let their guard down, with a natural tendency to trust this fierce, unpredictable, skittish pony.

During my first encounter with Tennessee, I thought she was one of the warmest, most genuinely cordial horses I had ever stroked. But such a greeting seemed a little too cozy for her. As I gently stroked her mane, I could see her disposition changing. Her large, protruding blue eyes danced and flashed puckishly. An unsettling grin played upon her mouth. Although short, she was tenacious and strong due to an unremitting exposure to riding and establishing a territorial position with other larger horses in the school corral. Her face divulged sadness, pity, trepidation, and a defensive alertness that was both surprising and terrifying.

One tranquil Sunday early summer afternoon, Tennessee escaped from the corral. I discovered her in the back of the schoolyard behind the greenhouse, chewing peacefully on a patch of grass. Seeing the harness over her preoccupied face while gregariously comforting her, I methodically reached over to grab the leather strap, when suddenly she swirled her sinewy back hips almost 180 degrees toward my chest and catapulted her legs straight up, one of them firmly targeting my belly. I instantly became short winded, gasping for air. The horseshoe imprint lay pressed between my ribs, but nothing felt fractured.

Providing solace to this horse was like attempting to comfort a great white shark. I stood unmoved, stunned, and truculent. This defiant, battered calico powerhouse nonetheless would not get the best of me. Tennessee galloped in the front of the schoolyard entrance to again graze amid a pleasant sparse patch of uncut green bunch grass. I could not imagine how this horse, who had nearly flattened me permanently on my ass, could be so erratically cruel.

Death-defying grievances directed to Tennessee triggered a death-defying confrontation. She stampeded unabashedly toward me, and, in a pure panic moment, I charged squarely into a front brick garden terrace wall along the school building façade. Swollen on both sides of my two-legged body, with a horseshoe printed on my belly, an idea arose that helped prevent any further injuries for man and beast while simultaneously capturing this intrepid pinto with an irrepressible adrenalin rush. Yanking some mature flowering wild asparagus stems in a remote section of the schoolyard, with a hidden display of rattled nerves, I steadily walked to the other side of a stretch of rubbly, pink, four-foot block wall parallel to the corral fence. Establishing a Maginot Line, my plan was ripe for implementation. By making a lasso from some rope I found on the ground, I firmly held the hardy asparagus bunch in front of the loop while Tennessee cautiously entered the realm of captivity. This equalizer proved remarkably effective. My benign tug over her neck precipitated a prompt kick to the wall and nothing else. After a few relentless futile kicks, her four legs became grounded again as I guided her along the wall on opposite sides toward the main gate. With her back sweating and her spirit despondent, Tennessee eased herself reluctantly into the corral as I threw the asparagus on the fenced-off ground for her to snatch.

My trust with this lethal pinto ended for all time on that explosive afternoon. The certified seal of equine distemper lay impressed upon my belly for several days. I had endured this agonizing confrontation and learned how to avoid the wrath of an abused horse in need of a Horse Whisperer. I also discovered a clever way to comfort the horse in the corral. It was the longest time I have ever spent with a horse without saddling up in my life, and one I shall never forget. I was jolted but not broken and taught a hard lesson by a tenaciously troubled pinto named Tennessee.

Chapter Eleven
One Night Is Enough

Stand up for yourself. Never give any one permission to abuse you.
— Lailah Gifty Akita

Sunday in Santa Fe in the late summer of 1976 when the aspen leaves are quaking with a tease of illuminating fall colors in the mountains seemed like a wonderful time to take a break and seek solace in the high country. But my 1971 Ford Falcon was not functioning well enough to endure the higher elevation, so I asked my community school neighbor Pat Martinez if I could possibly borrow his car. It turned out to be a 1969 powder blue Lincoln continental, which moved like a tugboat ascending up the mountains, slow and steady. When I reached a pleasant breezy spot about eight miles up from the Santa Fe ski basin, I found a lovely stand of aspens turning vibrant golden yellow. I parked the car, walked to a patchy glow of sun creeping into the grove, and sat down to smell the forest, feel the gentle winds, contemplate, and relax.

There's something pure and spicy sweet about the smells of moist aspen leaves in the early fall, which left me with a euphoric mellowness driving down the mountains. Entering the north end of the downtown plaza of Santa Fe, I stayed on the left side of the historic East Palace Avenue, not realizing the road had two lanes. As I signaled a left turn into Old Santa Fe Trail, a police car siren light appeared, and I pulled off to the side of the street. An officer came to my car and asked for my driver's license. I asked what was the charge. He said I was driving on the wrong side of the road on Palace Ave. I claimed there was no demarcated line to indicate what side of the road I should be on. That's when the conversation began to heat up.

"Officer, how am I supposed to know what side of the street to drive on when there are no lines? Can you please take off your sunglasses?

I can't see your eyes when you speak to me, and it's making me very nervous," I said, speaking loudly to compete with the jack hammer rattling and other road construction noise. I also had been suffering from hearing loss due to coming down off a few thousand feet elevation. I couldn't help but project the *persona* of this officer with mirror sunglasses to the shotgun honcho prison guard in *Cool Hand Luke*, who covered up his eyes with those deeply dark shades, so you are never able to read his emotions, keeping his anonymity and his power intact. However, I did get his name—Officer Tom Hill—only a young rookie cop, on the force for little over a year, trying to be a tough enforcer, making a name for himself on a little guy like me.

The officer slipped his glasses down his nose so I could see his eyes for a moment and then slipped them back up again. I wasn't pleased one bit.

"I don't feel I deserve this ticket," I said, my voice picking up in volume.

That did not go well with the officer. Can you please step out of the car."

"For what?"

"Please step out of the car now!" as he signaled for his fellow man in blue to come out of the car to assist him with this outspoken upset driver.

I became nervous and very emotional. I was told to put my hands behind my back and cooperate, but I resisted, so one of the officers grabbed my hands and handcuffed me. Only a few blocks away, I was transported to the Santa Fe County Jail, where I was stripped down butt naked and given a mug shot. I tried holding back my tears, but they kept pouring down my cheeks. The borrowed Lincoln Continental was towed to a city lot.

"Why are you treating me this way? I have my rights."

The officer assigned with booking the accused tried to calm me down, but I refused. I called my school administrator friend Ed Nagel, and, on my one entitled phone call, I asked him if he could come up with $150 dollars cash bond, or I would spend a night behind bars. It was Sunday, before ATMs existed, and he said he would have a hard time coming up with enough cash to bail me out on a Sunday. I decided to sleep overnight in the jail and not burden anyone with my first and only night ever in the slammer. I was escorted into a jail cell with a man on the opposite side of my bed wall. He was stone faced, staring at the ceiling, eyes wide open. I asked him what he was in for.

"I robbed a 7-11 store."

From that point on, we didn't say a word to each other throughout my entire stay in that wretched place. How could I be matched with an armed robber when I was charged for resisting arrest and crossing over into an opposite lane? My jail cell was steamy, hot, and oppressive. We were provided a wool blanket to sleep on hard, springless plywood-based single beds. A blinding spotlight was installed on the back wall to keep an eye on us all night. I heard a watchman play his guitar periodically singing slow whispering Spanish songs through the night. At the crack of dawn, I was awakened by the guardsman, who opened our cell and loudly said, "Breakfast, get up!"

I was treated to powdered eggs, a glass of Tang, and toast/jelly in a general, cell contained eating area adjacent to my single cell room. There was a TV on the other side of the general incarcerated area. I moved my hand between the bars to change the channel to watch the scintillating Public Broadcasting Station presentation of the opera *Carmen*. Only about five minutes into viewing this musical drama, however, a stocky tall gentleman switched channels, and I could only look up and smile to concede his dominant wishes.

I was livid, with an outrageous sense of injustice and humiliation about spending a night in jail. I requested a legal pad of paper to write my complaint. A guard was gracious enough to grant my wishes by giving me a pen. I went into a corner of the general cell room and wrote, single spaced on both sides of the legal sized paper, my case for why I was innocent of these charges. By high noon on Monday, I was released and headed to a local office for legal aid on Agua Fria Rd. They recommended a lawyer named Steve Herrera, who might assist me, knowing my funds were extremely limited. I decided to walk about a mile just to embrace the fresh air and collect myself before meeting up with this lawyer.

When I met Steve, he was very gracious and kind, and I didn't waste any time telling him how I was unjustly treated. When I mentioned that I worked with poor kids at the Santa Fe Community School, he immediately stopped me and said, "I know that school. They do good work with the kids there."

"I'm willing to do paper work, even clean around your office until I pay off your service."

"No, that won't be necessary. When your court date comes up to plead not guilty, we'll ask for a postponement and keep doing it until the case is dismissed. In a couple of years, you'll have a clean record again," he said.

I cannot describe how incredibly relieved I was to know this incident would be stricken from my record. But I was not done yet. The citation I received for driving on the wrong side of a historic street needed to be addressed. I walked down to the City of Santa Fe's office and met the mayor himself, Sam Pick, in a very contentious discussion related to correcting East Palace Avenue into a designated two-way street.

"Good to meet you," he asked. "How can I help you?"

"I'm here to address a problem that got me into trouble, spending a night in jail because I adamantly contested getting a ticket driving on the left side of East Palace Avenue, believing it was a one-way street."

"Well, you realize that is a centuries-old historic brick street that is purposely designed to remain that way," the mayor said.

"How am I supposed to know what side of the street to drive on when there's no demarcation?"

"What do you do for a living?" The mayor asked.

"I'm a teacher at the Santa Fe Community School by the airport, teaching children living in poverty. It's a very informal, caring place for kids to learn."

"I think I know that school. It's great that you're working with these kids," he added, not admitting if he really knew the school. "Okay, I'll see what I can do," he said.

As it was his first year as the mayor of Santa Fe, he was out to make an impression. Within three days, Mayor Sam Pick did something that completely stunned me. The streets surrounding Santa Fe Plaza were demarcated into two lanes. The one-way lanes were gone. I had my night in jail and learned the power of how to channel an unjust incident into one that brought vindication. But the story does not end there. Two years passed, and, around 4 a.m. on Cerrillos Rd., a few miles from the Santa Fe Plaza where I was arrested, an officer pulled a couple in a van off to the side and harassed them, eventually sending them both to jail. Little did this officer know that they were local reporters of a very reputable investigative independently owned newspaper, *the Santa Fe Reporter*. They wrote about this officer's police state tactics and how unjustly they were treated. That man in the dark blue uniform was a home-grown Santa Fean named Tom Hill. I wrote a letter to the editor of this newspaper, describing the similar treatment I received, comparing the arrests to how the police use such bullying tactics with people in an oppressive banana republic. Shortly after that story, Officer Tom Hill was demoted to working in the office and off the beat from abusing citizens in Santa Fe. He did, however, bounce back to return to action, eventually finishing up his career as a sergeant with the Santa Fe Police Department, retiring in 1999 and then becoming a commissioned Santa Fe County Deputy Sheriff. He died at 63 years of age in 2014.

The last time I met this abusive officer, he had a cigarette in his hand and was walking with a young attractive woman at an air show at the Santa Fe Airport in the summer of 1982. I walked right past him, and I doubt if he recognized me, but I sure knew who he was. To this day, I'll never forget what he did to me and the lives of others while wearing that badge of power and authority. I came down the mountain that day feeling relaxed and ready to face another demanding week with the kids at my hyperdrive, free-roaming, kid-centered school. But that was not to happen. My one night unjustly spent in jail by an abusive officer changed everything regarding my trust with local Santa Fe police officers—who are allowed to enforce the law like mini-dictators.

Noted legendary outdoor environmental wilderness writer Ed Abbey was a great enemy of terrorism in all its myriad forms. Maybe he would have something to say about such an officer as Tom Hill if he were alive today—with stinging added opinionated thoughts from yours truly.

"Climb the mountains, explore the forests, bag the peaks, breathe deep the lucid air, sit quietly for a while and contemplate the precious stillness, the lovely, mysterious, and awesome space. Keep connected to wilderness and I promise you *this one sweet victory over power hungry, arrogant, rookie cops, arresting innocent citizens just to earn a name as someone to fear.* I promise you this: You will outlive the bastards."

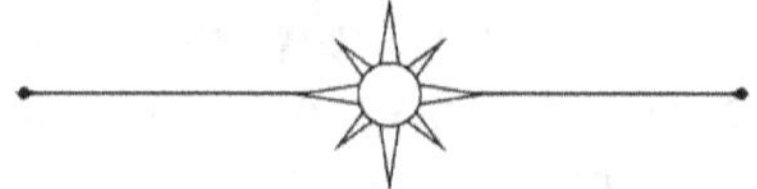

Chapter Twelve
Two Jolts That Changed Everything in January

*There is no path set for this kind of shock, and for the grief that
attends such terrible news.*
– Jacqueline Winspear, *To Die but Once*

Automobiles can provide an outlet for escaping one's immediate accustomed surroundings, expanding into a broader range of personal autonomy while exploring great distances inconceivable by modern foot. They are metaphorical symbols of power, action, freedom, comfort, progress, and individualism. Only one person controls the course of their fate. They are at the same time toxic allusions of decadent waste, chronic suffering, and death. Two individuals, who were deeply attached to my heart and soul, even to this day nearly 40 years later, experienced tragedy while in their cars in the still dormant month of January.

After just auspiciously returning from my festive annual family winter reunion in Chicago, a dear student intern friend of the community school and his slurpy mammoth dog Satchmo were discovered dead as a result of carbon monoxide asphyxiation while sleeping in his car in a closed garage off the coast of northern California. His name was Jonathon Chiensu Kim. He was a loving, princely big brother to many of the children and adults much older than him at the Santa Fe Community School. Jon used to exhibit qualities of exceptional compassionate volunteer leadership, tirelessly involving himself in the realm of unforeseen dangers, inspirational possibilities, searching to find deeper meaning in life by embracing all that the community school had to offer his body, mind, and spirit. He would confidentially donate hundreds of dollars to support the school's experiential travel-studies programs. I and maybe a couple of other staff members knew about his philanthropic generosity, but he insisted that the donor remain anonymous. Jon felt afraid that he would lose his genuine friendships with everyone at the community school if he openly admitted he gave that much money to our poor, struggling school. He added he wanted this contribution to guarantee him a lifetime pass for visiting the community school in between his personal journey to find himself. Oh, I loved his high-pitched, hearty laugh because it seemed to trigger such a wonderful atmosphere of comradery, fun, honesty, and spontaneity. SFCS meant a hell of a lot to Jon. Our school held a special memoriam for him. People who knew and loved Jon openly expressed the joy of being with him and the sorrow of his parting.

Living there for the past eight years, seeing scores of visitors, students, and soul-searching transients come and go, I have never seen people young and old accept someone with such open love and affection as with Jonathon Kim. The earth seemed to be his unspoken companion while searching to find himself. He relished making 30 pound adobe bricks and strenuously digging ditch lines to fulfill a community need. Whether sleeping overnight on the greens of a local golf course, the bed of a trampoline, or on a comfortable leveled plot of short grass prairie ground with his big, always-unleashed companion dog Satchmo, John enjoyed being close to the New Mexican earth. Perhaps, more importantly, he loved being with the kids he so warmly discovered when he arrived at the school as a young, somewhat self-assured idealistic adventurer. His smiles were wider, his voice more thrusting, and his vitality much greater when in the company of children and youth. He did not fret what he was going to wear, what he was going to say, or what he was going to do. He clearly wanted to live simply to avoid surfeiting his way up the ladder of success. But Jon had undisclosed needs and could not openly convey them, except to try to work out his inner secrets through the joys of playing with the children.

Moving up to the spiritually aesthetic land of ancient Taos, New Mexico, after completing his undergraduate degree in physics from Bennington College, Vermont, Jon wanted SFCS nevertheless to be his security blanket. All of us who knew him in between his traveling exploits for a brief time of three and a half years, wanted him to live here—except Jon didn't want to burden us with his inescapable presence. "Three more months living here, and I would be a pain in the ass to everyone," he painfully exclaimed, deeply inhaling his nonfilter Camel stick on an early November day just before heading back to Taos. Before he left, Jon threw a faded, teal T-shirt at me that had a hub cap logo and the words above and below it: "Wheeler Dealers."

As a way of remembering this dear soul-searching friend, I have a t-shirt he gave to me before leaving the Santa Fe Community School. A *wheeler dealer* true to this label, Jon Kim carried unforced natural attributes as a remarkable peacemaker and big brother conciliator. 2021

Less than three months after he declared himself a spiritual hard ass, Jon was gone forever, with his ashes spread around a tree. Somehow, our community school embarked on a different parallel journey, very deeply a part of his, but not totally reflecting his full desire to find his truer self. When Jon, a friend of his, and myself backpacked up to the cradle of Santa Fe Baldy during the monsoon season of 1981, an ominous afternoon thunderstorm from the west was rumbling on top of the summit, just below where we were planning to camp. From about two miles away, we could see the deep black purple clouds hovering over the mountain. I was very concerned about ascending any further and told Jon, "I think we should head back down the mountain, Jon. That storm looks pretty fierce."

"Bullshit," Jon asserted, like he was some defiant human god, knowing something most mortals can't fathom.

Jon, accompanied by his friend, Tom Keller, began to move up toward that ominous lightning tempest. As they hiked a few hundred feet from where I stood deciding what to do, you could see the clouds moving east further into the mountains and away from the cradle of our campsite. I joined them, knowing that Jon was fearless but also smart about his intuitively spot-on forecast. I never forgot that moment. He loved the mountains, the grandeur of open natural spaces, and the steep wilderness ridges where he could play his recorder. Wilderness nature was his best friend, right up there with Satchmo, catching the moments of beauty and wonder, essentially living in the moment with gusto, seldom wallowing in the mire. We would sometimes engage in long-distance running, but Jon would periodically stop to catch his tobacco breath, so we eventually ended that gasping workout routine.

The grubby, teal T-shirt with the hubcap that Jon wore constantly still stays with me on a shelf in a closet at my home in Conifer, Colorado. It was the same shirt he gave me as a farewell gift. Always a man in motion, searching for answers to fill his great mystery journey, he was indeed a generous "wheeler dealer," scheming to bring love, peace, and truthfulness to our community, and he sure won me over.

While overcoming the tragic loss of this kind, wonderful, noble young adventurer on that horrifying, hurtling moment in January 17, 1984, the acting principal of my school, Charlie Bentley, was driving his old reliable VW van along the historically meandering Agua Fria Road, accompanied by his petite dog Heidi in anticipation of picking up his 10-year old daughter and her friend from piano lessons. With an approaching driver facing a blinding sunset, he saw the car crossing over into his lane. He tried to swerve off the road to avoid the vehicle, aiming for a wall. Before hitting that stone partition, the oncoming car hit him, according to a state police report. Critically injured, with a minimum of reflexive communication, Charlie was lucky to receive immediate care because the accident happened across the road from *La Clinica de la Gente.* The medical staff performed a tracheotomy on the spot, assessing the numerous broken bones and brain damage. The dog Heidi was scared yet unscathed from the traumatic jolt.

No one seemed sure how long he would remain in a coma. As I visited him in the hospital for several weeks after, touching his fingers, telling him anecdotes of pleasant, past memorable incidents,

I was informed he was mostly in a state of unconsciousness, and that he had incurred an irreparable brain stem injury. His knees were shattered, and he would probably never be able to stand up again. For a month and a half Charlie was in a coma, but none of us who knew and loved him gave up on him. He eventually worked his way out of the hospital with a rigorous schedule of physical therapy and drugs and was moved to the Santa Fe Community School in a trailer home where he received 24-7 treatment as a live-in there by professional caregivers. But money was becoming scarce to support Charlie so people who lived on the property began caring for Charlie. For one and a half years, I was a caregiver for him. I watched his health plummet, feeling despair and hopelessness witnessing what he had to painfully endure to overcome his pre-crawling, quadriplegic condition. I was never really sure how Charlie felt about me, or if what I was doing made sense at all to ease his pain. My emotions became increasingly subdued, numb, almost forgotten, shaken by the slow dying suffering of a dear friend.

A distinguished friend of Charlie and the community school, Baba Ram Dass (born Richard Alpert) came by one day to sit down outside in front of one of the community's trailers and look him in the eye to ask him, "Hi, Charlie, this is Ram Dass, your friend. How are you doing?"

Charlie looked at him and then looked away. He could only whisper faint words, which were very difficult to hear. So, Ram Dass asked him to nod his head for answers.

The prominent spiritual teacher and author of *Be Here Now* asked him point blank, "Charlie, do you want to live?"

Charlie fussed a little bit, barely moving around in his wheel chair. Finally, he shook his head in the negative. Ed Nagel, a dear friend of Charlie and long-time teacher/administrator of the school, and I were stunned.

"Looks like he doesn't want to live anymore," Ram said, softly and sadly.

Three years after this meeting with all the intensive alternative and conventional therapies, seizures (both grand and small), anti-convulsant drugs, painkillers, so much loving care, and a dispiriting process of removing his most cherished value, freedom, Charlie Bentley died at the age of 47 on September 8, 1987, at a nursing home in Santa Fe, New Mexico. The very next day, the elderly school's mascot Shetland pony, Smokey, loved by all, was found dead at 37 years old in her corral. Charlie and Smokey were trusting kinship beings of love and gentleness. He cared for Smokey for many years, and they grew to appreciate each other's friendship. May their bonding spiritual journey be forever soaring and serene.

For 15 years, Charlie loved driving the school kids annually to a remote camping location off a bumpy US forest logging road close to the Santa Clara Pueblo Reservation, leading to the familiar hidden terrain of Garcia Canyon. He worked during the day as a principal/teacher, receiving just a pittance of pay, and he moonlighted at night as a plumber. These five-day overnight campouts really helped him relax and just be still in a place where he found much peace and tranquility, sitting around the campfire, playing his guitar while singing his folksy tunes, watching over the playful activities of the children in an amazing remote canyon hideout with commanding ancient overlooks. It was there in early October of 1987 that Charlie's ashes were prayerfully scattered in a solemn ceremony held by close friends and family.

Just as he was a "catcher in the rye" for so many children and adults, scores of people in the community-at-large were Charlie's "catcher in the rye" during his time of interminable suffering. That painstaking period in our lives touched us deeply—even to this day. His wife Merle and their children suffered dearly over the years, losing a husband, dear father, and a truly great exemplary teacher. As I write this memorial tribute to him, I notice it's January 17, 2021, exactly 38 years since his fatal car crash. Was I subconsciously cognizant about this day, or was there some other mystical force guiding me to write about him?

Both tragic losses of these two close friends from the Land of Enchantment have brought greater humility in my life, causing me to endeavor to comprehend the mystery of the world we live and die in. I'm so deeply grateful to have known them, and it's so painful to still feel their devastating loss.

Chapter Thirteen
Deserving a Red Badge for Boldness

*We are nature. We are nature seeing nature. The red-winged
blackbird flies in us.*
– Susan Griffin

There is a bird the size of a robin able to stand up to a hawk, eagle, and turkey vulture and chase them boldly away from their territory. That same bird could literally wreak havoc upon a runner, biker, or hiker. I can testify to a few relentless territorial standoffs.

Heading to the barbershop to receive a trim on my long, curly, unruly hair, a male red-winged blackbird began diving around my scalp while I peddled in panic for safety. He tried to pull hair out of my head, perhaps to use it to build a nest to impress his mate. I sped away from this attacker luckily with most of my hair intact. This incident served as a worthy reminder to not take Alfred Hitchcock's movie *the Birds* lightly.

On another instance, while running during evening twilight, a highly vocal blackbird with a stunning bold red patch on his shoulders began to swoop directly over my head, skimming my back as I was accelerating away from this territorial standoff. I ran a mile up the road and returned the same way only to see that same aggressive bird completely still on a branch hanging over the road. As the sun disappeared, this agitator in winged clothing decided to call it a day for dive-bombing intruders. Of all the wildlife present at Spring Valley Nature Center where I worked for close to 30 years only the red winged blackbird has been responsible for closing trails due to aggressive territorial attacks on innocent passing hikers and joggers.

Perhaps the greatest lesson I have ever learned from the red-winged blackbird is never ride no-handed while peddling along a marsh. At the cocky age of 43 years on Bull Valley Road in McHenry County, I was at the top of my cycling game on an early summer Century Run challenge, accelerating down a moderate slope with my hands to my side, when a female red-winged blackbird leaped out of a cattail bed in front of my bike and spooked me. Apparently, two male red-winged blackbirds were agitating the female on the side of the road, and she took off to escape from these aggressive pursuers. They followed her relentlessly while I was caught in the middle of this high-speed mating chase, trying to avoid slamming into the female, but she hit my front wheel, got caught in the spokes, and unfortunately was instantly killed. I lost control of the bike, flipped over the handlebars, and landed on the hard pavement, with arms extended. Fortunately, I was wearing a helmet.

I literally could not feel the severe throbbing pain since my adrenalin from all the pumping on the peddle was numbing the inevitable outcome of this moment. I couldn't find anyone on the road for help but saw a distant tractor tilling in a cornfield and walked about a quarter of a mile to meet up with the farmer. He shut off his old puttering engine and waited for me to speak.

"I hurt myself in a bike accident. Do you happen to have any ice packs for my wrists?"

"No, but my sister down the road on her farm might have some."

We hopped in his car and drove a couple miles down the unpaved country road to his sister's farmhouse, where she warmly assisted me with a bag of ice. I placed it on my wrists and asked to go back to the road where my bicycle was hidden in the cattail marsh. I asked this kind farmer to pick up my bike and place it on the side of the road for the flag vehicles monitoring the bikers to spot. When the farmer left, I was feeling a heavy, settling, throbbing pain from both of my wrists, as if a vice was pressing against my bones. A sponsored flagged vehicle picked me up after a short 10-minute wait and drove me back to my car.

"You sure you don't want me to take you to the Woodstock Hospital?" he asked.

"No, I'll be alright. Thanks for your help."

I drove home about 40 miles from Woodstock to Schaumburg, heading straight to Northwest Community Healthcare immediate care, believing I might have severely sprained my wrists. I received X-rays on them, with the orthopedist coming out to report, "Yep, you broke both of them."

No surgery was required. The doctor performed another effective treatment to ease the excruciating pain. He made me laugh just by being who he was. And it worked miraculously. Noted journalist and expert Norman Cousins knew what he was writing about when considering laughter as an effective upbeat approach for good healthy pain relief medicine. Both my wrists were realigned in his office and placed in casts, one up to my elbow, and the other halfway up from my elbow. The right one was broken in four places, the left in two places, and I was out for six weeks. No surgery was necessary. I drove to my fiancée's home, where I decided to chuck my painkillers, choosing to medicinally drink down a six pack of Corona and call it a night. The first two weeks were agonizing. Every little thing I did brought tears to my eyes. I still went to work two days after the injury, doing very little except to present interpretive nature programs, where I would be just talking and nothing else. I bombarded myself with large doses of vitamin E and had the casts removed in just four and a half weeks. After six weeks, I performed a two-night solo backpack trip in the high country of the Pecos Wilderness, New Mexico. Within six months, I was fully recovered, playing full court basketball twice a week with guys two decades younger than me until I was 68 years old. I'm happy to say I'm a persistent septuagenarian, still jamming away with my wrists on my percussion instruments, feeling no pain.

I never rode no-handed again on my bike, thanks to the red wings. But I must say those birds do have a sense of humor. While walking on an overlook deck during a nature walk with the children to observe the activity in the pond, I noticed something strange happening on a Canada goose. A bold, male red-winged blackbird was hitching a ride on the back of this honker, either for touring amusement or friendly bonding. All of us started laughing at this unprecedented scene, seeing this bold bird with red-winged badges of courage. It felt comforting discovering the lighter side of this tenacious intimidating bird.

Chapter Fourteen
The Two Lindas and I Face Steep Grades of Peril

Destiny is not fate, it's navigation.
– Richie Norton

In Chippewa traditional stories, there is a cruel, merciless winter spirit named *Gabibonike* that would seek to make life discomforting, even lethal, if given the chance. Many of the plants and animals were frozen by the relentless biting winds, uninviting frozen ground, and the deep sub-zero legendary spell of *Gabibonike*. Little did I know that two different Lindas would accompany me into the unforgiving world of *Gabibonike*.

On a cold, icy, gloomy mid-morning in February 2002, while backing out of my friend Linda's home in Algonquin, Illinois, I noticed the road was exceptionally tricky, but I still attempted to drive down a steep 9 percent grade sheet of ice. In my reliable, lightweight mini-pickup truck, I assumed there would not be much of a problem steering my way down to safety. I grossly miscalculated. As I began to descend, Linda appeared glued to her cell phone next to me, not paying attention to an imminent collision. I saw an elderly couple sitting in their car parked on the opposite side of the road about 300 feet from the initial point of view.

"Why are these people in their car not moving? My goodness, I'm about to collide head on with them. I can't use my brakes. Shit!"

Linda finally looked up as we both saw our lives slipping away in a critical head on car wreck. I tried using the steering wheel to stay on my side of the road, but nothing was working. We were sliding on a pure sheet of ice, with my foot off the gas pedal, lightly applying the brakes, about to meet the fate of *Gabibonike*. Coasting to a stop, we were parallel, looking directly across into the car and saw the couple appearing quiet, indifferent, and completely relaxed about where they were situated. After taking a few deep breaths of relief, I rolled down my window and said, "Are you two okay? Why are you still in your car not moving on this treacherous road?"

"Oh, we're just waiting for some help to come. Our engine died. We're trying to stay out of the wind," the senior gentleman ploddingly answered.

"I don't think you're in a safe place. Somebody could easily ram into you like us. You would be better off knocking on someone's door and asking to stay there till your help comes."

They agreed, putting their flasher lights on and walking ever so slowly to a neighbor's house until a towing service arrived. We all escaped injury, with Linda and I totally frazzled, and the ageing couple completely mellow. Maybe getting older for that meek duo meant that they had lived a good life and the grey winds of winter did not faze them that much anymore. It was an intergenerational reality hit that made me so grateful I was spared from a mortal catastrophic collision.

The other ominous experience I had with another Linda turned out to be the most chilling drive ever in more than one way—but quite entertaining for *Gabibonike*. I drove a 26 passenger mini-bus with the Schaumburg Park district for field trips. In mid-December 2002, my program coordinator, Linda, and I managed a 230-mile round trip for one day in Jo Daviess County to a sweet little historical town called Galena, Illinois, commonly referred to as *the city that time forgot*. The charming baseball classic *Field of Dreams* was filmed there. It was the holiday shopping season, and there were two park district buses bringing suburban shoppers to Galena, including a 50-passenger bus and my little bus I was always assigned to drive, affectionately named Gus.

Located in the unglaciated corner of Northwest Illinois, the spectacular scenic region has rolling hills, with the highest elevation in the state. It's a beautiful side of Illinois, resembling the serenity of a New England landscape. A wonderful holiday trip was anticipated. While people were busy shopping, I was trying to keep the bus warm and ready for deep cold trouble and headed to a local gas station on the edge of town, where I began to pump diesel fuel into the bus, only to have it freeze up, constantly foaming, causing me great agitation while filling up the tank. The days were short, and night entered with a deep bitterness, keeping me privately cursing as I held the metal pump bare handed through strong frigid gusts, dropping the wind chill temp to well below zero.

When I picked up the cheerfully festive shoppers, the engine shut off, but I didn't think there would be a problem. I assumed the engine was cold and just needed to be warmed up. The other bus had a full load, so I brought the remaining 13 passengers back with their shopping gifts. I forewarned my group to make sure their safety belts were fastened. As we made our way in the dark, through high blustery winds into the highest elevation in Jo Daviess County and perhaps the entire state, my living nightmare unfolded. Traveling down a steep, 7 percent grade, the check engine light went on, and my headlights began to dim and flicker, dim and flicker. Then complete darkness enveloped the bus.

The alternator had caused a complete electrical shutdown. I had no power brakes on an icy road heading down a steep grade for two miles. We had to hope that, when we arrived at an intersection with signal lights, the color would be green to go. Gus was speeding up while all I could do was keep my hands firmly on the wheel and try to keep a straight direction, coasting to wherever that would take us. People were holding hands in their seats while Linda was assuring everyone that we would get through this.

It was deathly quiet.

I tried to appear calm on the outside, but inside my nerves were rattling. Off in the distance, I could see commercial lights in a shopping center and signal lights just beyond there. Having no electrical system to smooth this treacherous ride, I turned the steering wheel with all my might and coasted into the parking lot of a mini-shopping center. Having no brakes to stop, I circled around the large open asphalt parking lot to slow down and eventually coasted off to the far side, pulling my emergency brakes up to come to an abrupt stop.

People inside the bus applauded. I was incredibly relieved. As the bus quickly cooled down from the outside frigid air, the passengers left Gus and headed into a food chain store to keep warm while Linda called the Park District about coordinating a way for the group to come home. It was Saturday night, around 8:30 p.m., and the park district supervisor Vince Kennedy told Linda to get everyone home, no matter what the cost for transportation would be. He added that mechanics would come out there to work on the bus the next day to replace the alternator and drive Gus back home. Linda and I began to search in the directory for any service that could take a group of 13 passengers back over a hundred miles. We couldn't find any conventional transportation service to meet our specific needs.

Finally, a fellow at the store suggested a funeral service. As the night was getting late and the shoppers were getting extremely tired, Linda and I decided to call that number. Linda talked to the owner and told him that we had 13 passengers stranded, needing a ride back to a Chicago suburb. He laughed about the offer and said, "Sure, no problem."

When he pulled into the well-lit parking lot, we could see he was driving a black hearse limousine. We all began laughing hysterically and ironically jammed ourselves into a car designed to honor the deceased. The driver was also a high school wrestling coach, and he spent a good portion of time talking about his high school team, especially his son's winning record on the mat. It felt so incredibly liberating and bizarre to be sitting in this warm limo, tightly boxed in with living people, laughing and relieved that we would soon be home unscathed thanks to the owner of a hearse company in the remote, rural, wind-driven rolling hills of Jo Daviess County.

Two Linda(s) partaking in life-threatening episodes on the road, jolting moments to make you grateful to be alive and still intact. It's enough to make *Gabibonike* sweat with disgust.

Chapter Fifteen
Humbling Lessons from *Gitchi Gami*

*When you're young you think that you're going to sail into a lovely
lake of quietude and peace. This is profoundly untrue.*
– Doris Lessing

It was the warmest day of the year in early October 2000 in the
quaint New England-like town of Bayfield, Wisconsin, off the
frigid shores of Lake Superior—or *Gitchi Gami*, an Ojibwe word
for "big sea." The mineral-rich shores of this amazing lake are rocky,
rugged, aesthetic, and mesmerizing. Craggy cliffs abound, towering
over timeworn smoothly pebbled water edges. The water was so
crystal clear that the pebbles could be seen from great depths. In
numerous areas, like our destination, the water immediately rose in
depth just a few feet from shore.

The winds were fierce, well over 25 miles per hour, and my
weekend outdoor adventure group was about to embark on a risky
kayaking adventure across the open Lake Superior waters to Oak
Island and back, close to the mainland. Waves were picking up at
about three to four feet. I was about to challenge myself in a slender
traditional 19-foot Inuit kayak, with no foot pedals to maintain
balance in rough waters. Having a wet suit was essential, with the
water temperatures around 48 degrees. Our rugged guide Ken
Peterson knew I had no experience navigating such a kayak, and yet
he gave me an optimistic false sense of security by saying I could *do
it. Do it* meaning I could paddle in these treacherous, rough wave-
infested waters, keeping up with the rest of the six expert maritime
adventurers and not worry about capsizing.

Pushing myself into these perpetual high waters under tempestuous
jolts with such a narrow window of error in this slender wooden
carved boat was a major forewarning that crossing over the bay toward

Oak Island would be gripping, even with the best eyesight. I sat in the middle of a totally open, primitive kayak and was hard paddling to the swirling winds of fate. I was only about 20 feet from the shore at about 10 feet in depth when strong north winds upended the kayak, flooding chilly waters instantly into the entire boat, flipping it over. I quickly swam out from under and headed to shore, but my eyeglasses sank straight to the bottom. I was completely humiliated. Meanwhile, the rest of the group began paddling with their state-of-the-art sea kayaks, disappearing off in the distance in the high undulating open waters of *Gitchi Gami.* Fortunately, Ken stayed back to make sure I could catch up with them in a similar sea kayak.

Distinctly near-sighted, with a 20/200 vision in my right eye and a 20/120 vision in my left, I could barely see the group about 200 yards away from me. And when huge unrelenting waves would pass by, I couldn't see where the paddlers were heading; they were totally removed from my vision. But I kept bearing down hard, paddling into these ominous, rhythmic waves till I caught up with them. A couple of these crazy human otters rolled over a few times in their kayaks with zest and laughter as I arrived among them. That totally freaked me out, knowing how hard a time I would have if I attempted to roll over in these forceful winds.

When we reached the island, I could only look out and wonder how I would ever enjoy, let alone endure, this weekend kayak adventure in such treacherous waters without my specs. On the backside of Oak Island, the winds were still, with whispering sea caves, and I gained confidence when we rounded the point and faced the gusty blast. All I could think while paddling back was stay focused, keep your eyes toward the mainland, paddle hard into the unforgiving waves, and stay calm and strong in body, mind, and spirit. Normally, paddling to and from Oak Island is relatively short and sweet when the winds are calm. Not today. The force of the waves underneath my kayak felt as if a phantom monster was rocking me out of balance. Eventually, however, we all made it safely and joyfully—maybe in my case gratefully—back to the mainland. I told Ken I wasn't sure if I could continue with this weekend adventure, having my vision greatly compromised.

He said, "Don't worry. We'll find your glasses."

I said, "Anyone who finds them will be treated to their favorite six pack."

I was terribly upset, having traveled 440 miles one way, spending several hundred dollars on a short getaway trip to know that, for the rest of the trip and the drive home, visually impaired, I would be extremely uncomfortable and worried.

That night, on the peninsula edge of the Red Cliff campground, I pitched my tent with the window totally unzipped, facing north straight across the calming *Gitchi Gami*. The stars were out; the sky was dark, with no moon, and the northern lights were shimmering a waving sheet of illuminating white. To me, it was a grand, glowing blur. Yet I was so disheartened not to see this vivid magnificent grandeur to soften my dreams. When I woke up around dawn, I came out of my tent, viewing the great Lake Superior as calm as glass. I sat on the shore where the Inuit kayak capsized, causing my specs to sink to the bottom. I headed to a picnic table by my tent and was feeling depressed about facing this day. My head laid dejectedly over my folded arms on the table, and I began to brood with my eyes closed. I started to feel drops of cool water over my shoulders and head, then a wet hand over my neck. When I leaned up to see who this intruder into my personal space was, I saw Ken had placed my glasses on the table beside me and said words that will jubilantly live forever in my memory:

"Sierra Nevada Pale Ale, six pack."

Ken was still in his wet suit and had found my glasses about 10 feet below the surface. The lake was as tranquil and clear as glass. The sun was sparkling through these waters, and he could see my metal rimmed specs shining from the stretched beams in the water. I was ecstatic, near tears. I promised to order the beer for pick-up through his local liquor store in Merrimac, Wisconsin. On that beautiful calm day, we devoted a full day to kayaking in and around the breathtaking ghostly cavernous calls of the whispering sea caves off Meyer's Beach near the Apostle Islands, and we were magically entertained by a kaleidoscope of migratory monarchs landing on our boat and our arms, shoulders, and hands. Carved out by the winds, icy conditions, and pounding of the waves, the caves invite a mumbling sound, as if the ancestors were conversing in a cryptic language that only they can comprehend. I was grateful to see the rich detail of these magnificent endangered butterflies thanks to Ken rescuing me from a potentially miserable weekend. *Gitchi Gami* has some of the most rugged landscapes on this Pale Blue Dot. To visit and take time to meditate motionless in our kayaks along her shores was indeed a sacred gift. Very few can resist the mysterious, powerful energy that radiates there. It demands respect and awareness to her temperamental ways of humbling those who dare to enter her great domain.

Chapter Sixteen
Breaking away from Bad Medicine

There is no such thing as an extraordinary coincidence. There is
only destiny.
– Robin Hobb

On a Friday morning in late May 2014, I set out to perform an earth-friendly program called *Journey from the Heart,* lugging all the production equipment, props, and costumes from my condo unit into an elevator, out of the lobby where my mini-pickup truck was parked in the back-loading entranceway. While setting up at the school, I noticed my medicine bag was missing. Where could I have placed it? I had to forfeit using it for my storytelling performance and became very preoccupied during the course of my show about the whereabouts of this important missing part of my act and life. When arriving back at my condo complex, I retraced my route. Could it have fallen through the crack by the elevator door, trapped at the bottom of the basement floor? Or maybe outside in the back entrance loading area? As a long-standing prayerful tool of honor, worn by many indigenous people of the Americas, medicine bags carry intimate sacred objects that symbolize personal well-being and tribal identity.

I searched extensively with no results. All my little personal kinship connections, like a 10,000-year-old wolf tooth, a beaver incisor, a kernel of corn, a piece of pipestone, a deer tine, and a marble of earth were in that medicine bag, along with a bead slipped in the leather necklace strand identifying my acceptance into the *Northern Branch of the Red Spotted Bead People (Lakota).*

A few days passed, and I was planting a mix of annual flowers in a raised bed on the back entrance to the condo complex where I lived

67

when a young man approached me and said, "Hey, can I help you plant. I love planting flowers."

"Sure, I'll get an extra trowel, and you can have at it."

His name was Jason, and he was to candidly share his life with me in that short period of time we planted these annuals. There is something about expressing your truer self when spring is awakening while planting flowers. He was the son of a neighbor who helped me relocate native plants and soil to another site on the condo property as a result of the infamous emerald ash borer killing off the green ash trees.

"I like planting. Makes me feel good." Jason said.

"So what do you?"

"I deliver pizzas."

"I assume that's not where you want to be for the rest of your life."

"No, I want to be a meth crystal chemist like Walter White in *Breaking Bad*."

"I never watched that program, but it doesn't seem to be my kind of entertainment. Kind of dark."

"Not at all. It's really a very cool program. You should check it out. So what do you do?" Jason asked.

"As you can see, I'm a gardener/native landscaper for the condominium. I work as a habitat restorationist-naturalist at a local nature center and also do Native American storytelling programs."

"Super cool. I found a medicine bag about a week ago in the building and gave it to my mom who's part Cherokee."

"Where did you find it?" I asked, as if divine intervention had struck me in the heart.

"Upstairs on the fourth floor by the elevator."

I stood up and explained to Jason that it was probably my medicine bag he found, and that I hoped he could return it back to me.

He said, "Okay, my mom is at a Ravinia concert right now, but I'll give her a call." Jason didn't have the keys to get into his mom's house, but she explained the bedroom window was open, and he could enter there. We drove to her home. The medicine bag was on her dresser. Jason returned the bag to me intact, and I gave him 20 dollars for his effort. I was so grateful.

There were times I would play my Native American flute in the stairwell, which had an amazing beautiful resonance echoing down the stairs. Jason and his girlfriend would occasionally sit on the stairs to hear me playing, listening to my soothing spontaneous melodies. We became friends. But Jason was an addict who fell into hard straits because of his fascination with meth crystals. Lacking ambition to pursue a life without chemical dependency was extremely difficult for him. His parents got fed up with his inability to confront his addiction and kicked him out of the house as an act of tough love. I received a call shortly after this eviction from him.

"Hi, Dennis, how are you?"

"Fine. How's it going?"

"I just got kicked out of the house. I've got to find a place to live for the next two weeks. Can I stay with you?"

"I don't think that's going to work out. My lady friend partner would probably not go for it." Having someone live with me with serious drug issues would be catastrophic. I'd be constantly worried whether any of my personal belongings would be sold off for meth crystals. Shortly after that conversation, within a few days, Jason died of an overdose. I'm not sure what the drug was, but I would guess the same drug glorified in *Breaking Bad.* People who knew Jason thought he was a really nice fellow. I thought so too, but his clinging on to demented TV heroes who dwell on the dark side of living cut his life short.

And yet he found my medicine bag. A couple weeks after Jason died, I had another gig at a KinderCare school in Palatine. I'm always invited there every year to perform my *Journey from the Heart* storytelling program. The teacher who usually has me come wasn't present. She had a substitute, and his first name was <u>Jason</u>. I had a hard time focusing on that program. I felt a great ominous spirit had come to haunt me because I didn't allow the deceased Jason to live with me. But maybe this was the *great mystery* helping me remember the gift he gave, finding my medicine bag. I eventually caught myself realizing the truer meaning of my time crossing paths with Jason. I now carry his spirit in that medicine bag forever in my journey.

The medicine bag honors not only what is in the bag but the bag itself. It is placed over the heart to honor balance and harmony in all of my relations. Traditionally worn under the shirt by indigenous peoples, I wear it openly over my decorative geometric native designed ribbon shirt during my storytelling programs to teach others on the personal meaning of the medicine bag. *2021*

Chapter Seventeen
Letting Go with the Help of Grandmother Earth

We must be willing to let go of the life we've planned, so as to have the life that is waiting for us.
– Joseph Campbell

A second marriage gone awry. Divorce was imminent. Samantha (pseudonym) had left me after five years ring-bonded together. I needed to let go and move on, not ask how could this happen. I needed to know where I go from here. It was time to return to where it all began. The Creator has given me guidance for my heart to release sadness, anger, frustration, and confusion to help me heal my wounded spirit. I trusted that I needed to follow this great unknown path. As I approached the sacred site of our vow, I began to notice on the steep, slimy slippery stairs of Trout Park in Elgin, Illinois, bright crimson maple leaves embedded on the steps. I could not hold my emotions back and began to release my sadness. It was as if that deep red color drew allusions of the emotional blood sacrificed in so many ways to keep our family and relationship going. I felt transported into a time and space beyond my own routine life, where incredible connections to my past and present merged together, and I felt so centered being there. I sage-smudged the area where the creek splits, moving in a circle to honor the seven directions. Then I kneeled down with a little wooden chest kept for many years to release a surge of grateful wishes for Samantha and I. It was a total rush of good positive wishes that were flowing like the little autumnal creek. Next, I opened the wooden box and saw the crimson sugar maple leaf I'd kept since we made our vows there. It was curled at two of the tips. I began to cry deeply, believing those two curls represented Samantha and I.

As I stood by the quiet streamlet, I saw a narrow veinous flow in the water that seemed to welcome the leaf. I placed it gently there, and the leaf took off with such a guiding force as if to declare it was time to move on and let go. I cried with joy and affirmation. When I looked in the wooden box, I saw two little pieces of leaf debris, which made me wonder whether I should release them too. I noticed they were pointing north and south in the box, which is the direction for following the Red Road, a guiding heartfelt path toward balance and harmony with everything.

After holding on to them for a brief moment, I decided to drop these two pieces of "us" in a thin flowing current, whereupon they seemed to touch each other gently off and on, disappearing down the creek. What a glorious purifying mystical moment.

With the smudge stick burning on an exposed tree root, I pressed the stick into the little wooden box to put out the smoke. The ashes were contained in the chest. I did another seven directions ceremonies with the ashes as an offering, and, with the remaining ashes, I said a prayer for Samantha and I, casting them off above the creek into the mild cool air. When that was complete, I dipped in the chilly creek with one hand and had a sip of water to taste the source of our sacred spot for the last time.

A huge weight seemed to have been lifted, and I drove to Glacial Park in McHenry County on a brisk, windy, grey overcast early November afternoon in 2009 to hike as a greatly healed transformed person in body, mind, and spirit. I started on the Coyote loop (totem animal for me) and ended my trail hike on the Deerpath trail (another totem animal for me). While at the base of a large, glacially tilled moraine, I looked up and saw two red-tailed hawks locking talons and catching the blustery winds of that day. Samantha was the Skyhawk up there, and I was her spiritual kin. We were freed up from our human bodies, playing with the sky together. Along my hike, I saw a wigwam structure from atop the hill and walked down toward it, watching a great blue heron walk ever so delicately on a fallen tree over the distant creek. It was heading toward the wigwam and then flew off down the Nippersink Creek.

I walked around a swale close to the creek and entered the wigwam, sitting there and viewing both openings. I loved the serene autumnal sheltered coolness of the moment. As I left the wigwam, I saw a pile of beaver-gnawed wood chips and picked up a couple of pieces to remember this day of letting go and moving on. Amazingly, the chips looked like a ruffled fragment of a bird of prey's wing—a hawk or perhaps an eagle. I have them in place in my prayer shrine in the living room.

When one puts heartfelt intentions of letting go with *wakan tanka* (Lakota for "great mystery"), the results are always humbling and amazingly beautiful. No need to dwell in the loss. I can only move on with unfolding a molting change for the better, bonding with all the bountiful cyclical dimensions of nature as my ultimate guide and healer.

Part II
Synchronicities

(Serendipitous encounters that have remarkably placed me in the
right place at the right time, catalyzing me toward the direction of
my destiny.)

Chapter Eighteen
The Grand Bliss of Soul Sacrifice

Only in spontaneity can we be who we truly are.
– John McLaughlin

One early, mid-summer Friday morning in 1975, on my day off from teaching at the Santa Fe Community School, I drove down to my friend Jerry Fisher's South Valley home in Albuquerque with a set of congas in my trunk. Outside a borrowed neighbor's powder blue 1969 Lincoln Continental, I took out of the trunk two mahogany buffed drums and began to jam away loudly, waiting for Jerry to come out. Rushing out of his house with no shirt, no socks, and just pants, he was laughing hysterically. We, along with another close friend, Jonathon Schwaber, who brought some Jack Daniels to share, spent the day wandering around the South Valley by the Rio Grande and decided to eventually check out a concert at the University of New Mexico's outdoor main center. The winds were extremely gusty, so strong that the free outdoor concert was cancelled. On the barren stage were sound systems shut down, huge speakers, and no performers. We looked around and saw students wandering around aimlessly, wondering what to do next on a night that seemed to be slipping away fast.

Then an idea dawned on Jerry. "Hey, Denny, why don't you get out your two congas in the trunk and start jamming up there on the stage."

"Fantastic!" I shouted with glee.

As I walked back to my car, I could hear the classic conga songs drumming in my head. I lifted the trunk and carried both drums up to the stage, stabilizing the legs from the frequent windy gusts. I looked at countless pedestrians scattered throughout the Smith UNM Plaza and felt this was a perfect time to play joyfully hard. The inward sounds of Carlos Santana were calling me to drum with tremendous fervor. The mind-blowing band proved how fast, how incredibly forceful, and how gloriously collaborative they could project collective joy through sensuous ethereal songs and soulful rhythm. The very first time I saw them was in one of the most memorable performances filmed in the 1969 documentary *Woodstock*. Under bleak, humid skies set in an overpopulated mud bowl of chanting, celebrating, primal shirtless sliders, you could hear the captivating African-Latino rock beat that changed my life forever: *Soul Sacrifice*.

My moment had arrived. I was determined to drum the hell out of the skins for as long as I could with my body, mind, and spirit. The rhythm was rising up in my soul. I tried to play the song exactly as recorded, except without back-up musicians. The crowd began to listen, some began to dance, and others assembled inside the Science Department to gather chairs to bring outside. They were not intending to sit as a sedentary audience, listening to my improvisational performance, but were setting the chairs in a row opposite of each other to play musical chairs. I caught their game plan and would stop periodically during the song to play along. Scores of chairs were set up, and nobody had any idea this blissful gathering would spontaneously explode with such communal conviviality. So much magic in the air, and I was there to replace the band that cancelled to initiate and orchestrate this unplanned once-in-a-lifetime happening. Spanish, Portuguese, and Filipino folklore have a word for what was unfolding. The word *duende* is traditionally applied in flamenco music or other art forms to refer to the mystical or powerful force given off by a performer to draw in the audience.

Jerry and Jon could only stand there in awe as I played for about 45 minutes facing a mighty wind that only ignited a soulful fire spreading throughout this campus plaza. When I was completely exhausted, I demonstrably postured myself like Richard Nixon, saluting to the crowd with arms outstretched and two fingers on each hand, making the V sign, yelling out in a classic tricky Dick Nixon voice, "Thank you, and I am not a crook!" The crowd of mostly young college students ate it up and wanted me to keep going. But my hands were shaking. I was completely dehydrated, barely able to get off the stage on my own. I have played on several global percussion instruments with several bands for hundreds of gigs over four decades, enough to make Grateful Dead drummer Mickey Hart wink with waggish approval, but I've never since had such a jubilant, natural uninhibited feeling of giving all I had in my musical drive to bring people together, albeit short-lived.

Chapter Nineteen
A UFO Takes Us for a Ride

I don't laugh at people any more when they say they've seen UFOs.
I've seen one myself.
– US President Jimmy Carter

In 1977, I saw a movie that brought enchantment and wonder to the dark skies: *Close Encounters of the Third Kind*. Directed by Steven Spielberg, it is a wondrous cinematic science fiction adventure about a group of people who attempt to contact alien intelligence. The lead character, Roy Neary, witnesses an unidentified flying object and even has a "sunburn" from its bright lights to prove it. Roy refuses to accept an explanation for what he saw and is prepared to give up his family and home to pursue the truth about his brush with a UFO. As a highly imaginative child back in the 1950s, movies seemed to create a very ominous impression of alien beings either out to get us, like *Invasion of the Body Snatchers, The Thing, War of the Worlds, and It Came from Outer Space*, or to tell us earthlings that we must live peacefully or be destroyed as a danger to other distant planets beyond our solar system, as in *The Day the Earth Stood Still*. But, after seeing *Close Encounters*, a more benevolent portrayal of outer space beings, I began to open my mind up to the possibility of actually experiencing a close encounter of the third kind, an actual sighting of alien visitors, preferably a good-natured meeting.

Star Wars was catching the grand imagination of American viewers, but I slept through the Jedi battle scenes. I couldn't suspend my intelligence about the fact there is no sound in outer space. I appreciate movies like *Close Encounters*, which draw a deeper possibility of connecting with highly intelligent, gentle, extra-terrestrials, and it certainly caught my imagination about embracing the stars and beyond.

A year after I saw that movie, my wish arrived. In the summer of 1978, I was hanging out with four young teen students at twilight by an open back door of the Santa Fe Community School. As a teacher, I just wanted to check in with these kids and enjoy the Friday night with them, shooting the breeze. Brothers Leon, Daniel, and Patrick Martinez and their cousin Tio Montoya were all relaxing in the mellow, fading New Mexico sunset, facing us, when I spotted a bright, metallic green, disc-shaped object about seven feet in width by four feet in height hovering over a willow tree at a local golf course about three blocks away. I asked the kids if they could see this sighting, and they all saw this highly unusual, suspended object. As hard as we tried, none of us could identify it, so, on a pay phone in the school, I called the Santa Fe Airport's control tower only four miles from where we were.

"Hi, we're noticing a strange glowing green disc-shaped object suspended above a willow tree down Airport Road and Agua Fria. Can you see it?" I said.

"Yes, we can see it," said the air traffic controller.

"What is it?" I asked, as the kids started to get nervously loud and restless. "Quiet, I'm trying to listen!"

"We don't know."

That was all I needed to hear. I immediately said thank you and *adios* to the air traffic controller. When I hung up, the boys were still and quiet, waiting to know what had transpired. I said we needed to drive to this UFO sighting and check it out. All of us were shaking with excitement and joyful curiosity.

We weren't afraid.

Driving up in my 1969 Ford Falcon to the willow tree, we could see the object about 60 feet above us. All the windows were open as we watched this mysterious sighting completely motionless. And then, as if Steven Spielberg was directing the next scene, it began to move onto Airport Road, slowly traveling east, away from the fading sunlight toward the Sangre de Cristo Mountains. We tailed behind this UFO and were totally hooked with consternation and delirious anticipation. As we crossed over Cerrillos Road, which is the main highway from Albuquerque to Santa Fe, sunset was long gone, and dark skies prominent, we could see stars popping up over the mountains. The night was young, and we were in the epicenter of a grand enchanting moment. This green, now-illuminated small spacecraft seemed to want us to follow it, moving slow about 50 feet above us, as if to guide us to some kind of unforgettable climax. Could there be an extra-terrestrial being navigating the craft inside? Driving along Rodeo Road in pitch dark sky conditions, the UFO stopped.

We were completely rowdy as I whispered emphatically for everyone to be quiet. We looked up, wondering what would come next. Then something that will be embedded in our minds forever happened. As if this glowing disc wanted us to never forget what we were about to see, we witnessed the craft accelerate in complete silence at an incredible warp speed, heading northeast into the Sangre de Cristo mountains. It was a close encounter of the second kind (third kind would have meant actual physical contact with the extra-terrestrials).

I believe there was intelligence navigating that UFO, though we were not sure if some being was inside the craft or not. We exploded with verbal affirmations.

"Did you see that?" I declared.

"Holy shit, yes," Leon shouted.

"I'm never going to forget this," Patrick said.

Their cousin Tio was laughing with hysterical joy. Speechless. After that arresting sighting, I became a member of the Center for UFO Studies, run by astronomer and ufologist Dr. Alan Hynek out of Northwestern University in Evanston, Illinois, who was the technical advisor to *Close Encounters of the Third Kind* (making a short cameo appearance in the film). I periodically received long data sheet printouts of sightings around the world, most of which occurred in dark skies continents like South America and Africa. Dr. Hynek claimed about 10 reports out of 100 are worth investigating and only 1 in 100 are worth keeping.

When I share this story to people, I tell them there were four other witnesses who experienced this sighting. I was not alone. We were there, and whatever that captivating intelligent encounter was certainly generated wonder and joy, not fear and belligerence.

New Mexico, since the Roswell UFO sightings and Project Blue Book studies conducted by the US Air Force in the late 1940s, has been a news media hotspot, drawing numerous reports of strange extra-terrestrial flying objects and debris. You can add my Santa Fe experience with witnesses to that list. I haven't experienced any UFO sightings since then. One was enough to convince me that we are not alone, despite our modern light-polluting world removing the dark skies, preventing us from ever witnessing such glorious mysterious phenomena beyond our solar system. However, this captivating disc-shaped flying object chose to visit us at the terrestrial level, among free, air-breathing humans, not in the heavens, perhaps to make sure we knew the universe was watching.

Chapter Twenty
A Tobacco Offering with Glorious Unimaginable Results

And the passing Comet, we wish-would cleanse our earth.
– Danikelii

The Tohono O'odham, formerly known as the Papago, are an indigenous Sonoran Desert people deeply akin to nature, with strong ties to Catholicism. As an outdoor environmental graduate school focusing on earth ethics with several academic and experiential areas related to living in balance with the planet, we included learning about indigenous ways as an important part of our education. Little did I realize that a ceremonial dance offering to thank the Bear Clan for healing someone gravely ill in their Coyote Clan would open up the opportunity for one of the most wondrous moments in my life.

At the San Xavier del Bac Mission south of Tucson, Arizona, the Tohono O'odham perform many ceremonies mixed with ancestral ways and Catholic traditions. In the case of what our school witnessed, we saw such a mix, filled with many shrines, prayer candles, and dancers wearing coyote and bear fur attachments. A man titled "uncle" came around to the visitors to offer each a cigarette as a gesture of gratitude for the Bear Clan healing someone in his clan. The Bear Clan is known for protecting the people and as the keeper of medicine knowledge. I accepted the modern tobacco gift, but, as he tried to light it for me to offer the exhaled smoke to the Creator for thanks, I told him I would break the filter and offer the tobacco as a prayer in a special place. He just nodded his head, accepting my wishes.

After we left the ceremony, we returned to our campsite on the outskirts of Tucson. The sun was setting, and I decided to move southward from my tent, finding a place where I could offer tobacco as a prayer of gratitude. I was thinking about the international global village camp experience the previous summer I participated in, where children, youth, and staff from around the world, particularly from war torn countries, came together in peace to celebrate their humanity through the arts and living together. The desert air was still as I said a prayer for international peace and understanding. A lucid night, the stars were exploding everywhere before I finally fell asleep. It was on February 9, 1986, when my camping partner Curt Welling woke me up around pre-dawn inside our tent.

"Hey, Dennis, check out the sky."

I woke up to a fresh, cool, southwestern, pre-dawn morning, smelling that wonderful damp air of creosote and sage, and decided to take a firsthand look at what Curt was raving about. It was a spectacular appearance of Halley's comet, with a tail leaving a stunning illuminating trail of cosmic enchantment. As its nucleus approaches the sun, it heats up and releases gas and dust that form the magnificent tail. This outgassing leaves a stream of debris around the orbit. Such a phenomenon happens once every 75 years. But, as I stood outside, staring at this glorious rare moment, I realized that, where I had spread that prayer tobacco was directly in line where the orbital comet was speeding.

Some inexplicable mystical force guided me in that direction, and Curt was there to awaken me for this unforgettable celestial event. Indigenous peoples understand the meaning of reciprocity because they believe living in balance honors the social, ecological, and spiritual interconnectedness that supports the vitality of their communities. The Tohono O'odham "uncle" knew it was important to give back through a sacred tobacco offering to the greater community, and this left a lasting, spiritual imprint on my journey.

Chapter Twenty-One
Newfound Home

Nature is not a place to visit. It is home.
– Gary Snyder

Sauntering in the mountain peatlands of southwestern Newfoundland, I became humbled at the incredible vitality our planet has to offer. Everywhere I stepped seemed to reveal some variation of life's theme. I felt a strong connection between my familial home and an eco-spiritual community. Abundant fields of fens provided affectionate spongy surfaces, hugging my feet with every step. I lavishly feasted in the copious offerings of blueberries and huckleberries, feeling as if Mother Nature herself was intimately sharing her livelihood with me. Distant barren mountainous rims momentarily demonstrated a striking resemblance to the Hopi mesas of Arizona. Glimpses of my biological roots carried me deep into the vast golden prairie lands I never knew in my home state of Illinois. Carnivorous pitcher plants hovered together, patiently waiting for the last few insects to digest before closing up for the season. Blooming cotton flowers melodiously danced in breezy, rippling, chilly pools. The winds were powerful, medicinal forces, blasting away any remnants of a sore throat I felt before entering this healthy bio-community. Caribou scat and tracks were in abundance. A rock with scattered colorful lichen was stained deep yellow from my dehydrated urine release. Boulders of timeworn polishing were animate, as if they were about to shake and bake at any moment. Innovative, huge ant mound constructed from dried-up spruce needle debris caught my eyes. Every ant was industriously at work, preparing for the subterranean season ahead. Activity abounded! Dense micro-cosmic worlds of dwarf-sized spruces and pines caught my falls, springing me quickly back up. The land was rich with support and mutual interdependence. Dehydrating mushrooms stood while Bog Rosemary and laurel flowers opened their colors in striking glorious splendor.

This was a time to welcome vulnerability to the fluctuations of the seasonal cycles. The delicate tiny star flowers reminded my hiking-booted feet to walk lightly and consciously. A colony of willow ptarmigans, tacitly camouflaged in the berry patches, gathered food together in the collective spirit of oneness. Birds of prey connected me to the mysteries of the sky. A rough legged hawk with its densely feathered talons was suspended in the air. With wings spread wide, it held back until the time was ripe to penetrate the earth with a captive rodent in its claws. Shortly afterward, the raptor united with a mate in a very vocal remarkable courtship display. They danced across the sky, both male and female, locked talons, and dramatically fell from a great height against a deep blue sky, while performing a series of steep undulations, often passing a small meal to its mate. Lichen flourished on every rock festooned with rich communities of colors and strong indicators for signaling high-quality air. Their unrelenting coverage has broken the biggest and hardest stones, decomposing and shaping new patterns of life from the complex symbiotic interplay between two separate organisms: a fungus and algae.

Clearly, this inextricably wondrous evolutionary ecosystem was anything but uniform. Life's most basic and complex impulses branched everywhere. Wherever I walked, I encountered tremendous depths of natural diversity. Each mat of lichen, each sunken patch of stunted woodlands, each lowland blueberry barren or mountain biome had a unique message to send to my heart, guiding me to a greater understanding of a super cooperative community. Such a solo hike on this day, attending a graduate outdoor environmental education program, created a momentary nexus of harmonious vibration with the earth. No fenced off demarcations or artificial barriers defined this unbroken untamed earth. I was home at last.

Chapter Twenty-Two
Awakened by Magical Plumage

It dances today, my heart, like a peacock it dances / it dances. It sports a mosaic of passions / like a peacock's tail / It soars to the sky with delight, it quests, Oh wildly / it dances today, my heart, like a peacock it dances.
– Rabindranath Tagore

After two years camping under the stars driving across North America in the Audubon Expedition Institute bus with a motley experiential group of earth-caring, consensus, decision-making graduate and undergraduate students, I was so happy to have accomplished such a rigorous outdoor environmental academic program at my actual Jack Benny age of 39 years young. I decided to celebrate by meeting up with my ex-school students and staff of the Santa Fe Community School at a homeschooling family home in Berkeley, California, joining them at a regional alternative education conference in Escondido. Berkeley is an exceptionally diverse, pedestrian-friendly, educated, wonderfully funky, progressive, and convivial town. It is loaded with cafes and bookstores, bringing joy and serenity for urban leisure living. I stayed with friends of our school and chose to sleep outside on the earth in the backyard because that had been my comfortable bed ground while attending the Audubon Expedition Institute (AEI) for two years.

The neighborhood was quiet, the air dry, comfortably cool, and was relatively dark, accommodating my night on a resting pad and sleeping bag. I slept solid straight through and was awakened by a shimmering sound by my feet. The sun was glaring off the side of my eyes, but I looked straight ahead and saw an image I will never forget. A peacock was spreading his dazzling, jewel-toned tail feathers with hypnotic eye spots at me, slowly swaying to one side then the other, looking directly at me. He continued to move 180 degrees so I could see his beautiful backside, shaking like a major, attention-seeking fan dancer. I was awe-struck by the poetic pride of this glorious, exquisite, mythical shapeshifter. What a wonderful sign of rebirth and renewal to wake up to after earning a master of science degree through the Lesley University-Audubon program in environmental education. Such an image is so inexplicable and irreproducible that all my heart could do was ache with gratitude, and all my youthful spirit at this fleeting illusionary moment could imagine was that I will live forever, love all the women, drink all the wine, seek high adventure, entertain the great masses for a healthier planet, and live robustly as if Mother Earth mattered.

Later, I was to discover that the peacock residing in the trees belonged to the neighborhood. The previous homeowners sold the house with the proviso that the new owners would have to take care of their peacock. Apparently, this flamboyant bird would not stay around their home but wandered around the neighborhood backyards, perched overnight on scattered local trees, roofs, and fences, and was thus loved and cared for by the neighbors. Berkeley carries a glorious urban communal vibe and is a place to accommodate visionary birds as messengers for pursuing a mythical vision of vitality, beauty, hope, and rejuvenation. I just happened to be in the right place at the right time with the right amiable transcendental bird.

Chapter Twenty-Three
Binos to the Rescue

To the question: Wilderness, who needs it? Doc would say: Because we like the taste of freedom, comrades. Because we like the smell of danger. But, thought Hayduke, what about the smell of fear, Dad?
– Edward Abbey, *The Monkey Wrench Gang*

Illinois is noted for its modest hills but mostly flatland terrain, quite suitable for casual cross-country skiers, which was my main source of recreational winter activity whenever we had enough snow on the tamed, disturbed ground. But I was always surrounded by sparse forest preserves; residential, commercial, and industrial landscapes; and a few golf courses with groomed trails. It was certainly not like skiing in the Upper Peninsula or out West, where the Rocky Mountains invite a wilderness fervor for engaging in the perpetual grandeur of solitude and spectacular beauty, undisturbed by trains, planes, and automobiles.

After returning to my hometown of Schaumburg, working as a part-time naturalist at a local nature center while starting my own earth-caring enterprise, Swiftdeer Paige, I was feeling drawn to the West for a quick getaway. My sister Janis invited me in March to join her and her husband Dan, their baby daughter Mallory and step daughter Michelle on a Colorado ski trip to Crested Butte. Downhill skiing was a bit challenging for me since I had only skied a few times while living in Santa Fe, New Mexico. Taos Ski Valley was especially challenging but absolutely wonderful, with constant moguls, steep slopes, and sharp turns to invite torn ligament injuries and broken bones for those who dare to speed beyond their ability. My brother-in-law had a few years earlier sped down the notorious, mogul-infested Al's run in Taos and met his fate, carried back on a stretcher with a torn meniscus. He was never to return to that accident magnet slope again.

As much as downhill skiing in Crested Butte was exhilarating, I was looking for a deeper experience to treasure before going back to the suburban world, where the wild things live in broken, fragmented natural communities. While returning to the lodge after a few runs down the mountain, I noticed in the lodge on the bulletin board a list of events and classes happening in the next few days. There was a cross-country ski class scheduled for the next day.

Crested Butte is one of the premier cross-country ski destinations in the United States, covering several miles of groomed trails in spellbinding wilderness areas. A ski instructor would guide a registered group on an 11-mile round trip Nordic run to the ranger station. I signed up and was so excited to face a breathtaking run, far from the lodges, chairlifts, commercial vistas, and crowds. When I showed up on the day of the event to register, there was a sign on the Nordic Ski Center door that stated, *due to the instructor becoming sick, the class is cancelled.*

I had rented the skis, boots, and poles and stared at them, wondering what should I do. The trails were groomed, and I had a map to show me where the Ranger Station was. Although an 11-mile round-trip ski venture might be a little too risky, the sky was bright, deep-blue, cloudless, and the temperature was in the low 30s with blustery winds. I looked out on the partially groomed trail and decided to go it alone, bringing water, an energy bar, and a pair of binoculars. There were no smartphones back then, and I didn't bring a compass. Figuring the run would not last more than three hours, I loaded lightly in my daypack a water bottle, a couple of energy bars, and an extra pair of wool gloves to insert into my mittens, if necessary. When I began during mid-morning, the wind was whipping around at 10 to 15 miles per hour. It picked up significantly after about an hour into the solo adventure, with the wind whipping up the powder. A fierce white out began speedily drifting over the groomed trails. The sun was blinding. Barely seeing beyond my nose, the snow constantly blasted across my face. I strayed off trail, sinking into snow almost up to my waist. At times, I had to dig myself out by reaching down deep in the snow to disconnect my skies, lifting them up and rolling to more solid ground to reattach them.

Off in the distance, amid an obstructive blizzard, I could see the ranger station. However, after struggling along this exposed rugged canyon ridge around 9,500 feet, I decided to turn back. But where should I turn back to? The trail was completely erased, covered by forceful howling winds that were almost deafening to my ears. The view was incredibly vast and blindingly white. All I could do was guess how to get back by skiing slowly and cautiously while stopping periodically to look at any signs leading me back to the trailhead. The vast powder and snow-packed wilderness was now a place where I felt beauty and death at the same time. I saw no signs of humans, buildings, or fences—no planes, trains, or automobiles. The winds sounded like haunting whispers. I knew I needed to keep going, but I kept falling into deep pockets of soft, drifting snow. Shaking off the winter dust, I felt the drifting, snow-laden ground for any possible groomed sensations to keep me on the right path of destiny. But I literally was not sure where I was going, especially without a compass, until I pulled out my binos in my sack while the blowing snow subsided. Panning around to see if there were any familiar spots, I auspiciously sighted off in the distance the original trailhead.

What a revelation! I had unintentionally skied in a loop, not realizing I was favoring my right leg as I was returning. I gave a deep sigh of relief and skied directly down a wide-open, unobstructed slope, leading to my final destination, where the distant sounds of downhill chairlifts could be heard. I didn't know who or what to thank, making it back, but I do know that experiencing that lone run made me so grateful to be alive, to find the courage and strength to press on, no matter the unknown risky obstacles, unscathed by the wrath of late winter's challenging, wind-swept squalls, putting my soul on ice.

Chapter Twenty-Four
When Skeptical Eyes Awaken

*Grown men can learn from very little children for the hearts of little
children are pure. Therefore, the Great Spirit may show to them
many things which older people miss.*
– Black Elk

When does one awaken to a deeper connection with nature, grasping the mysterious interplay of how we spiritually walk on this earth? I grew up traditionally indoctrinated in the tenets of the Russian Orthodox Church. I felt overwhelmed by regal-looking priests and Sunday School teachers telling me how and what I should believe and that I really didn't know who I was without falling back on some patriarchal Eastern European interpretation of Christianity to please the czars and czarinas.

I was simply born like so many other millions upon millions of children, forced to follow my parents' wishes in regard to choosing what religious path I should follow. It took a while for me to break the chains of this trapped upbringing to find what I was really looking for. I ultimately began searching for wise, indigenous ways of living with nature. For many years, I had been hooked into a small group, wanting to learn from the regional, tribal-affiliated peoples, but we never were close enough to explore the deeper spiritual sides of Grandmother Earth. I always found comfort in the great outdoor natural world but didn't have any solid transformational experience following any indigenous ways until a series of inexplicable events began to unfold in my life that opened the doors to spiritual enlightenment.

A friend of mine, Mary Hirose, in the spring of 1992, had encouraged me to attend a Spring Equinox ceremony held at the Theosophical Society in Wheaton, Illinois. Mary knew I was not set in any religious ways and thought I might consider this presentation most interesting. The gentleman conducting this ceremony was Dr. James E. Gillihan, known among the Lakota people as *Tatanka Ska* (White Buffalo). Jim was actively involved with Native Americans in Reburial and Repatriation and was a highly honored Lakota elder, even though he had a good mix of Cherokee and Irish in him. In 1972, Jim was director of the Natural History Museum of the University of South Dakota and was adopted by a Yankton Elder, Joseph Rock Boy, and given the name of *Tatanka Ska*. He worked with respectable Lakota elders, who stood up against government atrocities while corruption within the Bureau of Indian Affairs and Tribal Council was at an all-time high. He served as a peace-making liaison between these honored elders, representing the community and the FBI to help calm the tensions building up at Pine Ridge, South Dakota, in 1973. The confrontation ended in an armed battle with US armed forces, but Jim helped negotiate a peaceful settlement at the siege at Wounded Knee. Recognized as a man with good intentions and a kind heart, religious leaders such as Fools Crow, Lame Deer, Henry Crow Dog, and Joe Rock taught him their language, traditions, ceremonies, and ways of the Lakota/Dakota people.

In 1977–78, Jim was diagnosed with cancer. A series of operations and chemotherapy followed. In January 1978, the doctors told Jim there was nothing they could do for him, and he should make his final plans with his family. The Lakota/Dakota people remembered their peacemaking friend and adopted brother with prayers and ceremonies. Frank Fools Crow, the recognized medicine holy man, sent Charles Fast Horse and his brother Douglas to conduct a pipe ceremony at the hospital where Jim was staying. Charles received permission—with the doctors agreeing no worse harm could be done at this stage—to conduct the pipe ceremony in Jim's hospital room, as long as the door was closed to prevent smoke from entering the rest of the floor. Charles said to Jim, "This is a tough one; it'll take four days." Four days later, the doctors could find no trace of any cancer in his body, and it didn't return.

Once Jim regained strength and some weight, he wanted to thank Frank Fools Crow and drove out to South Dakota. Frank Fools Crow said "Jim, I need you to do something for me. I have had (*Hunkpapa Thatháŋka Íyotake*) Sitting Bull's Sacred *Chanupa* (Pipe) under my bed for about 30 years, and I haven't been a very good keeper of it. I would like you to take this pipe and pray for the people. If this goes to a reservation, knowing how the people may not respect it, it'll never be seen again."

Jim was surprised and responded by saying, "Why would you give that to me? I'm not even Lakota."

Fool's Crow responded by saying, "Spirit knows who you are, and the only wrong way to pray is to not pray."

Jim accepted this responsibility with total dedication and humility. But he chose to share the pipe with a greater community to help the outside world understand Lakota earth wisdom and power. He became the founding father of the Spotted Red Bead People (*Oyate*) to invite non-Lakota people into their sacred ways, following the Red Road (*Canku Luta*), which runs north and south as a unique spiritual path of life and enlightenment, having no end.

I had no idea how highly regarded Jim was at that time, except that he was planning to conduct a spring equinox ceremony to honor the great elders, meaning the rocks (*tunkashilas).* Jim requested to all those attending to bring a rock for the special gathering. Holding a special place in earth's true geological ancestral history seemed intriguing. I considered going but was leaning toward doing something else. The next morning on Saturday March 21st, my life mysteriously changed forever. Pulling into my condo home parking lot from a morning conservation work day at my nature center, I saw a young girl, around nine years old, chasing down a small, pink beach ball rolling to my car. I went around my car to fetch the ball for her and give it back. She said thank you and ran to the back entrance of my condo complex. When I met up with her once again, she had returned to a display table with her friend, where she was selling items. One exclusive item stood out like it was a gift from the gods. It was a rock the size of a grapefruit. I realized I needed to bring a rock for the coming of the spring equinox gathering. I offered a dollar to her, and she gladly accepted, after which I called Mary to come pick me up to attend this enticing ceremony in Wheaton. When she arrived, I decided to take the stairwell down from the 4th floor instead of the elevator. At about 1:30 p.m., Saturday afternoon, I could hear loud, echoing, child-like footsteps coming up the stairs. It was the little girl holding the pink ball as we crossed by each other. All I could do was smile and say thank you for the rock.

That late, mild, and calm afternoon, I met Jim, sharing this story with the rock in my hand among the circle group of very receptive participants. Although I was heartened by this sage-smudging pipe ceremony, with a firepit in the center of the circle—and the inexplicable events that led to coming there—the skeptic side of my mind was questioning this strange conjunction. In fact, 29 years later, I was to learn that what I had possibly experienced was based on a story passed down by Buffalo Calf Woman on one of the seven sacred rites of the Lakota/Dakota people: *Tapa Wankaye Yapi*, the Throwing of the Ball.

The ceremony is based on a dream that Dakota Chief Standing Buffalo had in the late 1800s. The following narration of this ceremony was given by Black Elk to Joseph Epes Brown. The playing field was marked off in four quarters, each of the four directions represented. A little girl who held a sacred ball in her hand stood at the center of the field. The ball was colored red, and it had two blue strips painted on it, crossing each other at right angles in the four directions. Buffalo people stood at each of the four directions (*just as a sidenote, I resided on the fourth floor*) on the playing field. The little girl threw the ball high into the air to the west. (*the little girl I encountered at my condominium complex moved west to receive the pink ball I retrieved for her in the parking lot by my car.*) As the ball descended upon the buffalo people, suddenly they turned into two-legged people. They caught the ball and returned it to the girl in the center. She threw the ball to the north (*As another sidenote of interest, I walked north to the back entrance of my condo building, where I met her at a table*). The same sequence was repeated. Then she threw the ball to the east and then to the south, and, each time in the sequence, the buffalo transformed into two leggeds and returned the ball to her. (*Additionally, as a sidenote I met her again east of my condo unit, coming up the stairwell as I was going down as I headed south to my car in the parking lot.*) The fifth time, she threw the ball straight up in the air (*the last time I saw her that day, she was walking upstairs with the pink ball.*) As the ball descended upon the people, they turned back into buffalo (*tatanka*) and could not catch it, representing ignorance and an illusion toward truth.

Black Elk said that this game represented human life. The playing field stood for the universe; the center of the playing field represented *Wakan Tanka*, the Great Mystery. The ball also represented *Wakan Tanka*. The little girl symbolized innocence and purity. The throwing of the ball to each direction showed that *Wakan Tanka* was everywhere. As the ball came down to the people, Wakan Tanka's power also came down; however, very few people caught it. Black Elk in 1953 knew the *Throwing of the Ball* (*Tapa Wanka Yap* in Lakota) was a sacred yet neglected rite but felt his people would return to a center of balance and harmony in being human. *At this sad time today among our people, we're scrambling for the ball, and some are not even trying to catch it, which makes me cry when I think of it. But soon, I know it will be caught, for the end is rapidly approaching, and then it will be returned to the center, and our people will be with it.*

Months had passed since this synchronistic encounter with the young girl at my condo, and *Tatanka Ska* was conducting another pipe ceremony at the Theosophical Society, only this time it would be honoring the coming of the autumnal equinox. Once again, I was considering going but seemed a little skeptical about attending such a seasonal event. After returning from a volunteer conservation work day at my nature center, I parked my car and headed to the back entrance of my condo complex. On Saturday September 19, there she was again. The same girl, minus the pink beach ball, who was sitting behind a table with a pad of manila paper and Crayolas. I asked her when was the last time she was there, and she said, "The last time I saw you." She didn't need the pink ball to get my attention.

"Really, can you color for me the earth and make it half white and half dark? I want to share this picture to honor the equal light and darkness of the season."

This girl, whose name I never asked, transported me to a whole new dimension, walking the spirit road. I gave her a dollar, and she happily received it. I never saw her again. She must have been visiting a friend or relative. When I shared this story in Jim's Sitting Bull pipe ceremonial circle group, people were in as much awe as I was.

But my deepening connections with this sacred mystical journey escalated even more. Spending an afternoon with my dad in mid-October on his bed, lamentably conversing over the recent loss of his sister, who was my aunt, I said, "Dad, looks like you and your brother are the only two remaining. The two sisters are gone. Seems like you got to stick around for a while."

He didn't say a word, but you could tell as he looked up at the ceiling in this somber space, he was deeply shaken by the pre-mature loss of his sister from a fatal neurodegenerative disorder. The next morning, he woke up and headed to a Dunkin Donut shop, ordered a donut and coffee, went to the bathroom, and, on his way back, he had a stroke, never to speak again. He died that same year on an early Saturday morning, December 19, 1992. By the time I arrived at the nursing care facility, only his body remained. Blood dripped from his nose. Outside I heard a black capped chickadee calling by the window on a leafless tree.

When I left my father lying there, motionless and gone, I realized *Tatanka Ska* was holding a winter solstice ceremony at the Theosophical Society that late afternoon. I definitely needed to discuss this powerful coincidence to share the *crossing over* of my father Henry Paige. My middle name was named after him. I brought nothing except my sad heart to share. But I knew then that I was on a spiritual path to partake in *inipis* (the purification lodge ceremony), learning to sing prayer songs in Lakota, culminating in a nine-day Sundance, serving as a firekeeper for the sun dancers. The spiritual journey I was embarking on was not fed with religious books of guilt-ridden salvation driven persuasion but mystical signs guiding me toward an indigenous wisdom connected with the earth. I was choosing to follow a journey, believing we are spiritual beings in a physical body. The full explanation of this Throwing of the Ball ritual is laid out in great detail here: Joseph Epes Brown, *Sacred Pipe: Black Elk's Account of the Seven Rites of the Oglala Sioux*, pp. 127–138.

Chapter Twenty-Five
Rising up to Earth's Tears

Strings of coincidence can strengthen us in the determination to follow our deepest intuitions even when they run counter to conventional wisdom and logic and cannot be subjected to rational explanation.
– Author Robert Moss

My graduate school director for the Audubon Expedition Institute once said to me, "Don't put all your eco-chips in one bag." Those words set the course for how I would earn my keep through the rest of my earning years. After graduating with an MS in environmental education, I decided to split my career aspirations into two categories: one was to make sure I had a favorable bread-and-butter job and the other pursuit was to have an unleashed passionate vision of how I want to give back to Grandmother Earth.

In 1987, I was hired by Spring Valley Nature Center as an assistant interpretive naturalist, subsequently to become a habitat restorationist and outdoor ecology summer adventure camp director. In 1989, I established an earth-caring enterprise titled, Swiftdeer Paige, *edutaining* thousands of young and old audiences on the important ecological issues of our times. Originally a book-distributing business, it morphed into a wide range of motivational talks on creating lifestyles that ensure a healthier person–planet well-being, expanding into native gardening talks on how to bring nature back to your land, while culminating with my favorite additions of engaging entertaining eco-friendly programs for adults and children. It involved understanding the existential ecological crisis we are in, adding storytelling workshops for children and adults that involve awakening the hidden storytellers from within, and rounding out these presentations with an indigenous storytelling program designed to enchant listeners into caring for the earth through songs, dances, and stories set within a captivating circle setting.

Such a challenging balanced journey has passionately brought me ever closer to understanding how spiritual a being I am. When I started to create these programs, I wanted to apply much of my comedic and environmental awareness skills. I came up with a lively program called, "The Dream World of Dr. Earl, the Crusty Earth Keeper." I performed this show in Massachusetts, Wisconsin, and mostly Illinois about a shy naturalist falling asleep under a tree and dreaming of becoming a feisty, outspoken, irreverent doctor to help heal the sick planet from pollution of all kinds, as well as reduce loss of habitat and combat the general disregard for nature. During the production of "Dr. Earl," I introduced my medicine bag, which contained personal pieces of importance related to the teachable lessons of becoming a better human being. Two of those pieces included a four inch grizzly bear claw and a wolf tooth, given to me by Jon Schwaber who lived on St. Lawrence Island, off the Alaska mainland. Those two personal items were in the permafrost for over 10,000 years and removed as a gift to me from my friend. It was while I was portraying this lively character in the backyard of the nature center at an Earth Day-Native Plant sale event in 1992, held at my nature center, that I knew the journey was drawing me ever closer to the Lakota way of honoring all beings as relatives to living in balance with the earth.

The volunteer receptionist, Judy Hannah, at Spring Valley Nature Center wanted me to meet a friend of hers, who was a Lakota jingle dancer. While I was showing the wolf tooth and bear claw to a small crowd, Judy's friend was quietly standing behind me. She heard me explain the purposeful meaning behind keeping them in my medicine bag. "I keep the bear claw to protect my vision in following a path to care for *Unci Maka* (Grandmother Earth) and to embrace the primal natural world. I also keep the wolf tooth to remind me about loyalty to the things you care deeply about and to trust my intuition and range of senses."

When I was finished, I was still holding these two late Pleistocene pieces in my hand. I looked behind me and saw a woman who introduced herself.

"Hello, my name is Barbara Wolf-Bear."

Enter the *Dream world of Dr. Earl, the Crusty Earth Keeper*. Dressed in a lively costume of intertwined native prairie grasses holding an inflatable earth, I wandered the backyard at a Spring Valley Nature Center Earth Day event. Only a few moments after this photo was taken while sharing my Pleistocene bear claw and wolf tooth from my medicine bag to a small audience, I was approached by a Lakota jingle dancer Barbara Wolf Bear who was referred to me by volunteer Judy Hannah. We became instant friends and would constantly see each other at local and regional Pow-wows. *1994*. Unknown photographer

Later on, we would occasionally cross paths at pow-wows between her healing jingle dances and catch up on our lives. Learning to go deeper in Lakota ways guided me to go deeper in my mystical calling to speak for the earth. When I arrived to perform at John Mills Elementary School in Elmwood Park, Illinois during Earth Month in April 1992, I couldn't believe how incredibly unsuitable the setting was for performing. Imagine an auditorium stage separated from an open gymnasium floor, with the packed audience sitting in caged, distant bleachers. I told the teacher and ecology program coordinator that I couldn't perform the show under such an uninviting setting. She agreed and had all of the 300 students sit on the gym floor, where I joined them, arranging my props and mini-stage in front of the audience. I knew I had to be wild and zany like Robin Williams before this restless group of early teeners to hold their attention to this important ecological message. The feedback by the teacher-program coordinator along with a hearty written shower of praise by the students showed me that I did indeed reach these seventh and eighth graders with a wonderful unforgettable performance.

She wrote the following review: *"What a CREATIVE PERFORMANCE! Thank you so much for the educational and entertaining assembly. To hold the attention of 300 students is no easy task, and your creative, unique performance did the trick. Weeks later, the students were still chanting 'Rainforest . . . Rainforest . . . and Earth Day, Every day!' Your contagious enthusiasm conveyed environmental issues in a way that was relevant to the students. The added bonus of learning about Native Americans fit beautifully into our social studies curriculum. The stories, the bongos, the bird calls, the puppetry, the costume, the music, the medicine bag, the corn were FANTASTIC. You are a valuable asset to the education of children and a talented, versatile performer. I highly recommend this program to any group looking for an extra-ordinary assembly on environmental issues."* – Coral Murphy, Ecology Coordinator, John Mills School, Elmwood Park, Illinois

Reading the ultimate eco-friendly book *The Lorax* by Dr Seuss as Dr. Earl, the Crusty Earth Keeper at a local Earth Day event held at District 54 Nature Center in Schaumburg, Illinois. 1993. Taken by Mary Ellen Knight

I was asked to just appear with my costume for special events such as participating in a parade through my local town of Schaumburg, Illinois at an All-Species Day Celebration. Amidst the bioregional banners designed by the Schaumburg High School students' art department, look carefully and you can spot Dennis Swiftdeer Paige with a red shirt without the beard wearing a tall grass prairie costume to honor a regional ecosystem along with other gathered contributing folks dressed for the occasion. The only authentic species not pretending to be what she was happened to be a llama slightly visible on the far-right corner of the picture who lead the parade. On the opposite corner are the panda bear Jerry Handlon, Director of the Schaumburg Park District and environmental and nature loving Mayor Al Larson next to him. I along with secretary of School District 54 Nature Center Mary Ellen Knight, volunteer parent Joan Dunne and director Jim Johnson helped organize and plan this auspicious event. *1993*. Taken by Mary Ellen Knight

Knowing how high maintenance "Dr. Earl" was to produce and set up steered me in a direction where I lightened up my load to a simpler, more intimate circle setting, creating "Journey from the Heart." The program attempted to spin a message toward understanding the meaning of reciprocity, learning to give back every day what we receive from the earth in so many life-affirming ways. The attempt is to enchant the audience's hearts with indigenous stories, animal impressions, songs, drumming, flute playing, and dancing, set within a captivating, authentic, colorfully drawn circle setting of native interests.

Performing an indigenous friendly program *Journey From the Heart* as Swiftdeer in a colorfully captivating circle setting at Riverside Library in Riverside, Illinois, I shared stories, songs, and dances through which the wisdom of the First Nations can speak in today's language. *2015*. Taken by Linda Baca

Two most memorable eye dropping moments of profoundly connecting with a great mystery through this program come to mind. While preparing for an evening summer program in 1994 at the Green Lake Christian Camp in Wisconsin, I was asked by the director if I could change my presentation to focus more on bats. I agreed, and she gave me some prep materials from Bat Conservation International to review while I headed back to the barracks to find a story in my *Keepers of the Night* book by Joseph Bruchac. It was warm and stuffy in the lodge, so I decided to open a shutter. On the outside frame of the panel, a shaken little brown bat flew quickly from the window and latched onto my ankle, walking ever so slowly toward my knee with its wings. Fortunately, I was wearing jeans.

This had never happened before to me—and will never happen again—especially during a program focusing on bats. I began to walk toward the office, where the director was, with the bat clinging to my leg until this friendly being felt safe enough to climb up my pants with its winged extensions. However, about halfway to the office, it caught the light of day and flew to the back side of the barracks, nestled on a window shutter upside down, catching up on lost sleeping time before the night. I realized I had to give back this wonderful gift with an *Anishinabe* story around the campfire on "How the Bats Came to Be." I may not have the nocturnal genes to embrace the night like a bat, but I do have the words to take the listener into a world so different than ours, one with a wondrous sense of kinship and respect. I have come to think of storytelling as an act of reciprocity with nature.

Another synchronistic moment to dearly remember happened while presenting a story to a Cub Scout pack in Glenview, Illinois, in the early fall of 1997. I had been accepted into the Northern Branch of the Red Spotted Bead People, founded by *Tatanka Ska* (White Buffalo in Lakota). He had a vision during an early frosty morning on top of Bear Butte, South Dakota, where he noticed, regarding the north side (*Waziyata*) of his circle honoring the seven directions, that the red flag had frosted little spider footprints dotting the cloth. His vision allowed him to start the *Pizhooto luta gleshka oyate waziyata* or Northern Branch of the Red Spotted Bead People. In other words, I belonged to a spider clan and still hold dearly to receiving the white speckled bead by Jim—although I lost it and graciously received another one by *Iktomi wawate ca washte* (Gentle Spider Man). Spiders spin intricate webs, reminding us about the inter-connectedness of all things, both dead and alive, teaching us to maintain a balance between past, present and future. They bring light to a greater awareness that much can be learned by staying close to home, weaving a nurturing sustainable relationship with the environment in which we choose to live. Spiders can teach us how to use written language with power and creativity so our stories weave a web of meaning around those who listen.

It was within this context that I shared a Muskogee Creek story on *How Grandmother Spider Stole the Sun*. Out of a storytelling bag consisting of small objects each related to an indigenous story, a young boy chose a colorful woven ribbon bundle bag. I told this story, closing with "And because Grandmother Spider brought the Sun in her bag of webbing for all to share, at times the Sun makes rays across the sky, which were shaped like the rays in Grandmother Spider's web. It reminds everyone that we are all connected, like the strands of Grandmother Spider's web, and it reminds everyone what Grandmother Spider did for all the animals and the people."

During this closing moment, coming down off the ceiling of the cabin nature center, was a small spider spinning a silky strand that reached the center of my storytelling circle, suspended at an eye-to-eye level. A complete hush came over the astounded sitting listeners. I signaled for everyone to be still and observe as I put my finger a couple inches below the captivating, eight-legged visitor, watching her sense my vibe and slowly return upward to the top of the ceiling, eating her silk for further use.

All of us who witnessed these mystical lessons carried a profound teachable moment regarding the people who walked the land and left old trails for following to honor all people—not just humans but also the bird people, the deer people, the bear people, the ant people, the bat people, the salmon people, the spider people and so on. And, by doing that, a great exchange of sharing differences in the web of life is heard and hopefully reciprocated.

Chapter Twenty-Six
A Surprise Visit from Chuck and George

That's the ideal meeting . . . once upon a time, only once,
unexpectedly, then never again.
– Helen Oyeyemi

It was a cold, windy, dreary morning at my nature center's Sugar Bush pancake festival in March 1988, and I was running an information booth at the entrance to this warm community event. People from towns outside of Schaumburg attended this highly anticipated early spring celebration. While waiting for the public to attend to pass out program leaflets, I noticed a man in a white trench coat carrying a walkie-talkie. I learned pretty quickly that he was a high security federal agent for the president of the United States, checking out the grounds to clear George Herbert Walker Bush and Illinois Governor Jim Thompson to attend this local pancake breakfast.

I was told the limo would arrive in about 10 minutes and would park right in front of my booth. I knew the president was campaigning and felt it was a perfect time to address some pressing questions on the environment. I thought up my question and stood ready to greet him. The black limousine with two American flags on opposite sides of the back pulled in, and there he was. At the time, I was not a Republican or Democrat but an independent, leaning toward the Green Party. With a couple of bodyguards in front of him, George looked a little disoriented when he came out of the car and started zigzagging on the trail toward the nature center, where the breakfast was being held. I called his name and he came quickly toward me.

"George, George!" I yelled while in front of my info booth.

"How are you?" he asked, as he shook my hand.

"What do you plan to do to protect our environment and wilderness areas?"

"Well, have you got your hands on *the President's Commission Report on Outdoor America*? It really does a nice job laying out the strategies for protecting the environment."

That was as far as the conversation went with the president, and he kept moving to other attendees, shaking hands and being very friendly. Later, I learned that other people were asking him the same question, and he gave the same practiced answer he said to me. Nevertheless, George turned out to be probably the best Republican environmental president, next to Teddy Roosevelt and Richard Nixon. He strengthened the *Clean Air Act*, arguably the most important piece of environmental legislation, and was the first president to raise climate change as a major issue of concern for the federal government. Not bad for a Republican.

Just six months into his term in June 1989, GHW Bush improved the air quality by reducing US emissions of ozone-depleting substances, as the ozone hole was widening to dangerous levels, and he tackled acid rain in the Northeast and mid-Atlantic, coming from mostly coal-fired power plants in the Midwest by capping the total quantity of sulfur dioxide that could be emitted—and reducing that cap over time. He did this by incentivizing ways to reduce the polluting industries emissions. He broke tradition from President Ronald Reagan in promoting incentives for energy efficiency and renewable energy. Lastly, he saw the emergence of climate change and vowed the United States would be a leader in the world in protecting the environment at the 1992 Earth Summit held in Rio de Janeiro. George wanted to instill the earth as a global village, where we were all in this together and couldn't escape the consequences of our collective toxic actions. We needed to tackle these threatening issues for current and future generations. Where did the Republicans go wrong regarding protecting the environment after George was defeated in office by Bill Clinton?

By midday the weather turned into a nastier chill, completely overcast with scattered snow flurries. I stood alone in the info booth, jumping up and down to keep from freezing. While I was staring into the half-empty parking lot, numbed by the cold, an older man approached the booth. He had the most amazing unforgettable cantankerous smile, no hat, hands in his pocket, and a weathered Terry and the Pirates leather jacket with the collar up. He was accompanied by his wife. I looked at him and knew who this legendary aviator hero of the 20th century was instantly.

"Oh my goodness. Are you Chuck Yeager?"

"Yep."

"I can't believe it. You're truly one of my all-time favorite heroes. And you don't even have a gallery of admirers with you either! You're truly the unsung lone wolf hero."

Once again, he gave a big appreciative smile while the flurries fell over his lustrous receding hairline. There I was standing next to perhaps one of the greatest daring aviators of all time, with not a single person standing around him to bear witness to this great American aviation hero. Chuck was campaigning for his long-time friend, George HW Bush, with his wife Glennis. A World War II fighter pilot ace and the first pilot to break the sound barrier, later to rise in rank as a brigadier general, Yeager, along with his equally tough and steady match, Glennis, were portrayed in the 1983 classic film *The Right Stuff*. As an exemplary gutsy test pilot for pioneering missions to perform safely and smoothly for the astronauts, he broke the sound barrier in the Bell X-1, which he dubbed "Glamorous Glennis." The name is painted prominently on the plane, which hangs in the Air and Space Museum of the Smithsonian Institution in Washington, DC.

The eagle-eyed West Virginia native was quite humorous, and there seemed nothing shy about him, as conveyed in the movie. I did feel he was an unsung hero, knowing how much he put his body, mind, and spirit on the line as an unheralded test pilot—while the astronauts received glorious media recognition for their mission flights. No admirers stood around him and Glennis the whole time I was with them. It was just us three in a short, momentary conversation but enough to last a lifetime.

Yeager was a member of the National Aviation Hall of Fame and awarded a special Congressional Medal of Honor in 1976 and ranked fifth on *Flying Magazine's* 2013 list of "The 51 Heroes of Aviation." Perhaps the awe-inspiring poem *High Flight* by John Gillespie Magee, Jr. encapsulates the reason why Chuck Yeager dedicated himself so much to reaching upward toward earth's atmospheric limits as an American test pilot: *Up, up the long delirious burning blue I've topped the wind-swept heights with easy grace, where never lark, or even eagle, flew – and while with silent, lifting mind I've trod the high untrespassed sanctity of space, put out my hand and touched the face of God.*

George HW Bush was the last president to serve in World War II. After the attack on Pearl Harbor, Bush decided he wanted to enlist in the Navy. He was just 18 years old when he signed up and started preflight training at the University of North Carolina at Chapel Hill. Ten months later, he was commissioned on June 9, 1943, just a few days before his 19th birthday. That made him the youngest naval aviator at the time in US history. Flying 58 combat missions against the Japanese forces, Bush's service during the war made him a genuine hero. Bush served until 1945, when he was honorably discharged after the Japanese surrendered. For his service, he earned the Distinguished Flying Cross, three Air Medals and a Presidential Unit Citation.

To experience shaking these honorable hands, sharing a short yet memorable conversation with the president of the United States and one of the greatest aviators of all time, both of whom were highly decorated WWII pilots, while alone in an info booth on a chilly, bleak blustery day in March certainly brought a tear of gratitude and joy that I was in the right place at the right time with the *right stuff.*

Now they belong to the angels.

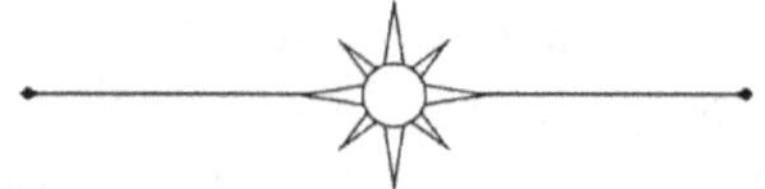

Chapter Twenty-Seven
Grand Radiant Treasures and More to Boot

*Thousands of tired, nerve-shaken, over-civilized people are
beginning to find out that going to the mountains is going home; that
wildness is a necessity.*
– John Muir, *Our National Parks*

In the middle of a six-and-a-half-day, 30-mile backpack trip at
Glacier National Park from Bowman Lake to Kintla Lake,
Montana, a storm was brewing. You could see deep purple clouds
building up off Thunderbird Mountain, forming a grand apocalyptic
sky, as if we could be hailed to death. Knowing how quick on my feet
I was back in the summer of 1990, the 130-pound female guide
Denise, who carried seventy-five pounds in her pack and wore low-
top sneakers, asked me and another middle-aged esoteric fellow Jay
to collect everyone's tent and set them up before the rest of the five
wilderness campers arrived.

We could hear the storm rumbling louder and deeper, coming right
toward the high ridge trail we were beholden to follow. Grabbing all
the tent gear, we began to hustle steadily downward to the campsite.
The trail was steep and narrow, with loose gravel debris that could
cause a serious fall several hundred feet down if you stepped off trail.
After jogging about a mile to the site, the thunder heads began to hover
over us. We immediately set up four tents while cold, heavy drops
rained down upon our sweaty backs. As we entered our individual
tents, you could see pea-sized hail coming down, stinging our faces
and exposed skin. Almost deafening, the pounding hail began to
morph into nickel-sized jolts. The group arrived in the midst of this
downpour and quickly jumped into their tents. We were all safe,
waiting out the hailstorm, surrounded with deafening thunder;
powerful, shattering lightning flashes; and strong gusty winds for

about 15 minutes. The air then became still, the drops were diminishing, and I could hear birds chirping. The sun was cracking through the clouds, and the heat began to rise. I exited out of my tent to view the fading storm and got some wonderful fresh after-rain, mountain-pine-scented air. The magnificent vista spreading down the valley radiated thousands upon thousands of moistened dwarf firs, sparkling with a glistening grandeur. Each needle was a four-sided parallelogram, multiplied millions of times, with a prism of glimmering colors of white, red, orange, yellow, green, blue, indigo, white, and violet. It was as if my life had crossed over into a paradise beyond imagination. The exhausted group just wanted to bed down for the night without eating, but I did manage to convince a reluctant Jay and his partner Diane from Philadelphia to get out of their safe, dry bubble and revel in the momentary glory of an unforgettable panoramic gem to treasure forever. They didn't regret it one bit. The other middle-aged couple, Al and Barbara from Lemont, Illinois, were sound asleep, recovering from altitude sickness and lack of conditioning.

"This better be good," Jay said inside his tent.

"It is."

When Yale graduate Jay looked out beyond his tent, he said to his wife in a monotone voice of wondrous disbelief. "Oh my goodness. Honey, you got to check this out!"

Diane came out as we all stood there, gazing with pure astonishment at miles upon miles of rainbow-colored moistened spruce needles as the sun sank quickly west, giving us just a few moments to savor the blissful, grand, illuminating, sparkling light touching our hearts, minds, and spirits. As we ascended to a higher subalpine elevation, we were joined by a family of four mountain goats for a couple of days. They even stayed overnight, wandering around our tents in the half-moon darkness, using their nocturnal vision to actually take one of Jay's hiking boots to a secret location for a salty snack. We spent a good chunk of our morning time searching around the campsite for that lost boot, but were unsuccessful. Eventually, we hiked further up the trail into a glorious wildflower meadow in the heart of the Hole in the Wall canyon, a fantastic basin perched below rugged cliffs at the head of the Bowman Valley. Fields of full blooming glacier lilies (*Erythronium grandiflorum*) carpeted the magnificent alpine landscape. That was where we found the family of mountain goats, munching down on these lovely yellow petals and licking salt from two dead trees. And, on the trail about a football field away from this herbivorous family, we found the missing boot.

Our trusting guide Denise said she was not planning to hike this far up the trail, and so we began to move down the mountain. Had the goat not removed Jay's boot outside the tent to this stunning wildflower paradise, we would not have left with a memory to treasure for a lifetime. It is very unusual for mountain goats to follow humans for that stretch of time.

As we trudged our way off the mountain, with the slightly chewed hiking boot retrieved, the family of goats rejoined us. But they eventually stopped on an overlook ledge and would not descend any further. We were moving downward, and they preferred to stay upward. We then parted our ways and wished them well, thanking them for leading us to a dreamy Elysian Field of bountiful wilderness glory.

Chapter Twenty-Eight
When Winged Lightning Strikes Twice

They travel at breath-taking speeds when they are in full flight
And to see them wheel above the cliffs is an amazing sight
The fastest birds on Planet Earth though some may not agree
They often cry out in full flight an amazing thing to hear and see.
— Frank Duggan

Awakening time. I was born an Aries, and my birth sign correlates to the falcon and the sun. I am skeptical about astrology, but my experience with falcons proves we're drawn to each other. I was assigned in 1986, at the Legacy International Summer Camp in Bedford, Virginia, to drive the foreign students back to Kennedy International Airport in NYC. We spent time touring through the United Nations, walking the lively streets around Columbia University, and enjoying the grand beauty of Central Park, where my encounter occurred. While sitting on a bench overlooking tall apartment complexes with a visiting high school student from Antigua named Dominque, I threw a commentary at him: "As much as this cultivated park is beautiful to look at, it really doesn't give me a feeling of wildness. I mean all I see here are sparrows, pigeons, squirrels, and if I were to stick around at night here, probably rats."

As soon as I finished flaunting my opinion, a peregrine falcon swooped down directly in front of us to unsuccessfully snatch an English sparrow for a mid-morning snack. We looked at each other with total consternation. We had just witnessed the fastest animal on the Earth including the cheetah, reaching unsurpassable diving speeds of over 240 mph. Evidently, there was a nest we sighted later on top a fancy hotel, wedged between two figurines on a frieze a block away from Central Park.

Jump to mid-March 2018. While retired in the coniferous montane beauty of Colorado, when the snows had subsided to ankle level, I decided to take a 12-mile hike up to a spectacular 9,450-foot overlook called Lion's head at Staunton State Park a few miles from home. This would be the last day that the trail leading to this breathtaking panoramic vista would be accessible until August 1st. The reason for this is because a pair of Peregrine falcons were preparing to nest there, and I wanted to see if I could experience them in a memorable, healing way. I was there as a solemn prayer for my brother-in-law, Dan Moylan, who was undergoing extensive treatment for stage four colon cancer.

Regarded by many raptor afficionados as the ultimate symbol of power and splendor, I hiked 11 miles round trip to the spectacular 9500 foot summit of Lion's Head, a most impressive panoramic peak at Staunton State Park, Colorado with tobacco and sage as prayerful offerings to encounter rare sightings of peregrine falcons. *2018*

I brought sage and tobacco to offer a Lakota seven directions prayer and made it to the summit without experiencing any setbacks. It was a bright, sunny, calm afternoon, and the grand scenery looking south was awe-inspiring, as I could see a wide range of modest mountains leading my eyes toward snowcapped Pike's Peak about 65 miles away as a crow flies. When I reached the summit, I cautiously walked along the steep edge of a 1,000-foot drop off with a pair of binoculars, attempting to spot these electrifying raptors.

No luck. I moved to a comfortable bed of pine needles hidden by a huge boulder and a wind-contorted ponderosa tree, eating lunch while keeping my eyes and ears out for them, with binos by my side next to my knapsack.

Still no signs. But the afternoon winds were starting to pick up. After leaving my trusty field glasses and food in my knapsack, I moved to an open area close to the edge of the cliff and expressed my circle prayer quietly honoring the seven directions. I gently sprinkled tobacco and sage as an offering to the great mystery (*Wakan Tanka*) honoring each direction. After the sixth direction, I honored the last one, referring to the heart, the center that connects all the directions into one's spiritual journey. Placing the seventh direction with the sacred herbs over my heart, I saw, out of the corner of my eye, a high-speed peregrine falcon flashing straight across the edge of the cliff. Off in the distance, this swift bird of prey did a circling swoop toward me so I could get a good look and see that, indeed, this protected rare bird of vision was a peregrine falcon. But the story does not end there because, just below me, down about a 100 to 150 feet from the edge where I was standing, I could hear the *kek, kek, kek, kek* sound of its mate. Some inexplicable force drew me to that spot along the side of Lion's Head.

I didn't need binos to relate directly to this memorable fleeting moment. I felt only my being in direct connection to all that brought me here to this moment, surrounded by a wide open azure sky, rocky foothills, soaring granite cliffs, and a great vision of grandeur. My prayers were answered. Dan Moylan survived another two years but could not endure the ongoing suffering of extensive chemo-treatment and weakening of his body. I'm so grateful to have this prayerful moment in my life to remember that the *great mystery* listens when your mindfully heartfelt intentions are pure and humbling to the mystical forces of nature that go way beyond our comprehension. I wasn't prepared to unexpectedly encounter the falcon in Central Park, but I became quite prepared for sharing my body, mind, and spirit with this exhilarating bird of awakening at Lion's Head.

Chapter Twenty-Nine
Star Making toward a Howling Bliss

Wilderness to the people of America is a spiritual necessity, an antidote to the high pressure of modern life, a means of regaining serenity and equilibrium.
– Sigurd F. Olson

It was my first time in the pristine waters of Quetico Provincial Park, considered to be the canoe paradise for Ontario, Canada. It is a grand, iconic wilderness park renowned for its rugged beauty, grueling portages, towering rock cliffs, red ochre petroglyphs, majestic waterfalls, virgin pine and spruce forests, and picturesque unscathed rivers and lakes. It is also a world-famous destination for backcountry canoeing, with over 2,000 sky blue water lakes, most of which are drinkable without boiling water, as well as over 1,100,000 acres of remote wilderness, sharing its southern border with Minnesota's Boundary Waters Canoe Wilderness, which is part of the larger Superior National Forest.

Hoisting a bear bag to anticipate the evening without any raids, Dave Brooks settles into a campsite to welcome the deep still darkness of a Quetico wilderness. *1992*

After a few days paddling and portaging, gaining strength while detoxing from the rat race urban scene, our senses were regenerated into a place of tranquil celebratory wildness. Fellow paddlers, Dave Brooks, Lisa Fabrizio, and Bob Virzi, and I were enjoying a warm, late evening by a fire on the shores of one of the Man Chain Lakes. The sky was lucid, with a thick blanket of stars and a slithering moon. The Milky Way stretched over our campsite like a nocturnal highway to heaven. The Andromeda galaxy could be seen. Distant loons were singing their haunting, ancient melodies. As the dead pine branches and kindling twigs, collected from the ground, settled into the little burning pile under the calm winds, the sticks began to crackle and spark straight up toward the sky, appearing as if the fire builder was a star maker, releasing sparks to conjure a wondrous starry blanket of nocturnal bliss and magical emissions. Our reflections from the active intense fire emanated an impression that we possessed shamanic powers.

Something happens to a wilderness camper when sitting before a fire. As the night unfolds into a glorious starry night at Quetico Provincial Park, loons call distant carrying tremolos, echoing ancient haunting calls, while the evening softens to a complete tranquil silence. On an open promontory, the small campfire shoots sparks to a lucid nocturnal abundantly stellar sky, inviting auspicious connections to embrace the call of the wild, beckoning the campers to explore a new moon mystery across the lake and into shadowy coniferous shores. *1992*

It was then that I asked Dave to perform his expert wolf calls across the lake. He said, "Sure." Putting his hands together over the side of his mouth, he faced the lake, looking across about a quarter of a mile into a silhouette of spruces shadowing the shore of a quiet lake and began to howl into the unknown. After a couple attempts, we heard a distant puppy bark and what will probably be the most beautiful haunting sound of the wild we will most likely ever experience. A single note rose sharply, followed by a crescendo of accompanied howls, harmonizing together, conveying an impression as if maybe six to nine *Canis lupis* were responding to Dave's imitative calling. Sudden dominant quick short barks by a lone wolf echoed across the lake, and then the world was still again. We were completely captivated, laughing in disbelief that this was really happening. I tested my wilderness vocal cords out, and with a deep, long, bellowing voice, I gave out a howl across the great unknown. A long responsive solo wail reaching higher pitches followed, tapering off into several additional escalating harmonics, accompanied by the same invisible pack along the dark forested shoreline, with quick repetitive barks to silence the howlers. We were once again hysterical and incredibly lucky to have this shared chilling moment to remember.

Dave reached out one more time to keep this encounter going. But there were no more calls. Nothing but complete silence. We remembered that the puppy barks and the pack of wolves were emphatically told by the alpha wolf to ignore this simulated impression of them. But Dave and I did catch them off guard enough to tell a great story of an unforgettably deep primordial encounter within the heart of the wilderness. As we were finishing our trip on the Canadian side facing across the lake that enters the U.S. border around sunset, we knew we had a rendezvous with the tamed over convenient modern world. The next day, we would be leaving this canoe paradise with magnificent ancient chains of lakes and land. I asked Dave to offer one more round of calls toward our country's border, as if there would be wolves to heed his sympathetic plea for responding to bid adieu. No stars were out, day was dimming, and the Canadian waters were still when Dave put out his final howl of the trip. The next thing we heard across the faint, gentle rippling shores of that border was pathetic and funny.

A distant, obtrusive voice directed toward us cried out across the lake, "Why don't you shut up, you bunch of drunks!" Anticipating an unwelcoming, boorish American reply certainly put a damper on returning back to the ever demanding fast paced highly materialistic driven culture. Nevertheless, I continue to receive inner strength and spiritual power by nature's wonders in pristine wilderness worlds, far from artificial consumer demands and cultural detachments from Grandmother Earth. Dave Brooks succinctly reaffirmed this sense of gratitude, describing his kinship connection with *Canis lupis*, "that moment remains one of the penultimate wilderness encounters of my life, and the only time I was able to experience a true connection to wild wolves." As a naturalist, outdoor adventurer, manager to my nature center, and someone who has visited Quetico at least seven times, that is saying something.

We, as hardy fellow paddlers and portagers on our first canoe trip together in these grand, sacred, pure sometimes stormy waters, where visions become lucid and real, couldn't agree more with him. Both our backs and spirits were stronger returning home, forever touched by a rare moment hearing the true lives of the ancestors to our domesticated dogs.

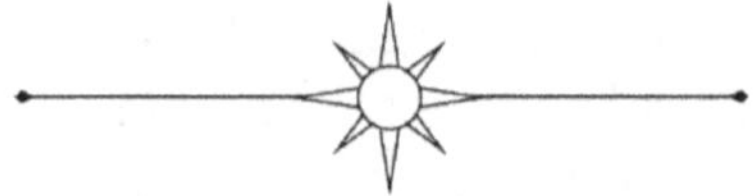

Chapter Thirty
So, Think You Have What It Takes?

*The music of all creatures has to do with their loves, even of toads
and frogs. Is it not the same with man?*
– Henry David Thoreau

I grew up possessing an amusing fascination imitating my family members, fellow students, teachers, and other grownups in positions of authority and celebrity status. My relatives would say at gatherings, "Dennis, do Grandma. Do Uncle Russ. Do your dad. Do John Wayne. Do Alfred Hitchcock. Do Marlon Brando." I learned to make sounds that would baffle people too. During one outrageous situation, students in my eighth-grade study hall insisted I blow my nose. Hearing my loud and uproarious nasal sound, the class would laugh heartily, agitating Mrs. Birchard, who kept me after class to reprimand me in a way that was equally as outrageous. She literally slapped my nose and told me to take that "noisemaker" out of my nostrils and hand it over to her.

"What are you doing? I don't have any noisemaker. That's how my nose sounds when I blow it," I said, as I moved away from the hand attempting to slap my nose a few times.

Vocal human impressions were a total challenging joy for friends and family to request of me. Listening to Warner Bros. cartoons with the *Man of a Thousand Voices*, Mel Blanc, was the ultimate experience to emulate. I later learned that, when I spent a great deal more time outdoors alone with nature, I could imitate animal sounds to many times draw them closer. Calls like the deep howling cry of a grey wolf; the high piercing call of a coyote; the irritating high-pitched buzz of a mosquito; the purring, cuddly sound of the raccoon; the low, growling *wah-wah* sound of the mountain lion; the rapid puffy exhale of an intimidated buck; the soothing cooo-AAH-oo-oo-oo-woo of the morning dove or the haunting tremolo calls of the common loon, both of which I perform by cupping my hands together and blowing into them; the *hu huhuhuhu hoo hoooo! hoo* from the great horned owl; the hoarse, screaming *kee-eeee-arr* call of the red-tailed hawk; the liquid gurgling *o-ka-lay* call of the red-winged blackbird; the classic *caw caw caw* of the American crow; the *whit dyeer dyeer dyeer* of the northern cardinal; the high-pitched whistling sound of the woodchuck; the nasal frog-like *bing* croak of the American woodcock; or the long drawn-out, high-pitched musical trill of the American toad. All of these animals above have responded to my calls, except for the mountain lion and mosquito, thank goodness.

But one calling exchange will forever remain dear in my archives of inter-species communication as the boldest, most outlandish challenging courtship showdown. No other frog carries such a dominant presence in North America as *Lithobates catesbeianusn.* The American bullfrog is the single most invasive amphibian in the world and the largest frog in North America. At Spring Valley Nature Center, especially in the still open, pervasive water lily pond, they are extremely adaptable and voracious, eating anything they can get ahold of, including worms, insects (terrestrial and aquatic), green frogs, chorus frogs, crayfish, small turtles, tadpoles, baby garter snakes, mice, voles, baby rats, salamanders, bats, small fish, fledgling birds that fall in the water, and other bullfrogs. Native to the Eastern United States, they can be held in check with such inviting predators as herons, turtles, snakes, raccoons, and humans to keep them from becoming the top of the food chain in their local ponds. But, make no mistake about it, by the time they change their dietary needs, eating algae and other plant material as tadpoles, and metamorphize into full-fledged bullfrogs, they become dominant predators with an insatiable carnivorous diet, not to be taken lightly in the aquatic food chain order.

A long-time friend of the earth, as well as a dear friend of mine, Mike Slawin, and his family came to visit me at Spring Valley during my work time. I took my lunch break early and hiked with him, his wife Margaret, and their two children Lauren and Ellen to the richly active pond, teeming with these aggressive amphibian bullies. One of the children spotted a large, muscular bullfrog on the side of the deck about 15 feet from me. I could tell it was a macho male by its size and by the very large tympanic membranes that covered his ears. I told them to be quiet and listen to see if the bullfrog would call back to my *Grrru, Grrrrrrrrm* impression. Within about five seconds, the male began to call back with a stone face as if a genetic robotic battery had kicked in—causing us to smile so widely we were on the brink of hysteria. Mike told me to do it again, and I returned the response as I kneeled on the deck, only to see this challenging bullfrog skip across several lily pads spanning over 12 feet and stop directly below me, by the edge of the deck, staring straight at my face without a single blink as if to say "So, you think you have what it takes."

Upon invitation by the bullfrog we commenced a calling contest, exchanging "jug-o-rums" for a few minutes, with Mike and his family reacting with uproarious amusement. Knowing I had to get back to work, I eventually conceded. All those female bullfrogs would be lucky to have such a bellowing mate as the one who defended his territorial courting ground. In nature, animals especially birds, are noted impressionists. Northern mockingbirds have been known to imitate at least 12 different species of North American frogs and toads, whereas jays are noted for imitating hawks to ward off their prey and signal to the other animals that a predator is in sight. I seldom apply animal impressions in the wild now, preferring to leave the jays and mockingbirds of the world to impress their communities with such evolutionary talent, and I only use them when animating my storytelling programs. However as an exception, as a result of several mule deer over eating the shrubs, native grasses and wildflowers in our yard around my retired home in the coniferous montane region of Colorado, I have been successfully able to reduce the daily flow of deer browsing by imitating a very assertive mountain lion roar. I never knew exactly how these animals interpreted my calls with their language, but they seemed to all respond with a sense of curiosity and the need to communicate. Now that my hearing is a little worse from all my professional drumming with various bands, I am inclined to focus more on listening to nature's calls than making sounds to attract wildlife. When we listen, we open ourselves to new, joyous affinities with species other than our own. By listening, we can preserve Earth's wild music. Without listening, how can it be preserved?

Chapter Thirty-One
Reaching for the Ocean Stars

The finest emotion of which we are capable is the mystic emotion.
Herein lies the germ of all art and all true science.
– Albert Einstein

My fear of the ocean goes back to my childhood and well into adulthood. Facing riptides and almost drowning a few times have certainly undermined my love of swimming in vast seas of wonder. But that slightly changed when I walked the nocturnal shores of Cumberland Island with my grad-school friend Jay McIntire. Jay loved to get up early before the other fellow students rose from their sleeping bags and catch a wild and blissful moment to share communally with the Audubon Expedition group. This could include staying up all night to watch a black bear sow and her cubs in Yosemite National Park invade nine food bags hoisted on tall ponderosa pine branches in recommended textbook fashion. Or, in this case, inviting me to a pre-dawn walk along the pristine shores of Cumberland Island off Georgia's southeast coast, which I gladly accepted.

When we arrived, you could hear the steady rhythmic waves coming to shore. It was pitch dark. The sky was overcast, but the stars were out by the millions, not coming from above but illuminating below us as we barefooted our steps into this coastal sea of enchantment. One of the most spectacular sights in the ocean is to witness the infinite explosion of tiny star-like bioluminescent phytoplankton, scintillating like grand kinetic constellations as the waves stirred this stellar activity into a coastline of pure, eye-opening wonder. During the night, a particular type of plankton called bioluminescent dinoflagellates lit up the water, disturbed by pounding waves or, as in my case, paddle stroking with a row boat a few years after this first blissful sighting.

Certain creatures both on land and sea can produce light through chemical reactions taking place within their bodies, which is known as bioluminescence. The bioluminescence results from a light- producing chemical reaction, also called chemiluminescence. Certain types of chemicals, when mixed together, produce energy that "excites" other particles to vibrate and generate light, which causes the glow. The group of chemicals involved in making plankton glow are broadly termed luciferins (same glowing chemical found in fireflies), and the light is produced by a series of oxidation reactions set off by a catalyst called luciferase. The bioluminescence in plankton is very high in several forms of plankton and is a form of cold light or luminescence.

Plankton consist of any drifting organism (plant or animal) that inhabit the oceans, and they provide a vital source of food to larger aquatic organisms, such as fish and whales. A vast range of plankton, both zoo plankton and single-celled animal plankton, are known to be bioluminescent. Bioluminescent phytoplankton occur in all the world's oceans. The most common of these are dinoflagellates, which are tiny unicellular marine plankton also known as fire plants.

Dinoflagellates are the most common source of bioluminescence in our oceans, and the chances are the sparks—not quite as bright as those made by high performance spark plugs for your car, but still bright— flying off your oar, bow, or wake of your boat are billions of tiny dinoflagellates or copepods. These creatures get their name by their ability to swim by two flagella, which are movable protein strands attached to their bodies. Bioluminescence is used to evade predators and acts as a defense mechanism in dinoflagellates. Dinoflagellates produce light when disturbed and will give a light flash lasting a fraction of a second. The flash is meant to attract a predator to the creature disturbing or trying to consume the dinoflagellate. The light flash also surprises the predator, causing it to worry about other predators attacking it, making the predator less likely to prey on the dinoflagellate.

Spending about a couple hours watching the radiant red sky sunrise over Cumberland Island, I could slowly see the infinite glowing stars in the water fade as a half-dozen, stone-faced, brown pelicans flew in line off in the distance parallel to the shore, their bellies grazing the surface of the ocean. Jay could only raise both his arms straight up to the sky with a big smile of a joyful dawn awakening. I felt the same. Looking at the ocean that morning made me feel so peaceful and not intimidated by the immense mystery below those distant waves. There is great beauty and endless wisdom to be gained by this grandeur. I became less apprehensive of the sea that day because of Jay, waking me up to a new dawn in my life.

Years would pass, and I would have the opportunity in the late summer of 2003 to fully embrace this illuminating world in Maine, rowing a quarter of a mile off the mainland to Hog Island in a night that shone both in and out of the water. The Audubon Camp for adults under director and graduate school friend Seth Benz invited me to perform my indigenous, eco-friendly storytelling program there, and I was given specific directions where to find a rowboat to use for paddling to this incredibly diverse bird sanctuary. It was a glorious night, with Mars approaching the Earth at its closest in 60,000 years. The next unique cosmic appearance wouldn't happen until 2287, and I was looking at a slithering crescent moon and the fourth-closest planet to the sun about 191 million miles closer than usual in its orbital pattern, with the reddish point of light appearing six times larger and shining 85 times brighter than it normally does.

Seth had mentioned that there would be a rowboat waiting for me when I arrived late at night to row a quarter mile to the island. I could see the spruce-pine-fir silhouettes of my destination, and the oceanic waters were extremely calm. Nevertheless, the thought of paddling in these waters still made me nervous, even with a life jacket securely fastened around my chest. It wasn't until I sat in the boat, extended the oars, and started to stroke evenly on both sides that I felt at home in these mysterious unfamiliar waters. Every time I dropped my oars into the water, there were dripping twinkles of aquatic stardust, illuminating the sides of my boat. When I would skim across the surface with my hands, there were streams of glittering magic, guiding toward an enchanting, peaceful trusting comfort. I took it slow, rowing to the island. I wasn't afraid. The Japanese have a phrase they use whenever something profound happens that will probably never happen again in our lifetime—*Mono no aware*—which is commonly translated as the "ahness" of things. It is the way in which something affects us immediately and involuntarily before we are able to put that feeling into words, whose emotional impact is both powerful and obscure to us. In the midst of the night, I confronted my fear of not feeling comfortable on the ocean, and I found the light from above and below from a beautiful illuminating dimension to guide my wild soul out of darkness.

Chapter Thirty-Two
Loons, the Moon and Randee

No one who has ever heard the diver's music – the mournful far-carrying call notes and the uninhibited, cacophonous, crazy laughter – can ever forget it.
– Oliver Austin, 1961

A loon mug sits on my windowsill to remind me of a magical moment that brought the light of love among my partner Randee, the moon, and a family of loons. Traveling over 2,100 miles around the entire loop of Lake Superior in the mid-summer of 2015 to celebrate Randee's retirement from her academic teaching career at National Louis University, we came toward the Canadian end of our camping trip to the lovely Marie Louise Lake, overlooking one of the country's seven wonders: Sleeping Giant Provincial Park. Ojibwa stories tell of *Nanna Bijou*, the Spirit of the Deep Water, being turned to stone for betraying the secret of the silver found beneath the rocks.

On the tranquil Marie Louise lake close to the city of Thunder Bay, Ontario one can view off in the distance a sleeping geologic giant floating on his back in Lake Superior.

The early moonlight evening in a borrowed canoe invited a haunting loon magic of romantic beauty and blissful wonder so fleeting yet soulfully absorbing, *2015*.

After setting up our tent in a remote site visited by a family of 11 mallards and a stunning large circular spider web glistening with dew along the shore, we decided to walk along a primitive road, encountering a Canadian doctor who had been coming to this area for years with his trusting, amiable Labradoodle. We had a wonderful conversation over a beer or two, and he offered his canoe, with state-of-the-art paddles to match, for exploring the lake that early evening. With the clear waters calm as polished glass, we slowly paddled our way across this seven-mile lake, listening to the haunting tremolos of the most primal drawn calls of the loons that it brings you to tears of ancient elemental joy. They are one of the oldest bird groups on earth going back 50 million years. We couldn't see them close to shore, as the sun was setting, shadowing out their images. The sky was lucid, with stars popping out through the course of our time in these serene waters. No one except us could be seen in the lake, as far as the eye could see. There were no motor sounds. No other voices except *Gavia immer*. I cupped my hands and performed a dynamic tremolo call to the distant loons. Randee told me to keep quiet and just let the silence sink in. We paddled, hearing the calls and the gentle droplets of water dripping down into the sides of our canoe.

The moon was almost full and rising from the east, coming up over the mystical terrain of the Sleeping Giant. A strong beacon of lunar light reflected off the subtle, rippling lake, heading in our direction as the loons were crossing our path. We lifted up our paddles to come to a complete pause in the middle of the lake. A family of six loons began to softly call to each other, moving ever so close to our canoe. We were about to burst with ecstatic giggles but watched and absorbed this beautiful passing moment. Each loon cut through the moonbeam waters only a few yards from the tip of our canoe, with the rising moon directly behind them over the horizon.

And we were there to absorb this tranquil, harmonic convergence, with a stunning sunset sky, fresh pure cool water, and loon magic. I never drink from that loon mug. It has a crack on the handle and would fall from the grip. I only look at that mug on the windowsill and remember.

Chapter Thirty-Three
Getting Rattled with Lieutenant Dan

He laughs best who laughs last.
– John Vanbrugh

In the summer of 2018, my sister Janis and brother-in-law Dan Moylan paid a visit for a few days, so we decided to hike in one of the most beautiful ecological parks in Colorado: Roxborough State Park. No dogs are allowed—to avoid disturbing the wildlife. Neither is mountain biking allowed, which could tear up the fragile fabric of the pristine front range foothills ecosystem, teeming with flowering meadows. Gigantic tilted intense, and colorful red, white, and yellow sandstone uplifting formations, interspersed with scrub oak forests and conifers, dramatically showcased the terrain of this magnificent, preserved front range. Dan had been under remission with stage four colon cancer and felt great being out, stretching his imagination and loving every minute vacationing in the great Western landscape.

We decided to pursue the north-end loop of the park, revealing spectacular views of red and white rocks, interspersed with the green foliage of Gambel oaks and aspens. As we moved away from the trailhead and headed onto the path, I shared with Dan a forewarning to watch out for rattlesnakes. This was the prime time of the warmer season for them, and they tended to swiftly slither over exposed trails into shadier hideaways. Immediately after this warning, a large rattling engine from a Bobcat tractor could be heard a few yards away, which sounded like a Godzilla rattlesnake. That shook up old Dan pretty good, and he put his hand to his heart as a sigh of relief. As I got deeper into my conversational thoughts, I stopped concentrating on what we could encounter. At six foot two, Dan had a better vision of what lay ahead. He put his big hand over my chest, and, without a word, stopped me from taking one more step onto the back half of a passing three-foot prairie rattler (*Crotalus viridis*). We both watched this venomous snake quickly slither across our path and disappear into the short prairie grasses.

Only a few yards ahead on the trail from where this photo was taken my brother-in-law Dan Moylan pressed his hand over my chest and stopped me from taking the next step on a three-foot prairie rattlesnake (*Crotalus viridis)* by the dramatic red rock uplifts of Roxborough State Park, Colorado, *2018*.

We stood speechless. A few yards ahead, we were equally humored to hear once again the rumbling of that roaring tractor kickstarting. This time Dan got the last laugh, and I was so glad he did. Good old Vietnam fighter Navy pilot vet Lieutenant Dan later promoted to Commander was my catcher in the rye, keeping me from stepping on a bite that could have cost me dearly. As much as we were on opposite ends of that "dirty little war," we genuinely became good in-law friends toward the later years, and I'm grateful we reconciled our strong differences on what it means to serve our country. That was the last time Jan and Dan visited me, for he passed away two years later, succumbing to his illness. He loved the West, rattlesnakes and all.

Chapter Thirty-Four
A Vision of a Great Lost Voice

I ask no favor for my sex. All I ask of our brethren is that they take their feet off our necks.
– Ruth Bader Ginsburg

Between Shafer Crossing and Meander Overlook on the West Rim Trail at Dead Horse Point State Park, Utah, I saw a soul-stirring vision on a canyon wall of a ghostly white face with eyes but no mouth. It was as if a voice had been removed. The date was September 18, 2020. When my soulmate Randee and I finished our sauntering five-mile hike, we drove out of the park, and I noticed by the state park's visitor center the American flag flying at half-mast. Within seconds, I said in a calm, monotoned voice, "That must be Ruth Ginsberg."

By the overlook on the West Rim Trail at Dead Horse Point State Park, Utah, I came across a stirring evocative vision off a remote canyon wall having a ghostly white face with eyes and no mouth as an eerie premonition that a profound voice had been removed, *2020*.

I pulled into the parking lot to find out who this mourning flag served. And indeed, it was dear Ruth. Randee and I felt a deep silence in ourselves. We lost a great feminist icon for civil liberties, someone who held an esteemed rank as a warrior judge for gender rights from the highest courts in the land, one of which was the U.S. Supreme Court. A couple of days later, we drove to the Arches National Park, viewing numerous exquisitely carved out arches gracing the park, paying a special visit to one in particular, the Courthouse Towers. We brought our Native American flutes out and played, offering tobacco to thank Ruth Bader Ginsberg for her tenacious perseverance toward minority and women's rights. As I looked up at these monumental towers, I noticed a fissure split right down the middle of the upper level. How symbolic to know that Ruth's loss just a few months before a Democratic president was elected had been replaced by someone who takes a very conservative, restrictive, originalist posture toward human rights compared to RBG. That crack down the middle of this prodigious monolith reinforced for me how such a serious blow to civil rights and social justice had been done, most likely tipping the courts in favor of a far-right, top down, conservative, discriminatory ideology.

My soulmate Randee Lawrence and I brought out our Native American flutes and played before Courthouse Towers at Arches National Park, offering tobacco to thank Supreme Court Justice Ruth Bader Ginsberg for her tenacious perseverance toward minority and women's rights. One flute stands alone as a lone symbol of Ruth's dignity and courage to speak out for gender equality, the rights of workers and the separation of church and state. As I looked up at these monumental towers, I noticed a fissure split right down the middle of the upper level reminding me of a great lost voice once holding the court accountable with those important issues for our time. *2020.*

Compared to the late justice RBG, Amy Comey Barret's appointment created the largest ideological shift caused by a single seat's replacement during her 40-year period. In fact, Barrett, whose mentor was the late Justice Anthony Scalia, shifted the high court rightward even more than the appointment of Clarence Thomas, a conservative appeals court judge, did when he replaced the liberal stalwart, Justice Thurgood Marshall. When Norwegian artist Edvard Munch painted his anxiety ridden maddening vision in *The Scream*, there was a bone-chilling figure with a howling mouth, exclaiming the unthinkable horror of modern life. The ghostly vision I saw on that canyon wall had no mouth. The dark crack in the upper area going down the middle of that monolith at Courthouse Tower symbolized a lost voice, causing a serious gap in ensuring the full rights of women and minorities are protected.

All of us, men, women, transgenders and people of different colors, faiths, and ethnicities must pay attention to proactively standing up for equality and inclusive justice. Denying the rights of one group puts everyone's rights at risk. But that canyon wall, with an evocative topical vision, conveyed an intuitive mystical message about paying attention to the ancient carvings of time and space. No mouth, just eyes on a pale white face. When a sufficient number of contemporary, intuitive, right-brain thinking people have reentered nature's flow of kinship connections and become conscious contributors to the evolving drama of the world, our modern, industrialized, high-tech-driven planet might re-awaken to a new, interwoven global village inhabited by passionate, wildly creative, imaginative, adventurous, curious, empathetic, joyous, and cooperative members of an exciting promising future. Such a collective vision can only enhance the quality of our existence and save us from further dehumanizing our species.

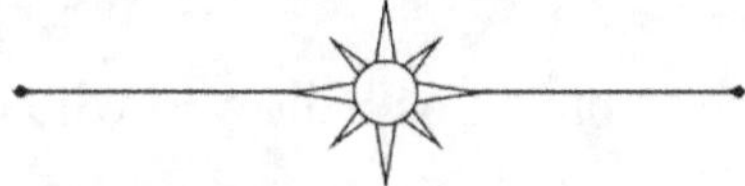

Chapter Thirty-Five
Towering Crowned Twig Eater Enchants our Home

When moose comes into your life, the void of life is being awakened.
—Ted Andrews

The moose is an animal of contradictions. It is strange yet majestic. It seems awkward, but there is a profound gracefulness to its cautious movement. While it makes us smile upon seeing this rare four-legged giant, it also causes us to catch our breath. Despite the mammoth size of the moose, it does have a unique ability to move silently and speedily.

They have superb depth perception and can accurately judge the negotiability of an area. One bull moose chose to speedily roam our front yard and awakened a magical awakening on September 14th, 2022 in our retirement Rocky Mountain setting.

Our refrigerator clunked out the day before, so we distributed food in a cooler, our trailer's frig and a neighbor's home freezer. The following mid-morning I went downstairs to get the orange juice out of the cooler and when I returned with the juice, I decided to lighten up the moment by asking Randee "Think of something that rhymes with juice." Her answer matched mine.

"Moose." We were in sync. Shortly thereafter, Randee goes outside to water the plants on the deck, and cries out, "Oh my god, oh my god! There's a moose in our front yard."

I immediately ran out of the kitchen, down the stairs with my camera, only to see the moose trotting away from our front yard. Unbelievable! First time in six years we have spotted a moose on our property and it turns out to be the very moment Randee and I were in sync with the "juice-moose" game.

To many indigenous peoples of the woodlands when a moose appears unexpectedly in your life, it is a special, sacred gift, opening up unique energies to awaken the power of paying attention to new depths of awareness and sensitivity within yourself and within your immediate environs.

We were so blessed to have this hallowed wild converging magical moment by our home.

132

On several occasions Randee and I are in sync with our thoughts but in this case we were even astonished to encounter our first moose in our yard after playing a guessing game that included this passing wonder. 2022

Part III
Dream Catchers

(Inspirational people and nature revelations, instilling compelling
lessons of eternal wisdom.)

Chapter Thirty-Six
A Wurlitzer Monolith Serves as a Dream Maker

Then she spotted in the corner, glowing wonderfully, a Wurlitzer jukebox. 'Holy shit!' It was like being on a commuter train through the Bronx and seeing among the piles of crushed cars a pasture with a lone white horse.
– Garth Risk Hallberg

For the first five years of my life, I lived in a three-flat apartment on the north side of Chicago, located in the Avondale neighborhood, sandwiched between my father's parents and his brother's family. We all lived exclusively above the Spring Mill Tavern, which my uncle, aunt, grandparents, and parents owned. They all worked hard, keeping this lively Eastern European drinking hole going, with my mom and aunt making sandwiches, my grandma and step-grandpa running the conversation in Russian and Polish, and my dad and uncle serving the drinks. My tough yet loveable bootlegging Ukrainian-Russian Grandma Pauline Macko owned three bars during the 1930s, 40s, and 50s, where, unbecoming at the time, she encouraged women to openly drink at her taverns. We were an extended family, living in very close quarters to each other.

Outside of playing with my older cousin Lee, who turned me on to animated cartoon characters like Tweety Pie and Sylvester the Cat on Capitol Records, and my friend Billy, who played marbles with me, I would repeatedly come downstairs in need of something to do, whereby my parents would direct me to what would be my surrogate parent: the iconic Wurlitzer jukebox. Simply enchanting in so many ways, the arching colorful, illuminating bubble tubes were dazzling to watch, even when the songs were silent. Everything seemed to blend into a swirling captivating motion. Granted it was a machine, but, as a young child, I could care less if my fascinating ornate attraction was human or not, just as long as it dazzled me, sending me off to a place where music, visual ecstasy, and a reliable non-human automated baby sitter awaited my visit, stationed to where my mom and dad, aunt and uncle, and grandparents worked. I can still recall the richly detailed, flashy jukebox, flipping pop 45 disc hits while customers shouted, laughed, danced, and sang through the wee hours of the morning. I loved singing "How Much Is That Doggie in the Window" by Patti Page and "That's Amore" by Dean Martin. Sometimes, strangers would drop coins for me to keep on singing my favorite tunes. Having that collective unconscious experience embedded in me a love for music and gave me the confidence to take that passion to another level. I was a protégé to that jukebox, launching me on a path toward entertaining the masses.

Sporting a red checkered coat and neatly cut hair before an audience of festive attentive families, at five years old with a firm grip on the mic stand, I test out my *calling* to forever entertain with the holiday favorite "I Saw Mommy Kissing Santa Claus," by Jimmy Boyd, who became a big hit at 13 years old., *1953*. Photo taken by Lucille Paige (deceased).

My first-grade teacher, Mrs. Mueller at Wilson Elementary School in Bellwood, Illinois, knew I couldn't sit still and loved to entertain fellow student peers around my assigned desk, so she wisely channeled this irresistible hyper-ball of talent into a regular TV show, consisting of a large refrigerator box with a 20 square inch cut-out, TV screen-sized opening, so I could present a wide range of songs, slapstick antics, and comedic impressions to the class. My teacher would introduce me, "And now are you ready for Dennis?" Shows would occur weekly. I was so entertaining with my slapstick pratfalls and class clown antics (inspired by noted comics Red Skelton and Buster Keaton) beyond the cardboard TV screen that my teacher had me perform to the second- and third-grade classes during monthly Sandwich Sale events held in the classes.

Mrs. Mueller was truly my favorite teacher during my 12-year public-school sentence because she caught my love and passion to make people laugh and channeled that gift to feed into my need for making me happy and feeling gratified. This I believe is what the secret of life is all about. Each of us has a gift, and, if someone in a position of authority or influence helps you nurture that exceptional passionate ability, no matter what it is, to make people feel good or improve their condition in life, then you're blessed and on your way to a life worth living and remembering. My parents knew I had this uncanny gift to perform constantly, no matter the setting.

Unquestionably, my favorite and kindest teacher from kindergarten through high school, Mrs. Mueller found a way to tap into my restless creative outgoing gifts which catapulted my love for entertaining fellow classmates. I was truly the happiest student in first grade thanks to her gifted willingness to think out of the box on empathetically understanding my true calling, *1954*. (Class Photos) Unknown photographer.

But there was another person who saw a potential celebrity in the making: my flamboyantly feathered hat neighbor Mrs. Zaki, who liked to act like the unconventional individualist socialite Broadway eccentric *Auntie Mame*, and who warmly took me under her wings.

When I was eight years old, she invited me to the incredibly popular Fritzel's restaurant on State St. This Second City landmark, operating for 30 years, catered to the celebrity, politician, athlete, and upper crust of society in and visiting Chicago. Famous sports names such as Yogi Berra, Whitey Ford, and Mickey Mantle would visit when the Yankees were in town. Mrs. Zaki knew I was quite an entertainer and told me a story that stuck with my entertaining, outgoing personality. As she was exiting the restaurant on a cold blustery winter afternoon, her head was down, ready to anticipate the heartless Chicago biting winds. She began to push the revolving doors, but they were stuck. As she looked up to see what was jamming them, there were legendary comics Dean Martin and Jerry Lewis holding the doors from moving, being as zany as ever. She nearly had a heart attack, needing to catch her breath from so much laughter. I knew Mrs. Zaki loved the world of glamor and entertainment, and I had such an inspirational time feeding off this joy of theatricality. Music during my childhood was a blessed vehicle for bringing my extended families together. Our festive gatherings usually consisted of alternating accordion-playing cousins, a chorus of other cousins, sisters, brothers, and aunts and me on whatever I could get my hyperactive hands on for drumming, like pots and pans, not to mention even using my fingers and cupped hands over my cheeks and mouth to make rhythmic complimentary sounds. Through the years, I never gave up being a percussionist or singing my heart away in a private space, where I could lively perform my favorite Broadway, motion picture and pop tunes.

I always had a passion to entertain in a lively manner. Decades would pass, and it wasn't until the mid-1980s that I began to seriously revive the inspirational time I had with that magical Wurlitzer wonder. I helped start a contemporary professional folk band called Prairie Smoke, where I was a backup singer, harmonicist, and global percussionist, inspired by the Grateful Dead's Mickey Hart. I played with the band for over 20 years and also founded a storytelling performance enterprise in 1989 called Swiftdeer Paige, focusing on ecology, indigenous people, and earth ethics through stories, dances, and songs. I have professionally entertained enough people to easily surpass Chicago's Wrigley Field's seating capacity.

Playing in a contemporary folk band Prairie Smoke for about 20 years I was so grateful to perform with a myriad of wonderful settings but my favorite place of all was at the Acorn Folklore Center in Naperville, Illinois. Packed with 60 people young and old immersed in enchanting spooky fun décor during the Halloween season of 1999, Dave Margolis, Donna Anderson Brooks and myself felt such a joyful appreciation from the audience coming from our happy magical time humoring each other while effortlessly harmonizing original and familiar American folk melodies. It was a warm blissful night to remember for everyone.

As I was alone again as a onesome, ailing from a sad, irreconcilable divorce, biking down the Fox River Trail, I entered the quaint town of Dundee, where *Road to Perdition*, featuring Tom Hanks, was filmed. I was thirsty and needed a juice kicker to continue on and came across a multicolored, Harley-motorcycle-friendly pirate bar around high noon. I walked in, and the first thing I saw was a jukebox. Somebody heard me enter and came out of the kitchen. He looked tired and grumpy.

"Can I help you?" he asked with a gruffy voice.

"Sure, would appreciate a glass of orange juice," I said.

"We don't have any orange juice," he said, agitated over the fact that he was in the back kitchen working and had to leave his task for this guy ordering at a macho bar a glass of orange juice.

I requested just a glass of water, so he grabbed one and began to fill it up while I moved over to the jukebox. I knew the man was awfully tense, so I looked at the selections and saw a song that could completely change the mood: "Peaceful Easy Feeling" by the Eagles. When the song blasted across the room, you could see this grumbling bartender come to life. He began to bellow the words, and I joined him. We were mellowing out together alone in this early afternoon waterhole, and then he came around the bar. We put our arms over each other's shoulders, and we both began to sing the chorus. "Cause I get a peaceful, easy feeling. And I know you won't let me down cause I'm already standing, I'm already standing, yes I'm already standing on the ground. Hoo, hoo, hoo, hoo."

Music is the only true liberating thing that can enter your psyche without permission, and we both dropped our defenses to appreciate the jubilant comradery of the moment. He then went back to the kitchen and came back with a tall glass of orange juice. All this happened within less than 15 minutes. We were instant buddies thanks to that jukebox and the Eagles, although I never got his name. I pedaled away, never forgetting that moment, which happened in the early fall of 1999.

Jump to May 18, 2021. Driving home on Interstate 76 from Chicago with my soulmate, Randee, to visit family and friends through the short grass prairie plains of eastern Colorado, near the quaint town of Crook, I was listening to a classic rock station play Joan Jett's *I love Rock n' Roll.* When she started bellowing out, "so put another dime in the jukebox baby," I began to remember my "easy peaceful feeling" moment with the pirate bartender in Dundee. To my utter consternation, the very next song played on 99.7 FM at 11:31 a.m. was "Peaceful Easy Feeling" by the Eagles. Need I say more? Pure magic.

Retiring to Colorado in the small, coniferous foothills-montane town of Conifer, my dear partner Randee and I discovered a Green Bay Packer friendly Midwestern style bar called The Well that constantly had live music, with all kinds of styles like classic 60s–70s rock, bluegrass, folk, country, and blues. Owned by Leslie Murray who I later learned was raised in the Black Hills of South Dakota on the Standing Rock Indian Reservation with her mom and step dad as an honored Lakota medicine man. Entering this mountain neighborhood bar for the very first time, we heard a bluesy trio singing *Sweet Home Chicago.* My eyes lit up with such a comforting assurance to see Midwesterners and Coloradans mingling in a warm, intimate atmosphere of music and instant friendliness. I knew we found a second home in our town. I couldn't hold back but approach these musicians of different genres with complete confidence in my ability to play for nothing if necessary, possessing the fullest zest to make the customers feel happy about social drinking and having a good time.

You might say, being retired, I was performing a greater volunteer service to the community. For the first two years playing, I found a magical performing niche, fitting to my vison for being at the right place at the right time with the right musicians—with even a CD jukebox without any dazzling effects fastened into the wall. Every time I played with these different combinations of musicians brought me closer to my roots. I would occasionally go into a blissful trance and remember when I used to stare into the monolithic enchantment of that Wurlitzer jukebox, bringing me more than a joy in the moment but a calling to make people happy while I spontaneously accompanied whatever song came my way. The apartment, living with my extended family, and the tavern of my early childhood years are long gone, but I have come full circle in this journey and know that peace and happiness come when you remember what made you happy during early childhood.

To help me recall where my love for music began, I gave a replicated framed copy of a tavern ad my Grandma Macko had back in the 1930s to The Well's owner Leslie Murray to hang on her business wall as people enter through the front door. It reads, using the seductive words of Mae West, *"You must come up and see us sometime! Ladies especially invited. Pauline's Inn (imported and Domestic wines and liquors; tables for the ladies)."* That pictured drawing of young women drinking liquor at a table unbecoming for its time triggers a lot of fond memories of music and wonderful times with my family. Although the Spring Mill Tavern has been torn down, along with the rest of the building where I lived, later converted into an elementary school, I feel at home again full circle from where I began this journey, very grateful to catch the *milagro* of those life-affirming, rooted connections. Ironically, the school where the tavern once stood at 3231 Milwaukee Ave.is named Federico Garcia Lorca, after a renowned Spanish poet, playwright, and theater director. He was a true lover of the performing arts and so am I.

Playing for a local full house benefit in Conifer, Colorado at the Venue Theater, artisan musician Norm Hughes, noted Cowboy raconteur musician Rex Rideout, both of whom are professional historic reenactors, and Swiftdeer-Paige pull off a festive evening of Christmas past in the West. Norm is playing is playing a helicon, Rex is on one of his many fiddles of different sizes and styles, and Swiftdeer on a bodhran Irish drum shouldering a weight of sleigh bells intended for horses. *2022.* Photo taken by Elaine Rideout.

A personal lifetime collection of global percussion instruments spanning over 6 decades including a cajon, conga, bongos, boron, chimes, tongue drum, a diminutive Taos drum, along with harmonicas and a Native American flute that have graced my journey and provided a strong life force of rhythmic joys from childhood through my greying years with several bands, group drumming, informal jams, Lakota *inipi* purification lodge ceremonies, storytelling performances and personal spiritual connections with nature. *2021*

As a bootlegger in the 1930s, devout rose gardener and Russian Orthodox Church patron, divorced twice, married three times, with an extended family that reveled in drinking, eating hearty Polish-Russian dishes and generously celebrating holiday gatherings at her home, my affectionate, sweet yet shrewd, tough business woman Grandma Pauline Macko took pride in bringing the bars to life through music and conversation for both men as well as women. As a 1st generation immigrant she never looked back from returning to her Mother Russia but she never forgot her Vodka roots or her ancestral faith. B/W. Taken in the early 1950s by unknown.

To help me recall where my love for music began, a replicated framed copy provided by my brother Wayne Paige of a tavern ad my Grandma Macko had back in the 1930s hangs by the entrance at The Well bar in Conifer, a reminder to understanding the full circle journey of my roots. 2017

Chapter Thirty-Seven
What's in a Totem Name?

*Every animal. Every plant. Every time an animal or plant becomes
extinct or threatened, the world loses some of its beauty, and we, some
of ours. Every time we see the uniqueness of one animal or plant, we
also discover something new and unique about ourselves.*
　　　　　　　　　　　　– Ted Andrews

Away from the immense oppressive concrete landscape of the
city, I remember spending precious vacations during the
summer with my extended family in Tomahawk, Wisconsin,
where my grandparents, uncles and aunts, cousins, and of course my
family would come together at a rustic lodge in the wild, northern
woods.

One early dawn, while vacationing there in our quaint log cabin, I
awoke before my mom, Dad, older brother Wayne, and baby sister
Janis. Sneaking out the door just a few feet from the cabin, I was
greeted on a dirt road by a fawn, who took an instant liking to me. At
five years old, we were roughly the same eye-to-eye level height.

Trust at first sight. That fawn walked me into the woods. I was an
urban child from Chicago, where forests were nonexistent in and
around my neighborhood, and that gentle spotted yearling slowly
walked across the road while I tailed along. We seemed to belong
together, like kin. Scores of tall pine trees and their shadows did not
scare me one bit, knowing I had an accepting wildlife friend of the
woods to guide me into this new, unsullied natural world. Call it a
profound case of *Bambiphilia*, an unconditional love for fawns. I was
forever hooked with this kinship connection. I wanted to keep this life-
changing encounter a secret, but the next morning, at the same time,
the same fawn was waiting for me on that dirt road in the same spot.
We stood quietly together until my mom came out with a camera to
shoot pictures of us. As I look at those photos today, I am struck by
how happy I looked. Later, I was told that the reason the fawn was

alone was because the mother had been lethally struck down by a car, and the father was killed by a hunter. My family called the fawn Honey because of its gentle sweetness, and it stayed around our lodge as a place to find food and attention. My mom and I bottle-fed the orphaned victim while we were there from my baby sister's milk bottle.

I never forgot this story because my parents would bring it up throughout the years well into my adulthood. My personality evolved with the character of that deer. Always energetic, seldom feeling comfortable sitting down for a while, I loved to run everywhere. My first-grade teacher once said about me, "Dennis is a little visitor who enjoys visiting other friends while the teacher is conducting class."

Like the deer, I am extra-sensitive, quick, and can't sit still. Intuitive with many stories to back it up, I can readily sense the feelings of others and fall into the trappings of losing myself in other people's lives. Because my mind, body, and spirit were always on hyperdrive, I had a tendency like the deer to not always be attentive. My thoughts would race so quickly that, what I heard often started off as a train of thought within my mind, stirring up my emotions, so I feel the impulsive need to express these immediately.

One illustrious example of that reflexive spontaneous tendency was when I turned four years old, I randomly appeared on a local ABC daily talk show in Chicago called "The Tommy Bartlett Show" to sample taste a spoonful of Kosto pudding. With my spiffy, immaculate white shirt, and every seat filled in the studio theater, not to mention thousands of viewers watching throughout the Chicago area, the charming master of ceremonies and creator of the world-famous water skiing shows, Tommy Bartlett himself, asked me what I thought of it. Spitting the chocolate pudding over my shirt and face, I exclaimed "Yuck!," which brought a roar of laughter from the live audience and the rest of the Chicagoland TV viewers probably heard all the way up to Kenosha, Wisconsin.

So goes the price of having live TV commercials.

As a result, I have developed what to some is an annoying tendency to interrupt a conversation and not allow the person talking to finish what they're trying to share. Since 1986, I have added a totem title to the name I was born with: Dennis *Swiftdeer* Paige, keeping me aware of how that innocent fawn lived on the edge of the forest between lightness and darkness, curious and vulnerable yet open to the kindness of another species responsible for that fawn's loss of both parents. I had a friend that was not of my kind, taking me to an unfamiliar forest that made me feel right at home. It wasn't until after I became Swiftdeer that my brother told me my father's original last name, Olenicz, which, when translated from the Russian, means *deer*.

Welcoming the deer to my journey, I have embraced the quiet intelligence, beauty and stillness. But it is not always beauty that lies beneath the skin. Deer are highly resourceful, which makes it possible for them to produce something attractive out of simple, basic materials. They will step into each other's footprint to conserve energy and create a scented trail to avoid deep snows. My need to be resourceful expresses itself not only physically but emotionally as well because I am able to draw together community affinities, emphasizing a balanced interwoven relationship with plants, rocks, animals and waterways.

Unfortunately, like the male deer, I seem to have a problem holding on to any females or raising young. Having been educated with a master of science degree in environmental education, I understand the importance of having no children to help put an end to our modern reckless consumption of the planet's limited living systems, especially as humanity faces the Sixth Mass Extinction of life on the earth. I have always preferred to be alone or in the company of my own sex, and I have a willingness to share with both genders what I have learned via performing solo as a professional storyteller, playing in a band, although with limited female accompaniment, working as an environmental education/conservation staff or as a professional educator with children in open learning outdoor settings.

Married twice, with few female relationships and no children, I found it difficult to settle into a single, permanent relationship until I began to feel the heaviness of getting older. Yet, I have never been unfaithful in all my relationships with the opposite sex and have had little problem associating with women away from the complications of living with them. I cannot say that about my dad, who was a Playboy wannabe womanizer throughout his marriage, which undermined my mom's ability to have a healthy relationship with him. My mom considered me a nature boy who wanted Mother Earth to be my ultimate inspirational backbone. Now, I have distanced myself from what I used to be, moving over the years toward an interdependent feminine side of "becoming," as though the doe was always in me, waiting to unfold a purposeful balance in all my relations.

As the deer bounds from one place to another, so do I frequently leap from one idea or situation to another, and I have tried to work hard over the past several years to set out what I intended to accomplish. I do have a restless, uncontrollable side to my nature, which makes it difficult for others to understand me. Part of the purpose of my life is to learn the value of discipline, consistency, and persistence. Over the years, I believe I have learned to overcome these problematic issues, incorporating other totems along the way in my life journey. I have many lessons to learn from my totem names as I grow grey into the next phase of my grateful life.

Chapter Thirty-Eight
An Outfielder of Dreams

Defense to me is the key to playing baseball.
– Willie Mays

Baseball was always a part of my life up until my preteens. I loved the game, no matter the setting. Wiffle ball in front of the home, sand lot with my local buddies in the streets, open fields or "strike out" on a chalked strike zone wall at a bank or local school when they were closed, the game was a major interactive pastime during the summer. My dad was a South Sider. He hated the Cubs and always belonged to the Chicago White Sox. He attended high school and worked on the South Side at the produce mecca South Water Market Street, nurturing a distinct loyalty to the American League's Chicago team. One day, my dad received tickets to attend a Chicago Cubs–New York Giants game in the summer of 1955. I wondered how he could attend such a game, knowing how much he hated the Cubs. But he was not there to see the North Siders play, but to see the NY Giants play against them.

My brother Wayne and I had the privilege of experiencing one of my favorite moments ever: standing in the playing field by the dugout of the New York Giant's team at the friendly ivy walled confines of Wrigley Field, thanks to my dad's flimflam boss Mickey Houston knowing the rambunctious celebrity Manager Leo "the Lip" Durocher. It was a bright early summer fair weather day forever embedded in my memory because, sitting in the dugout just a few feet away from us, rattling out words like he was spitting out a mouthful of sunflower seeds, smiling as wide as the brim on his hat angled to the open sky, was one of the best if not the best center fielders ever to play the game: number 24 Hall of Famer, Willie Mays.

Willie played in 24 All-Star Games and four World Series and is the sixth all-time legitimate home run leader, pushing the boundaries as a spectacular center outfielder who could turn his back running on a deep fly ball and at waist level, with his palms facing upward wait for the ball to drop to him. Additionally, he possessed an incredible throwing marksman arm to nab the runners at home plate. As a seven-year-old avid Topps baseball card collector and aficionado of the game, I knew I was in the presence of such greatness. There he was, the "Say Hey Kid," as he was nicknamed, sitting by himself on that dugout bench. I was speechless. All I could do standing above the dugout only a few feet away from Mays was look at him and say nothing. I was nervously in awe of his presence.

Playing in the little minor leagues as a kid who loved to play the game at any position, I was chosen to play in the all-star game a couple of years after I met Willie Mays. I was assigned as the starting center fielder. It was a day I'll never forget. My Dad, who rarely showed up at my games, appeared sitting in the bleachers with the other parents and fans. Diehard Chicago Cub fan and Coach, Bill Keller, who lived a few doors from my family, hit balls out to the players, warming us up for the big game. One high pop-up was heading my way. As I stood under the descending, hard-stitched sphere, I lifted my Charlie Maxwell Detroit Tiger outfielder mitt into the air, but the ball skimmed the tip of the glove and popped me right in the middle of my forehead. I was on the ground, seeing stars. The manager knew I'd been shaken but didn't call for any medical help. I had a small goose egg that was being treated with an ice pack. I wasn't going to start the game, which I had looked so much forward to playing, especially with my dad present.

As the game progressed, the coach could see I was fully conscious and so anxious to get out there that he said "Paige, grab your glove. You're going out to center field." I had two innings left in the game, and we were up 3 to 1. No balls were hit to me until there were two outs, a runner on first base, and it was the last inning. The coach signaled to me to play in closer to match the hitter's range. I was anxious, perhaps so nervous that my judgement was clouded by the moment, seeing my dad watching me and hearing the crowd cheering so loudly.

Then it happened. A long fly ball skyrocketed toward me. I ran in to catch it, but my overzealous anticipation got the best of me. I could see the ball sailing over my bruised head. I turned my back, completely removed from seeing the ball, and was desperately hoping to make a basket catch, as if possessed with the gifted athleticism of Willie Mays during that classic World Series moment at the Polo Grounds against the Cleveland Indians in 1954, where he made such a sensational catch about 465 feet from home plate in deep center field. Not a chance.

No time to spare, I threw my glove down and ran with fury to chase the elusive ball down. The runner on base had already scored, and the hitter was rounding third, heading home to tie the game. With all the power reserved in my body, mind, and spirit conjured up in my arm, I threw a long strike on one bounce to the second baseman, who relayed a bullet to the catcher and tagged the tying runner out. We won the game on a dramatic finish that Willie Mays would have loved to have witnessed. And my dad was there, still sitting on that bench through the entire game, seeing his son's glorious comeback. On that very special day at Wrigley field, my brother and I received a handwritten baseball from the New York Giants, with four Hall of Famers, including the "Say Hey Kid."

Many decades have passed, and I handed that ball as a graduation gift over to my nephew, Corey Moylan, who was an outstanding baseball player for the University of Vermont and Butler University. I may have relinquished that treasured souvenir but never the memory of spending inspirational time with one of baseball's monumental legends.

Chapter Thirty-Nine
The Head of His Class

You can jail a revolutionary, but you can't jail the revolution.
– Fred Hampton

The high school I attended consisted of extraordinary individuals from a diverse range of backgrounds. Proviso East High School in Maywood, Illinois, back in the 1950s and 1960s, produced such talent as TV actor Dennis Franz, the All-Pro Green Bay Packer monster linebacker Ray Nitschke, Broadway performer Carol Lawrence, astronaut moon walker Eugene Cernan, the first Black female billionaire and co-owner of *BET (Black Entertainment Television)* Sheila Crump Johnson, NBA all-star/head coach Glen "Doc" Rivers, country folk singer/composer John Prine, and a classmate friend who I knew before he became the Illinois Chairperson for the Black Panther Party. His name was Fred Hampton.

With a razor-sharp tongue, amazing leadership qualities, an outrageous sense of humor, and a photographic memory, Fred was so much fun to be around. We were opposite linebackers and wrestled in the same weight class our freshmen year and attended a couple of classes together. One was chemistry, where he loved throwing spit wads on the back of an unlucky white dude's neck—who seemed to be slightly irritated but never reported this slimy attack to the teacher. By the time Fred was a junior in high school, he belonged to the local chapter of the NAACP (National Association for the Advancement of Colored People) in Maywood. He learned about the founder and poet James Weldon Johnson. Our English teacher that junior year gave us an assignment to memorize a poem to present to the class. Fred chose a poem that totally made our mouths drop in awe: *The Creation (a Negro Sermon)* by James Weldon Johnson, written in the early 1920s. Like a bible belt preacher attempting to convert the nonbelievers, Fred took off with that poem and stunned us all, including the teacher, by memorizing about 800 words with such articulate fervor and conviction.

1966 Proviso East High School yearbook, Fred Hampton posed in a graduation class photo. As a promising leader in the community becoming chairperson for a local NAACP chapter in Maywood, he seemed destined to serve his town well. Known as "the Head" by his fellow classmates, Fred was a pure delight to be around. When Martin Luther King was assassinated after graduation, his militant activism took on a dynamic sense of urgency that addressed cultural and physical genocide against peoples of different racial colors, particularly African-Americans in poor living conditions. Class photo

People who knew Fred had a nickname fitting for his character. We called him "The Head" not only because he had a large forehead but because he was so incredibly quick witted, with a sharp memory for detail and purpose. In that same English class, our teacher was going to keep the entire class after school for a behavioral issue. Fred stood up and said "We need to take a bus home. Ain't no way you're going to keep us here missing our bus." Instantly, as soon as the bell rang, we all began to make a mad dash to the door, kicking over a garbage can filled with scrap paper. The teacher yelled "Where do you think you all are going?" It didn't matter to Fred and the rest of us. He led the way with such gleeful conviction and purpose that we didn't care what the consequences would be. You could sense there was growing rage under that sharp-tongued wit.

The next day we were lectured but not reprimanded by the teacher. As a senior majoring in social studies, having taken courses in African American history and racism in America in November 1969 while attending Northern Illinois University, I met up with Fred Hampton right after giving an explosive speech on the need for the oppressed to carry guns. Invited by the Student Activity Committee to present a lecture on "American Imperialism and Racism from 1900 to the Present," his presentation was electrifying and powerfully militant. He passionately rapped about social, economic, and political oppression as an intolerable, unjust human condition, citing historical examples of organized resistance among Black, Yellow, Brown, and White peoples of the USA. Years of explosive civil unrest had unfolded, and I was about to meet a high school friend I hadn't seen for about four years, coming off a politically ruthless Chicago Seven trial, dramatically changed into a militant community organizing "preacher with a shotgun on a mission" to address the growing fascist crackdown of political dissidents in a questionable democratic republic that proclaimed liberty and justice for all.

Despite the two Black bodyguards with black berets and black leather jackets to match at all times, I approached Fred outside the lecture hall after his radical sermon at the pulpit. He was wearing his Panther beret, blue jeans, a faded corduroy sport coat, a T-shirt, and gym shoes. "Fred, I just thought I'd say. . ."

Immediately, the bodyguards stepped between Fred and I.

"Denny, Denny Paige? He's cool. Let him be. How ya' doing?" Fred auspiciously asked, with a rather raspy, quiet voice that sounded much different from the boisterous tone of old. He was upbeat but tired from his inflammatory revolutionary speech with a predominantly lily-white, middle-class student body.

"Just great!" I replied. "Man, you made me want to be Black like you. Your speech was eloquent, with a whole lot of fire to inflame the cause."

"Right on. Thank you, man. Why don't you stop by our Panther Headquarters sometime soon? Just let me know when you're gonna be there or maybe call the office. I'll tell them your name, so it's cool and everything. Right now, the brothers and sisters are getting the poor people in the streets on the West Side of Chicago organized. We got free breakfast programs to feed the people and free medical clinics to help the community get their act together. You know, a lot of consciousness-raising activities are going on over there."

"Sounds great! My church isn't too far from your headquarters. Maybe after my service I can drop by. I can't wait to rap with you then. We got a whole lot of catching up to do, bro. Keep the faith, Fred." As I walked away, I gave him the classic peace sign. That was the last time I ever saw this dear radical high school friend, for he was shuffled off quickly by the local student press after speaking briefly to me. Originally, Fred was an active chairperson for the NAACP chapter in Maywood, but he became bitterly disillusioned after the assassination of Dr. Martin Luther King Jr. He felt it was time for non-white people to grab a gun to defend themselves. Such a national, tragic death radicalized Fred enormously.

One month after my brisk, warm encounter with this confrontational dynamic ball of humanity, approximately 99 shots were fired through his front door on that infamous December morning, 1969. At first the police claimed they had responded to the shooting fire of the Panthers. It was quickly determined by the local press that such an accusation was clearly false. Despite law enforcement claims, it was eventually proven the "bullet holes" supposedly left by Panthers' gunfire actually were nail holes. Fred Hampton, one of the most gifted orators and promising leaders of an oppressed America, was brutally gunned down in a pre-dawn raid while lying asleep in his own bed. It was later proven in court that he was assassinated in his apartment by a tactical unit of the Cook County State's Attorney's Office, in conjunction with the Chicago Police Department and the Federal Bureau of Investigations.

Later, the family brought a multimillion-dollar civil rights lawsuit against the Chicago Police and the FBI for allegedly engaging in a national counter-intelligence program known as COINTELPRO (Counter Intelligence Program), which led to gestapo-style murders of "threats" such as Fred Hampton and activist Mark Clark, also present in the apartment. The disclosure of the intent of this covert operation divulged further political assassination plots and illegal wiretapping by the higher US intergovernmental authorities in the name of "national security" to go after leading dissidents critical against the US policies in Vietnam, as well as racial discrimination, poverty, the lack of Native American rights, and social injustices. Malcolm X, Martin Luther King Jr., Dennis Banks, and Russell Means of the American Indian Movement were examples of such intimidating unconstitutional investigations.

In 1982, the City of Chicago, Cook County, and the federal government agreed to a settlement in which each would pay $616,333 to a group of nine plaintiffs, including the mothers of Hampton and Clark. The $1.85 million settlement was at that time believed to be the largest ever in a civil rights case. Fred Hampton's radical changes through the turbulent 60s in pursuit of a "better people world order" transformed me into an outspoken, angry, conscientious critical social and political thinker, ready to take to the streets in protest of such blatant injustices. His friendship, although short lived, raised the bar in regard to understanding how our government really works against those disenfranchised from the system and those wanting equal inclusive justice under the law.

Today, we're witnessing a similar movement, where people are rising up against police brutality; the militarization of law enforcement agencies, where communities are treated like domestic war zones; systemic racism; xenophobia; voter suppression; and misogyny. Extreme economic disparity, alarming climate change, and a global pandemic are bringing us to a stark realization that we're all in this together to some degree and need to stand up now with our disadvantaged fellow human beings to address these pressing issues. I'm so saddened about what happened to Fred, meeting his fate so early in life, but I hope his lessons will not be lost in the historical dust of indifference and ignorance.

A statue dedicated on December 17, 2006, named for the young, Black, 21-year-old revolutionary Fred Hampton lies in front of the nonsegregated public swimming pool in his name, with a quote by "The Head" underneath the bust: "If I leave, I'll be back, and when I do come back, I'll be back to stay and join the Revolution."

GoFundMe donations have raised enough money to establish a permanent Fred Hampton House Museum at his childhood home in Maywood, Illinois, which will serve not only as a museum but include a community garden and recording studio. Hampton's relatives are seeking landmark status for the building, so the property will be protected from demolition. Maywood will always remember the bold, compelling humanity Fred brought to us, despite his tragic murder, which did not go unnoticed but instead is honored in his hometown. I will always carry his courageous, jolting story with me.

Chapter Forty
Close Encounter with the "Greatest" Conscientious Objector

Service to others is the rent you pay for your room here on earth.
– Muhammad Ali

In the fall of 1967, I was facing a real crisis in my early adult life. I had buried myself in deep trouble. As a party animal away from home attending Northern Illinois University, I violated every academic rule in the book except flunking out. I was away from my parents' rules and liberating myself by working during the summers to pay off my schooling—yet clearly becoming an irresponsible adult. I was staying up until the wee hours playing poker during school days, drinking Southern Comfort, guzzling down Schlitz malt liquors, using up my grandparents' and parents' pocket change they gave to me for my education—what a shame to see such a gift of generosity gambled away among fellow dorm students. I was self-inflicting a toxic pre-occupation with underage drinking, smoking cigarettes, and partying like there was no tomorrow while engaging in endless talks about how unjust the Vietnam War and the "establishment" was. There were panty raids, and enough wild dorm activities to make an *Animal House 2.*

Consequently, I was on the verge of flunking out and losing my student deferment. I was imminently bound for Vietnam and starting to feel extremely depressed and worried about my future. My parents didn't need to lecture me. I knew what was ahead, and it wasn't pleasant. As a sophomore, I had to get my grades significantly up to avoid a fate fighting an illegal and immoral war in Southeast Asia— or choose to either leave the country or join VISTA (Volunteers in Service to America) or possibly the Peace Corps. I pondered and brooded these options, frequently walking alone in a daze during my free time throughout the campus, preferring to linger around Glidden

Field, where pedestrians were rarely seen. One day in early fall 1967, I was sitting on hard, barren ground, overlooking the sports turf practice football field, wondering about my future in a dead-end street when a shiny black Cadillac coasted to the end of the street and parked about 40 feet from me. Leaping out of the car was one of the most outspoken critics to the Vietnam War and probably the greatest boxer ever to fight in the ring: Muhammad Ali.

In June 1967, Ali was convicted in federal court for refusing induction into the US Army when he claimed conscientious objector status because of his Islamic faith. The act was considered by various states' boxing authorities as "detrimental to boxing," with each stripping away his title and license to box. Federal authorities took Ali's passport, and he faced five years in jail and an expensive appeal process that quickly depleted the Champ's savings. Ali had much to think about and needed to be by himself, so he took to the road with a couple of bodyguards and began to lecture throughout the country about his faith, the war, the fights, and his love for humanity.

Ali stood up to stretch and take in a fresh deep breath of Dekalb County hog farm air. He looked around to check out this rural campus before heading back into his luxury car to prepare a speech for the university students that evening. His 6-foot-3-inch presence wore a formal, white, long-sleeve shirt partially rolled up, with an open collar, black pants, and a beautiful princely aura that could only be described as "completely mesmerizing." It certainly got my attention, especially when he extended his arms toward the sky to take it all in. He was bigger than life, as if there had been a divine intervention, striking me right through my heart, mind, and spirit. Call it a transformational knock-out (TKO).

That moment, perhaps lasting no more than 5 or 10 minutes, was enough to spark a dramatic change, shifting my attitude for the need to grow up and face the consequences of my actions. I chose to stay in school by studying like my life was on the line. I majored in history, focusing on American and Asian studies, with a minor in sociology, and I rose my grades up to complete undergrad school in four years. Eventually, I earned two master's degrees, one in social studies from Northwestern University and the other in environmental education at Lesley University.

During the summer of 1968 I drove to the Southwest with childhood friend and college roommate Jerry Fisher in his brand new red hot mustang purchased at a rock bottom price from my parents. During our adventurous youth travels, we met up with an extremely amiable, highly energetic man while waiting in line at a Dairy Queen in Colorado. He introduced himself as Julius Menendez, who just happened to be the legendary US Olympic training coach for Cassius Marcellus Clay, aka Muhammad Ali. He treated us to hamburgers and shared a few interesting details about "pretty boy" Cassius Clay getting ready at the University of Michigan for the 1960 Olympics held in Rome, Italy.

"He was a mama's boy. His mom would sit on the side of the ring and watch her son train all the time."

Ali's mother Odessa was a Baptist and a strong believer in her faith. She would take him and his brother to church to learn her idea of what was righteous. She taught both her sons to love people and treat everybody with kindness. Little did she know that benevolent code of behavior would end up by the ropes of the heavyweight boxing ring. Cassius Clay won the gold medal in the light-heavyweight division and went on to not only become Muhammad Ali, one of the world's "greatest" boxers but also an outspoken, fierce anti-war critic, a very high-profile figure of racial pride for African Americans during the Civil Rights Movement, poetically as fast with his words as his fist, and eventually becoming a committed humanitarian as a faithful member of Islam.

Likewise, Julius Menendez also had a profound influence on my life. Before we parted our ways, he said something that has always stuck with me after all these decades. "Always be in motion. If you can take the stairs, take it. Don't slouch on life" He then ran back to his car to meet up with his wife, patiently waiting for her food. No way could I achieve the greatness of Ali, nor did I want to pursue a career punching people's brains out, but I could achieve those wise words from legendary Coach Menendez by staying healthy and in shape.

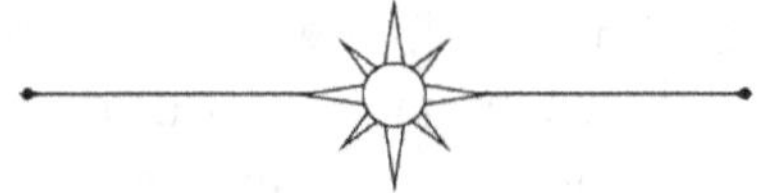

Chapter Forty-One
Training for Improvisational Living

I wanted a perfect ending. Now I've learned, the hard way, that some poems don't rhyme, and some stories don't have a clear beginning, middle, and end. Life is about not knowing, having to change, taking the moment and making the best of it, without knowing what's going to happen next. Delicious Ambiguity.
– Gilda Radner

After a serious break-up with my first young adult love while enduring a highly paid non consensus-based formal learning public middle school teaching job in Skokie, Illinois, in late 1973, I sought refuge in pursuing a dream of becoming a performing humorist and writer at the acclaimed Second City School of Comedy. I also suffered from sexual shyness and was determined to resolve my feelings toward women by lightening up socially and perhaps professionally. Through a year-long training with the Jo Forsberg Players Workshop, I overcame my quiet desperation and acquired plenty of hearty compliments for my whimsically off-the-wall and inventive routines.

As a child, I always wanted to be funny and sought comedic ammunition for making people laugh at and with me. Now, in search of a professional life, I was testing out the waters to fully plunge into the light-hearted entertainment world, which could lead to continuous laughter and wickedly insightful truths about the human condition. I studied under the gifted improvisational ensemble master teacher, Josephine Raciti Forsberg, who trained such actors and writers as Harold Ramis, Peter Boyle, Shelly Long, George Wendt, Bob Odenkirk, and Bill Murray.

Players Workshop was incorporated in 1971—and was the first school of its kind. Its charter was to teach people how to improvise over a course of five terms, prepare them for the Second City stage, and offer them opportunities to perform. With a space of her own, Jo was able to hold classes in the evenings at branch locations like church halls when people who worked during the day could come. Suddenly, a new influx of students started to enroll: working people who just wanted to have fun. Jo saw this as an opportunity to turn masses of people on to the stage.

And that was her ultimate goal. Jo would often say "I want a theater on every corner." Even though she had her own space Josephine was still an integral part of the Second City family. She continued to teach many of her more advanced classes on the main stage there; her Players Workshop sign was hung on the Second City wall by the stairs for all to see, and her Children's Theater was going strong every Sunday, offering original plays and musicals with audience participation and free birthday parties. However, most of all, Jo's students and graduates were selected over and over to be in the Second City companies—because they were talented and because Jo trained them well.

Whenever we, as potential future Second City paid players, would finish our workshop training, most of us would head over to someone's home and brainstorm new comedic ideas and routines. I loved triggering improvisational scenes in close quarters with a dynamic intimate audience of receptive peers. However, one serious setback that made me very ill at ease was the casual use of cocaine in all its forms of intake. As a teacher, that troubled me deeply. Yes, this drug can bring out the Richard Pryor or Robin Williams' brilliance of spontaneous hilarity, but it can also kill you. Performers, especially in the comedy field, have the need to "be on" all the time, and so cocaine was an ephemeral, yet lethal, vehicle to keeping that upper drive going.

As the days were numbered with this workshop, I was able to critique one superstar Second City performer who went on to become probably one of the most successful students to come out of the school: Bill Murray. As workshop students, we would be allowed to stand on the side of the main Second City Stage behind the curtains and critique the satirical skits. One memorable scrutiny dealt with "Boss Daley," based on a book by *Chicago Sun Times* columnist Mike Royko about the city's ruling Mayor Richard J. Daley. At a thin 6' 2", Murray was outrageous trying to portray a pudgy 5' 8" man who was acting more like a laid-back Florida Keys slacker than the stout no nonsense mayor of a tough city. Less than two years later, Bill Murray made his debut on *Saturday Night Live*, and the rest is history.

Josephine Forsberg was my favorite teacher while living in the Chicagoland area as an adult, providing important improvisational skills for living in the moment, taking the theater of humanity that's in us all and bringing home a wonderful sense of collaborative trust in the process of performing. When I was attempting to create a scene with a small cast of improvs, Josephine stopped the act and said, "You're acting in your head, not with your body. The audience doesn't see what kind of funny brain you have. Bring it out." Although I wasn't able to conquer my sexual timidity, I at least discovered a creative format to fulfill a dormant dimension, that being my insatiable drive to break down the barriers of personal ego and pride to make people from all walks of life laugh at their own inadequacies. No matter where I go, taking those improv skills opens my journey to a greater community through warmth and humor.

Eventually, I dropped out of teaching in public school and chose a different path of learning based on experiential, multi-aged, non-graded, more informal, non-coercive, consensus-based learning. I decided to choose a job at a poverty-based alternative community school in Santa Fe, New Mexico. I was told later by someone who partook in my Player's Workshop that records of my comedy schooling there were kept until 1978, roughly four years after I completed the program. There was a slight degree of hope that I would return, and my schooling would continue till I made it big time on the main stage at Second City, the world's greatest comedy theater. Improvisational techniques really helped me endure the rough times and embrace the glorious teachable moments at the radical Summerhillian, poverty-based Santa Fe Community School thanks to, in Bill Murray's candid words, "Jo Forsberg, the best teacher I ever had."

Chapter Forty-Two
A Fortuitous Vision Quest

*I dream of a hard and brutal mysticism in which the naked self
merges with the nonhuman world and yet survives still intact,
individual, separate.*
– Ed Abbey, *Desert Solitaire*

Sometimes when you lose yourself in the great dark unknown, you can find yourself. Every spring, my rugged little private school of spirited, independently guided children and adults loaded up our camping gear and water supplies in old reliable clunkers and headed to the colorfully weathered mesas of north central New Mexico. Pottery shards dotted the timeworn landscape while well-preserved secrets of ancient pueblo legends remained in abandoned cliff dwellings. A five-day food and water supply sustained our basic needs. This remote annual destination campsite along an obscure bumpy US Forest Service road in the heart of a pristine ponderosa forest was always a welcoming getaway sanctuary from the struggling, impoverished conditions of the school. People seldom visited this hidden region known as Garcia Canyon, which is a few miles from the ancient Puye Cliff dwellings on the Santa Clara Pueblo Reservation. On a clear night, the illuminating lights of Los Alamos can be seen from atop the higher mesas, causing one to imagine the coming of the *aurora borealis*, the spectacular northern lights.

A student from the Santa Fe Community school tosses a frisbee among his free-spirited adventurers on the cliff edge of Garcia Canyon only a few miles south of Puye Cliffs, one of the historic ancestral villages of the Santa Clara people on the Parajito Plateau, New Mexico. At the base of that overlook was our remote campground where I began my unforeseen transformational hike toward an ascending personal destiny. 1982

Each time visiting this richly wild place, with its pueblo remains, I took a partial day off to hike alone during the week. Low-impact camping and outdoor living demand constant attention, especially when one is responsible for testy children on playfully challenging terrain. In short, I sought a break from teaching and watching over these little experiential fireballs. Mountain lions, golden eagles, rattlesnakes, and coyotes continue to prevail with their gifted, wild wits, reminding me to have all of my senses on high alert. I cherished this solo time immensely, embracing the unfolding mysteries of natural dramas with every concealed trail I followed. The deep blue sky, windswept whispering pines, smoothed out mountains, gentle, short, undulating prairie grasses, and cool, clean, bubbly streams imbued a sense of joy, simplicity, and wonder.

All those blissful connections over years of being there seemed to feed into an unforeseen *vision quest* in that early May morning of 1982, forever leaving me with a growing heartfelt appreciation for human kinship and a sharper understanding of my life's calling. Charlie Bentley, the acting principal of the Santa Fe Community School, carried a deep affection and respect among the many who were fortunate enough to know him. For over 10 years, Charlie did these annual pilgrimages to the promised campsite, though he rarely ventured beyond the familiar terrain of Garcia Canyon. Aside from keeping an eye on the children, he had another good reason for staying put this particular year.

As the fire cracked repeatedly over a chilly early morning dew, Charlie told his story, unaware that this was a forewarning for what I was about to face. "There's a monk from a local Franciscan order who was found face down dead last month, a few miles north of here. He had a broken leg and was apparently stretched out, with his hands deep in the sand, desperately attempting to find water from a dried-up arroyo."

I was shaken by his warning and reconsidered hiking the backcountry this time around. However, the next day, I briefed Charlie that I was going to hike for most of the morning and possibly into the early afternoon over a few mesas straight south from where we were camped. The hike would not be expected to last more than a few hours. However, if by any chance I could not make it back before sunset, a fire would be built on top of the first mesa to signal my safety.   With a small daypack, lightly loaded, containing a hardy yucca root, a couple of PB&J sandwiches, a plastic gallon jug of water, an orange, a paperback on the genesis of Native Americans, and a book of matches tucked in my wallet, I trekked my way to the summit of the first mesa. It was 8:30 in the morning, with a slight frost on the tents, when I briskly walked away from the quiet campsite of restless sleepers and deep dreamers. The dry, swift winds passing through the Ponderosa pines and along the steep cliffs were momentary reminders of a breathing, ever-changing earth. Assuming the hike would last until the peak of the day, I dressed lightly, wearing a pair of cutoffs, a T-shirt, a long-sleeve flannel shirt, a baseball cap, a pair of cotton socks, and low top sneakers.

Looking back from the apex of the first mesa, I saw and heard the children waking up, while Heidi, the principal's petite, chatty schnauzer, scampered around the campground with her high-pitched piercing bark. The vast Southwestern landscape was intimidating for a *flatlander* growing up in a Chicago suburb—and strange in its geologic, moon-like grandeur—but the familiarity of still seeing Garcia Canyon instilled a hearty vote of confidence to pursue unknown vistas ahead. To avoid getting lost, I decided to veer in the direction of a distant, illuminated white-water tower in the shape of a gargantuan golf ball. The tall, pronounced tank seemed to stand like a permanently embedded hot air balloon off the main highway leading to Los Alamos.

Walking up the second mesa was exhilarating. Thermal updrafts could lift a raven's playful spirit and mine as well. A meandering stream cut through the side of an extinct volcano, hidden from loggers and campers. Verdant, heart-shaped-leaved cottonwoods spread along the edges of these crystal lucid waters. Immediately, I made my way down, feeling the loose red pumice break from my unsteady steps, while disturbing several blue belly lizards basking on sunbaked primeval solid dark rocks, performing push-ups, like warm-up exercises to start their day. I was losing a sense of conventional time, oblivious to the moment.

In this valley surrounded by early spring awakenings of open, regenerative high desert New Mexican landscape, I was at peace. It was time to purify myself in the cool, shaded, bubbling stream of soothing undulant aquatic grasses. I cut scraps of fresh yucca root given to me by a friend and dropped them in my plastic jug of freshly filled, spring-fed water. After setting the container in the radiant sunshine of a nearby wet meadow, I began reading my packed book on the origin of Native Americans perched from a strong cottonwood limb suspended several feet above the ground. After barely reading a few pages, I was surprised to witness a rumbling procession of cattle directly below me, following these wonderfully shady cottonwoods, avoiding the intensity of a midday sun. As the head bull nudged the herd, moving like a flowing linear stream, I was reminded of the need to move on to embrace all I could in the short amount of quality break time I had.

Celebrating the preciousness of solitude among nature's glorious affinities, I prepared for a joyful washdown. The water in the jug was tepid enough for bathing. I shook the solution and watched an explosive surge of yucca suds rising to the cap. Naked, I stood staring up at the bright sky as if to boldly proclaim, "Great to be alive for all to see!" Once grown and harvested by the Pueblo people and Dine' (Navajo), the native plant-derived soap ran gently down my salty, smokey-smelling body. It was purifying and incredibly refreshing. Whatever yucca root water remained in the jug would be swallowed as a nutritional drink high in vitamins and minerals. I sat on healthy patches of grama grasses to dry my skin and watch the winds dance with the trees and birds.

The sun was directly over my face. It was time to get dressed and move on. I followed the stream through a thicket of willows until the flow disappeared into the underground mouth of a canyon. I ascended to the top of a mesa and saw the serenity of a splendid cove. The subterranean waters merged into the glittering, ever-so winding *Rio Chama*. I carefully and nervously walked to the edge of a promontory. There I sat eating a PB&J sandwich, viewing all that was above, around, and below me. Painted on a wall using natural pigments were petroglyph inscriptions, indicating the merging of these precious waters. It was a *sacred, hidden confluence.* The stick-like drawings showed a man and a boy, perhaps a father and his son, standing by a creek that lead to a river with four fish figures face down and placed tail up. I realized that this drawing conveyed the very same underground creek I followed to get to this spot, and the river must have been the place where bountiful fishing most likely occurred. I was so excited I wanted to cry out in jubilation, but I chose not to disturb the wildlife. I sat still with a tearful smile, endeavoring to comprehend the temporal ancient beauty of the moment. The earth and sky were speaking to my heart like great wise elders.

Skipping down the backside of the overview, I decided to not backtrack and create my own trail to the campground as a wishful shortcut. Obliviously bushwhacking for miles through short growth pines and scrub oaks in hurried anticipation of sharing this wonderful petroglyph discovery with the motley school campers, I recklessly ran to another unknown huge mesa, scraping cactus pears, yuccas, and jagged cliffs. I realized, to my greatest fear, that the vista beyond this mesa was completely unfamiliar.

I was lost.

The sun was sinking fast, but fortunately a half moon was shining over the horizon. Struggling to reach the apex to another mesa to gauge my whereabouts, I fearfully noticed my plastic water jug was leaking profusely from a cactus pear puncture, and I had to guzzle down the remaining source of yucca ablution before spilling it into the red sandy soil beneath my swollen feet. I was without food and water. The crisp evening winds were cooling while the fading light was seriously altering my perspective. I lost my baseball cap and faced an increasing chill. It was a critical situation. I needed to make an emergency plan while my senses were still intact. A shocking moment arose. Could this be the same damn mesa I trekked over earlier today? I climbed a steep slope in an attempt to reconnect with my afternoon footprints. Breathless, cold, hungry, and frantically running out of options, I sensed the earth I walked on could be my burial ground. Although on the brink of pure exhaustion and defeat, I refused to collapse.

Ascending to another unfamiliar mesa, I remained there with the remote hope that a rescue team would spot me the next morning or possibly sooner. It was becoming hard just to think. I wondered what Charlie was thinking at this moment, especially since he would not see a fire on the first mesa signaling my safety. As my hands trembled, I attempted to build a fire with dry grass and all the business cards stuffed in my wallet. I only had six match heads in the book to trigger a blaze. They were all damp from my sweaty pockets. The evening wind was biting, gusty, and ominously unforgiving. Every time I tried to light these crumbling cards, the wind extinguished the embers. With one stick left, I was able to light a small pile of grasses, only to have the wind swiftly blow the embers out. All of my matches were gone. Hope was fading. Darkness was feeding into my despair. I was suffering from a severe case of hypothermia, producing a chilling effect of diarrhea in my cutoffs. I vitally needed warmth. Even though my body was curled up like a Siberian husky in a blizzard, I became deathly cold and rapidly short of options. The temperature hovered around freezing. Conscious alternatives were depleted. I decided to let Mother Earth will her destiny upon my life. Such a precarious surrendering allowed a mix of hallucination and vision to unfold. I heard a puppy bark a few yards away. Could that little loyal canine be Heidi, the principal's dog? My heart awakened. A sudden cool breeze passed up my spine under my untucked shirt as a forewarning of what was about to unfold. An unforgettable call permeated the night. It was the deep, prolonged, echoing, piercing cry of a coyote. I felt an incredible, primordial rush for survival—a million-year-old national anthem, sung to the stars and planets and me.

As these momentary silhouettes on the open plateau ran across a fading blue lunar evening haze, I could hear and see their heavy, vaporous, palpitating breaths. The parent coyote and her pup sensed my silent desperation. They suddenly stopped about 50 feet from where I lay, keeping an acute eye on this unusual visitor in need of help. The sky faintly glowed with a sinking moon while bunch grasses and sage blended snow blue into boulders and starlight. The night awaited me with shades of darkness, mystery, and powerful hidden beauty.

As we went our own way, I felt an ache of longing to share in this embrace, to commune and be forever grateful for all the powers of life and love waiting to unfold. A coyote song heard from the illuminating moonlight could sustain a vast high desert terrain in its wondering. Despite our separate realities, I sensed a compassionate kinship and vitality from the coyotes, a spiritual bond to follow a path in this crazy, fragmented modern world, as if nature mattered. Moving down the mesa was easy. I leaped over slippery edges of loose rocks and tussled my way to the opaque, unknown bottom with relentless determination. While scratching and crawling out of several unmapped mesas, the moon disappeared for the evening. Slowly and methodically, I walked in total darkness. Nearly exhausted yet completely reluctant to bow to the *Grim Reaper*—and without water, the ground began to waver. I was hallucinating but had to keep going. I refused to stand still and freeze to death. Frigid temperatures accompanied my fate like a ghostly all seasons 24 hours 7 days a week outdoor friend, nudging me to keep going.

I latched onto tenacious branches of centuries old junipers and pinyons, projecting off steep cliffs to hoist me up over mesa ledges. I would not stop. As I heard distant cars buzzing down an unseen highway, my eyes caught a flashing beacon of radiating light between two closely adjacent mesas. The road was definitely nearby, perhaps less than three miles away. It must be the Los Alamos Highway! I knew this road. My body was warming with much joyful anticipation. Coyotes barked, yelped, and howled in celebration of the early spring nocturnal sensory awakenings.

I wasn't afraid.

A grand truth of time and space was calling me to come home. Cactus pear needles stuck into my bare flesh from a few falls, puncturing my knees to the point where I felt the blood dripping down to my ankles. I kept going, remembering when I first bit into a cactus pear, not knowing that several spiny diminutive prickles on the fruit skin would be embedded in my lips. I tripped and fell again, sliding down a sandy slope, staring face to face with a boulder the size of four bowling balls. Spitting desert granules out of my dehydrated mouth, I made my way to the road, grateful that the big rock did not crack my skull.

Feeling the heat of the pavement, cars hummed by every few minutes in the middle of the night to and from the maximum-security, 24-hours, 7-days-a-week Los Alamos scientific Lab, an insular community that produced such secretive world-changing creations as the atomic bomb. My thumb became a free ticket to water, food, and rest. Being such an accelerating, hard-driven, high-tech culture, toying with secretive research, no one was picking me up. A driver looked back over his shoulder, brake lights dimming as he sped away. I appeared disheveled and wretched from head to toe: a feral derelict, reeking with blood, shredded clothes, and unkempt grit.

I kept on trekking.

Drivers simply would not stop. In some cases, cars accelerated as they passed by. I was comforted by the distant street lights and telephone poles. My senses were still faintly together. I knew how to get back to the campground. Following the asphalt road through the heart of a pueblo village, an impressive black mesa stood boldly in the background as the incredibly lucid dark skies illuminated my vision, with a glorious display of countless stars, the Milky Way, and familiar planets. Dogs barked territorially at me from their nearby adobe homes. A Western diamondback sidewinded across my path, liking the heat of the road as much as I did. I let the venomous rattler humbly pass with trembling respect. Dawn was spreading over the Rio Grande Valley. I was entrenched with a bone-weary *death march* state of mind to get back, unfocused on paying attention to crucial directional highway signs and turnoffs, trudging with my head down right by the junction that led to Garcia Canyon.

"Holy shit, sonofabitch, I took the wrong goddamn road!" It was the main highway heading to Espanola, a town 12 miles away from where my worn wobbly feet stood. I needed to turn back two miles to the intersection. The road to the Garcia Canyon turnoff was graded steeply upward. Gritty and exhausted, I ascended with just a few miles remaining. The sun cracked through the Sangre de Cristo Mountains. The meadowlark sang with a soft, cheerful greeting while the stillness of the air was making me sleepy. Collapsing off the roadside, I caressed the gravel surface like a welcoming mattress as the heat of the sunlight slowly crept along my weather-tormented legs. Cars zipped by like hornets, buzzing as if to convey a meditative highway lullaby. As I began to sleep, a pick-up truck came to a screeching halt, nearly sideswiping me by a few inches. With my eyes closed, I heard two doors open and shut, followed by gravel crunching footsteps heading my way. Two Pueblo Tribal Council rangers from Puye Cliffs, home to the ancestors of today's Santa Clara Pueblo people, tried to wake me up.

"Hey, man, are you alright?" Nudging me on the shoulder, he repeated, "Hey, are you alright?"

"I think so, but can you get me some water fast?" I pleaded with a slow gravelly voice.

"Sorry, we can't do that. You see, we're bound by Tribal Council law not to pick up any non-Indians. Will you be okay?" the ranger calmly said.

"I guess so."

The park truck was gone before I realized what the hell I had said. How could I be so completely inept at expressing my need for help? With my mind seriously drifting and foaming saliva showing signs of severe dehydration, the rising, pulsing sun warmed my body, awakening my desire to press on. Reaching the US Forest Service Road to Garcia Canyon was like entering a familiar street, leading to a long-lost home. Everything was falling into place. I could hear Heidi barking. The last mile was exhilarating and memorable only because I knew my unintended *vision quest* was complete. My feet dragged and stumbled but would endure. Charlie's wife Merle saw me about a football field length away on the beaten logging road and ran with her two-year-old daughter Amella with welcoming warm hugs, escorting me back to the campground. We cried heartily along the way. It was one of the happiest, most grateful moments of my life.

Sitting around a quaint fire on comfy logs for breakfast, Merle offered a heaping glass of orange juice, but my swollen gritty dehydrated throat instantly rejected it. I couldn't swallow any acidic drinks, albeit nutritional. She offered me water instead. It was a simple joy, gulping down this precious, life-giving essence. I slowly tasted the fried eggs and buttered toast, savoring each bite while telling Merle the story of my perilous hike through the night in the high desert plateau wilderness. Charlie arrived in the middle of my personal, gripping tale, giving me one good brotherly hug. He had been organizing an early morning private search and rescue party to find me.

"We were going to call a search and rescue team by noon today if you didn't show up. What happened?"

"I can't talk now, Charlie. I need sleep, and, when I wake up, you'll hear one of the most powerfully telling experiences in my life."

After plopping on a self-made pine needle mattress, I slept instantly in my mummified sleeping bag under a shady ponderosa pine for seven undisturbed hours, listening to the inner winds of my dreams. When I woke up around midday, everyone gathered around the campfire, not saying a word, just waiting for me to tell them what happened out there.

Within 24 hours, I had hiked over 40 miles through incredibly rugged, yet starkly beautiful visionary terrain. I walked through the night, mostly in pitch darkness, without food, shelter, water, adequate clothing, a compass, or a map under freezing hypothermic conditions. I encountered many lessons about remembering the meaning of gratitude, determination, feeling awe under severe stress, and honoring all the experiential affinities that made my journey memorable. But the part of this unintended *vision quest* that made me a better human being lay within the true nocturnal voice of the mesa, *el coyote, Canis latrans.* Years passed and I was to later discover a side of the alleged four-legged canine trickster fitting for my profound awakening encounter. According to the Pueblo, Zuni, and Hopi traditions, the presence of *the coyote gives the lonely man in trouble new courage, new heart to fight for his life until help comes.* I am forever grateful to the lunar calls of this elusive wanderer for helping me embrace the great mysteries of the animal within. You have opened my heart to the life-giving, life-affirming spirit of the planet. For it is the primal self that dwells closest to the undomesticated natural world, drawn toward deeper affinities, communing with the non-human world and understanding all the forces that escape logical minds.

Paying attention to nature has been my *calling* ever since. Many cultures and traditions honor or despise the coyote, but, for me, I'm drawn to the incredible survivability and eco-wisdom this prairie wolf has to endure and adapt over thousands of years with humans. I have a shrine in my house honoring the coyote in my journey as my first totem animal inspiring me to learn about my deep-rooted kinship connections with the deer, and I have shared this compelling, transformative experience over the decades to scout gatherings, outdoor adventure youth camps, and family programs at state parks, libraries, schools, and nature centers. As long as I am breathing and mindful in my life, I will continue to give back to Grandmother Earth, professionally and personally remembering there is no separation between anything that is part of the sacred light and water. Blessed or cursed with the coyote imprint as a "wise-fool" years before encountering this wilderness awakening from the tribal elders of my Peace Corps assigned village, I can never surrender my pursuit to find the balance of wisdom and folly that makes for a fulfilling life.

Chapter Forty-Three
A Mensch for All Seasons

A teacher affects eternity: he can never tell where his influence stops.
– Henry Adams

For 8 years, from 1975 to 1983, I chose to take a vow of poverty at a little, impoverished, struggling alternative community-as-a-classroom school outside Santa Fe, New Mexico, where children were allowed the freedom to move around the school property, exploring their serious playful interests for learning or not learning. Under such a difficult setting, where these feisty children test the teachers in crude ways to gain trust, there was one man who gained undivided trust with them, possessing one of the greatest gifts for delicately engaging in the lively realm of motivational inquiry. He led by example. Charlie Bentley was the acting principal. Graduating from St. John's University in Annapolis, Maryland, with a degree in philosophy and math, he studied for four years the *Great Books of Western Civilization* thinkers. He was superbly intellectually equipped to work with the best and brightest students in the country. He chose to put his children in an underfunded, freedom-based private school, where those academic works he studied would essentially collect dust on the bookshelves. But what he shared with the children was forever priceless, a lifelong value for living and enjoying the art of critical thinking and loving what you do.

His soft-spoken, light-hearted, quiet demeanor of phrasing speculative possibilities with gentle inflections as provocative friendly persuaders often left me with an insatiable, curious quest to pursue other sides of the learning cube on practically any subject. I'd never worked with such an erudite and refined gentleman in Woody Guthrie proletariat clothes and a Will Rogers Stetson style hat before, and I wholeheartedly appreciated his empathetic view of children and their world.

"It is all a matter of faith in children. Some adults have it, most don't. And if you do not have this faith, the children feel it. They feel that your love cannot be very deep, or you would trust them more," Charlie once said.

And this wonderful, inspirational teacher wouldn't give answers to his math riddles, which would aggravate the hell out of the students. He would only ask questions. Students frustrated with Charlie's game plan would try to bribe him with a small gift of coins, only to receive a definitive "Nope" for an answer. The man rarely swore too. Students would try to coax him with coins to just say a swear word, and Charlie once in a great while would accept it, saying such nasty words as "damn" and "shit." Big deal. That would make the children aghast and yet laugh because he was human after all.

As the years unfolded getting to know him, we were becoming real, if distant, friends. He sensed I didn't like strapping kids, knowing my dad used that expedient tool for discipline, nor forcing them into academic subservience, nor reprimanding kids for being genuinely honest. I enjoyed the open peacefulness that tended to reign during most of the field trips to various remote locations of natural recreational beauty throughout north central New Mexico. Charlie didn't divulge many personal opinions publicly, though he was elected by the school board as the principal and pronounced unofficially by most Santa Fe Community School members for many years, both young and old, as the most trusting figurehead of the kids, by the kids, and for the kids. He would rarely if ever raise his voice, or give students homework, unless they so desired. Occasionally, Charlie would bring his folk guitar in his rightfully earned territorially claimed back classroom and serenely toy around with his limited collection of folk songs that he learned in Greenwich Village at the ripe old age of 13 years. Or, as an accomplished origamist, he enchanted viewers with his succinctly folded, paper bird presentations. Children loved to be around him.

Sometimes, he would just talk things over with the students, usually on a one-to-one basis. I had a history of not responding well to incompetent or callous school boards, and though he tried to tell me that electing officers for the school was simply protocol for forming a legal corporate body and nothing else, I could see in the children's behavior, and even a few of the rooted adults living there, that Charlie was indeed eternally pronounced as the central E.T. heart light for SFCS and all it stood for. Moreover, he would never give lectures to the children but devised other means for showing disapproval through the art of exemplifying an effective silent language. By acting indifferent, Charlie Bentley could alleviate the anxiety or aggression in the child. His presence alone emitted an atmosphere where people listened to the heartbeat of themselves.

In one explosive episode, Charlie entered the school library while I was angrily confronting a student Patrick about his fisticuffs with his younger brother Daniel. I spewed verbal venom in his direction, and he spit fire back at me.

"Who do you think you are, kicking your brother in the face like that?" I roared.

"What damn business is it of yours? He's my brother, so stay out of it!" Patrick demanded.

"Anytime you have to hurt somebody to prove a point in this school, I'm not going to stay out of it!" I declared.

"Then fuck you!" Patrick mutually retaliated.

Meanwhile, Daniel profusely cried his guts out. With Charlie hearing the resounding confrontation and outpouring of misery, he methodically walked into the room and quietly brushed by us without saying a word. The altercation and assertive tears dropping ceased immediately. What did this fair-minded human being have that other mortals did not? Perhaps, this gifted teacher possessed the quality of unspoken kindness within a familiar continuity of loving this man's proven commitment to listening to them. Each day during school time for several years, this indefatigable person offered an attentive ear with a benevolent heart engaged directly with the children to open their curious eyes to a wondrous world of creative thoughtful learning no matter the subject be it bee keeping, horse tending, guitar instructing, chicken raising, reading stories, tuning up car engines, plumbing, making math puzzles, and most importantly putting the burden on the learner to find the answers to their questions by guiding them toward a direction where they must pursue the answer by themselves.

As mounting financial concerns threatened the future of the school, Charlie took a 3 month pay cut despite supporting a family of six, still teaching full time while moonlighting as a plumber to make ends meet. His fierce commitment to see his children actively involved in an education based on freedom, happiness and love was a beautiful process to behold.

Having a world-traveling father who was Dean of Education at Columbia University in New York, a family tradition of Utah horse ranching, and highly literate parents, Charlie exuded an illustrious background of noble gentility. His spunky grandfather once served as a Mormon bishop in Mexico during the era of Pancho Villa's raids into southern New Mexico. In fact, he was once captured for a few days by the invincible general and interrogated as a suspect for cooperating with the "enemies of the revolution." After a short leave of absence due to rebel looting and requisitioning of their once claimed land, many Mormon families returned to settle in northern Mexico. Mexican Mormons were not mountain men or cowboys, but essentially family ranchers. Then, in 1916, came Pancho Villa's raid on Columbus, New Mexico, in which 20 Americans were killed. Brigadier General John J. "Black Jack" Pershing was ordered to enter Mexico and get Villa dead or alive. But Villa was too elusive to be caught. Pershing, having paid in good American dollars for supplies, found the Mormon families so receptive to his troops that when the United States finally retreated and called him back across the border, the Mormons might well have predicted Mexican reprisal. This did occur when General Salazar rode into Colonia Juarez and told the Saints that all their able-bodied men would either join his Mexican army or be shot. He added that they would not only have to fight against the Mexican *Federalistas* but also against US troops in reprisal for Pershing's interference in Mexican matters.

Bishop Bentley, who had succeeded Junius Romney as the Mormon stake president, thought over General Salazar's demands and then he presented a short, courageous speech. Mormons, he said, were a peaceful people, devoting their lives to working and educating their children. They did not wage war. If Salazar wanted to shoot them for that, let him do so. Bentley was a small man, who was oftentimes mistaken for the Mexican revolutionary martyr Francisco Madero, and quite possibly his tenacious spunk tickled Salazar's Mexican sense of humor. At any rate, the last great threat against the *colonistas* had been averted.

Charlie Bentley seemed to carry that inherited fierce principled trait of facing stormy situations with bold, honest gentleness. More than anything else, Charlie represented security and continuity to the children and youth attending the radical little school of experiential learning. Many times, he would adeptly point out the paradoxes of life—sometimes comically, extra critical about his own actions. One time in his multipurpose, math-art room, when everyone appeared to be actively mellowing in some interesting, self-directed activity, Charlie and I would begin discussing the political nature of democracy in our daily lives.

"Some people have a hard time living up to rules, even though they may be equally a part of the decision-making process, and even though they may agree with the rules in principle. They want other people to comply with these consensus-approved guidelines, but they're reluctant to follow such decisions because such restrictions can stifle the freedom to be yourself. Sooner or later, a 'nagging inconsistency' arises," Charlie explained, attributing such a term to noted de-schooling educator John Holt.

"What do you mean?" I asked.

"You essentially begin to feel a conflict that does not go away, that it's okay to have other people live by your agreed-upon rules, but not okay for you to abide by them."

"I tend to be like that occasionally. I want others to act accordingly, even though I'm not sure I can live up to those self-imposed expectations," I added.

"But this is different. You see, there's a difference between a self-imposed rule and a group-imposed rule. If you live within a particular group, living up to any rules or understandings is crucial for the sake of comforting and protecting everyone's limited freedom. The 'nagging inconsistency' happens when the person senses the conflict between the need to organize certain cohesive group rules and the need to avoid such rules as they personally apply to you," Charlie elaborated.

"It's actually a conflict between authoritarian and democratic sides in oneself," I added.

"Exactly!" Charlie expressed in a rare moment of emotional assertiveness.

However, Charlie seemed to avoid his own "nagging inconsistency" in addressing an education designed to emphasize community schooling where people live and are educated on the land with experiential, consensus-based, small-group learning yet actively encouraging respect for each person through highly individualized instruction. He shunned the thought of moving his five children and wife to the community school, choosing instead to raise his family in a quaint, established Santa Fe neighborhood. Yet he was more of a community-minded person in action than anybody else in the school. By commuting from his home each day as a lone individual parent–teacher in quiet pursuit of freedom and responsibility, he nevertheless assumed much more interdependent connections with the greater community and the ongoing process of the school than people who lived day-to-day on the community land.

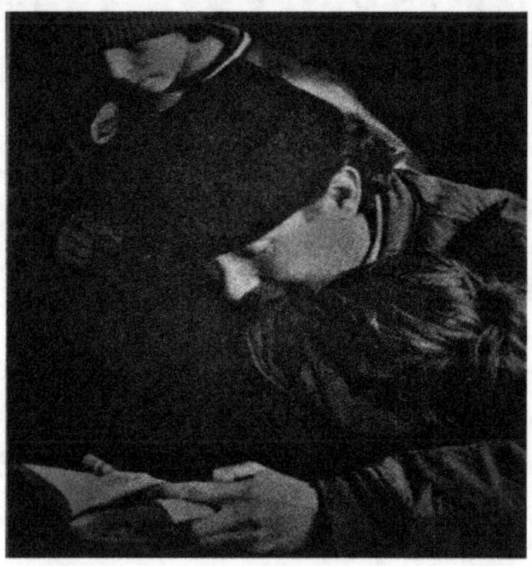

Charlie Bentley brought such an intimate perspective on learning to make the words come to life. 1973. Taken by Ed Nagel

Charlie Bentley with a child enjoying a nice conversation over an open auto engine world. 1972. Taken by Ed Nagel

A spontaneous moment where a visiting Japanese photographer interested in alternative community schools named Yasushi Onuma photographed a handful of staff and students at the Santa Fe Community School. Charlie Bentley is seen on the far-left side next to a student Patrick Martinez, while I am on the far-right side with fellow staff member Ed Nagel and Julia Meeks a student intern both in the front middle. 1981

Shortly after having this conversation, Charlie offered me a special birthday gift that completely moved me. He handed me a signed copy of a book dated 1908 titled *Debs: His Life Writings and Speeches*. A written signature of Eugene V. Debs was on the inside first page. Charlie knew I didn't openly advocate or espouse socialism to the children or adults. And he also knew, based on how I lived and related to people, that I believed in democratic socialism, so I treasured this book dearly. A great teacher is someone who sees your journey heading toward a greater humanity and nudges you ever closer to that thoughtful aspiration. But Charlie possessed a calming quality of agape, which is understanding goodwill for all. It begins by loving others for their sakes and making no distinction between a friend and stranger; it is directed toward both.

However, keeping up with all the demands of operating a private struggling school of mostly poverty-based students, multi-age, non-graded, and filled with a kinetic ball of playful energy to openly explore the world beyond the classroom, Charlie was getting tired. On a field trip to White Rock Canyon, a few students got lost in the dark, and the staff and the kids went out to try to find them. Hours into the night, we found them: cold, bone-tired and quite relieved. The three older boys had lost their way but heard our calls and came back safe and sound. It was simply exhausting for us, but particularly Charlie, who leaned on my shoulder in tears saying "I'm getting too old for this." Two years later Charlie was in his critical car accident.

Chapter Forty-Four
Accosted by Spiritual Clowns

Behold this day. It is yours to make.
– Black Elk Oglala Lakota

Stretching along the top of the first mesa on the southern end of Hopi land lies a village continuously inhabited for more than 1,100 years. They have the longest authenticated history of occupation of a single region by any indigenous tribe in the United States. The ancient home of Walpi stands above the vast desert grandeur, surrounded by awesome vistas of the sky and distant horizons overlooking the San Francisco Peaks. It is one of the most inspiring places to leap into a world of living in balance with the earth through richly performed cyclical calendrical ceremonies and time-tested, kinship-connecting agricultural practices.

Located on the northeastern corner of Arizona, my graduate and undergraduate school students from the Audubon Expedition Institute spent a few days walking the ancient grounds of other Hopi villages, but Walpi affected me the most through a ceremonial event that will forever strike a deep note in my spiritual quest.

Understanding how to live in balance with nature is crucial to embracing the pre-spring dances to invite rain upon the sacred nurturing blue corn earth. Corn Kachina dancers chant in a narrow, open plaza facing the distant San Francisco Peaks to welcome the coming of the rain while Clown Kachinas provide ethical amusement lessons to becoming better human beings in the Hopi way. The clown ceremony is concerned with life from the age of innocence to the age of maturity and profound awareness. I witnessed the cycle of human consciousness, where Hopi clowns popped out of the womb of a kiva, crying like newly born babies, only to spread their irreverent Marx Brothers antics with outrageous humor.

In the Hopi tradition, the Sacred Clown Kachina frequently disrupts and makes a *holy* mess out of some of the most vital and fundamental rituals. The clown satirizes Hopi life by acting out and exaggerating improper behavior, sometimes quite graphic in nature. Many times, the actions of the clowns are meant to portray a lesson on waywardness apparent in a tribal member like a Rastafarian pot-head member in the village. Other times, the clowns will appear obese and are often loud and boisterous in their conversation, grabbing villagers' food in rampant acts of gluttony. I watched them enter a store and shut off the electricity, grabbing food items without paying and unloading logs off a truck, resting them on the side of the road. But it wasn't until they came for me that their antics hit home.

I was standing next to my grad student friend Brian David Steinberg along the path of the *Koshari Hano* clowns, when one of them chased me down and grabbed me. As sacred and profane kachinas, they are highly amusing, but you do not want to get caught by them unless you wish to receive a gauntlet of verbal and physical humiliation in public. They are the ultimate example of overdoing everything they set about doing. I did not resist but played along. I was accosted into a group of zany, profanely sacred kachinas, who loudly embarrassed me before a crowd of spectators. One shouted for me to take my pants off. I stood huddled between them and refused. They began to try to pull my pants down, and I didn't play along. Then they insulted me as their pet *Bahana* (white person or outsider).

When they were finally finished, one of the clowns whispered to me and said something that made me laugh with gratitude, "When you're caught by Hopi clowns, it means two things. One, you're a fool for being caught and two, you'll live a long, good life." They then thanked me for participating in this ancient ceremonial practice. On the outside, the Hopi clowns satirize Hopi life by overtly acting out and exaggerating improper behavior like drinking alcohol or taking drugs, but they're meant to magnify a lesson on good behavior in a tribal member. Their purpose is to demonstrate how overdoing anything puts life out of balance, not only for the individual but for the people as a whole as well. Like the more serious Kachinas, but in a humorous way, the clowns help maintain community harmony by reminding people of acceptable standards of behavior within the Hopi way of living.

I was in a total daze, walking away from this rattling captive moment, leaving my friend Brian to just look out at the vast desert space beyond the mesa and wonder what just happened. I felt an eternal moment where the forecast for living a long good life seemed much more imminent. I can honestly say these Hopi clowns gave me a boost of confidence to follow their prognostication.

As a young septuagenarian on the mystical winding road to finding balance in my life, I have a strong bill of health, an ecologically friendly landscape, a beautiful passive/active solar home, living with a lovely soulmate with a green thumb, and a gentle cat. I'm happy to be where I am in the dense coniferous montane region of Colorado. Hopi people clearly believe we are spiritual beings in a physical body, having a profound sense of austere values to back it up. Called the *Peaceful People*, they carry a fiercely proven sense of self-determination to honor grandmother earth and have forever jolted my quest to do the same.

Chapter Forty-Five
Who Listens to Thunder Beings?

Once again, the tangible recognition of Black Elk's power by the
Thunder Beings in the form of thunder and rain validates the reality
of his power and the efficacy of his prayer.
– John G. Neihardt, *The Sixth Grandfather*

Occasionally, I participated in a few seasonal, circle pipe ceremonies honoring *Wakan Tanka* and the sacred seven directions with Jim Gillihan (*Tatanka Ska* - White Buffalo), the fourth Keeper of the Pipe of Sitting Bull. Each time I planned to attend, I experienced powerful inexplicable awakenings that guided my heart toward a oneness with the great mystery. Sharing these magnetic events with Jim, I asked that he wed me with my first wife to be, Rosa Lee (pseudonym), through a sunset pipe ceremony to be held at my nature center by a Lakota tipi overlooking a splendid reconstructed prairie landscape. *Tatanka Ska* agreed to perform the Lakota *Wakan Kiciyuzpi* (Traditional Lakota wedding ceremony). This would happen on August 4, 1995, and would entail an unforgettable range of spiritual affinities with the sky and earth never before witnessed by the 120 family members and friends who attended.

During the early afternoon on that Friday, *Tatanka Ska* walked the grounds of the ceremonial site alone. He asked about the Pottawatomie garden, where I grew the three sister crops of corn, beans, and squash from authentic indigenous seeds on the east end of the Lakota tipi. He spread tobacco on the ground, honoring the seven directions. After giving him space for a silent prayer to honor all the relations (*Mitakuye Oyasin*), I approached him about the oncoming weather forecast that predicted severe thunderstorms at the time of the wedding ceremony.

"Hi Jim, how does it look for tonight, knowing they're forecasting severe thunderstorms."

"I think the thunder beings (*Wakinyan*) will not disturb your wedding."

"Okay, Jim, let's go with what you say."

With all the planning and out-of-town guests scheduled to show up, I personally was a little frazzled by this great unknown about to unfold in a matter of a few hours. The *Thunder Beings* are the creators of all grasses. Living in the west, they're winged, bird-like creatures and patrons of cleanliness. They are known to have a voice of thunder and a glance of lightning, and they are enforcers of divine law, offering protection from famine, hard times, disease, and misfortune.

As the invited guests began to attend the circle ceremony, Rosa Lee and I, along with our family members on opposite ends, were assembled on the east side. I wore a ribbon, muslin shirt, honoring the four directions sewed together by Rosa Lee. My medicine bag had a special red, spotted bead to honor what clan *(tiospaye)* I would belong to: the northern branch of the Red Spotted Bead People. Rosa Lee had a long, flowery, brown-toned dress, with a half-dollar-sized round silver medallion necklace. We offered tobacco and a special gift to Jim. A Pendleton blanket of the Lakota *morning star* welcoming the coming of the sun and light into our hearts was worn around both of us. Our fingers were pricked by Jim, with blood shared between Rosa Lee and I, followed by an Apache prayer of coming together. We each had Hopi rings to honor the circle of our journey as we shared our wedding vows.

There was an inner circle of close friends and family, with an outer circle for the remainder of the invited guests. You could see looking north that the sky was darkening and rumbling. Two of Rosa Lee's children wore black clothes, almost as if they wanted to invite the Thunder Beings to be present during the ceremony. Accompanied by his wife, Medicine Hawk, Jim removed the pipe of Sitting Bull from his parfleche and pointed the tip to the sky to allow the great mystery to spiritually smoke from it, and then he turned it, following the movement of the sun. The storm began to rumble, spreading to the West, and deep black purplish clouds began to swirl ever closer toward the circle gathering.

Rumbling *Thunder Beings* with immense dark clouds surround the wedding ceremony. For a Lakota way, the circle of gatherers is a sacred symbol representing every aspect of life coming together as a whole. Having no beginning or end, the powerful symbolism permeates into every aspect of Lakota life as it appears in the tipi, a pipe bowl, a round purification lodge (inipi), a tossed stone rippling in the water, a bird's nest or a sky hole coming from the center of our wedding circle. *Tatanka Ska* (White Buffalo) performed an unforgettable mystical ceremony on the east end where the grandest circle of our solar system rises, the sun. *1995*. Taken by Lynn Eikenberry

A fire was lit to open the ceremony in the middle of the circle, as the winds began to pick up. We watched two monarch butterflies dance around the open fire, shortly followed by a couple of Canada geese flying directly over the top of the fire at the height of the tipi. The wedding invite card, designed by my noted artist brother Wayne, illustrated two geese flying over a tipi. Jim then had everyone in the inner intimate circle smoke the pipe as a prayer offering—but to only exhale—for all the smoke needed to be given to *Wakan Tanka.* As he entered the south end of the circle, starting from the east and moving in the direction of the sun, the wedding photographer zoomed in on the pipe. Jim mentioned before the service that it was forbidden to take any close-up pictures of the carved bison head made of pipestone, which once belonged to *Tatanka Iotanka.* Rosa Lee's sister, Barbara, tried to brush away the photographer, only to have him take a close-up of the pipe anyway. Lakota tradition has it that the White Buffalo Calf Woman brought the *chanupa* (pipe) to the people, as one of the Seven Sacred Rites, to serve as a sacred bridge between this world and *Wakan Tanka* (the Great Mystery).

As *Tatanka Ska* rounded the final stretch from north to east, there appeared above the fire pit a stunning sky hole, where you could see an open, clear sky surrounded by extremely dark, swirling, ruffled, feathery-like clouds that looked like a grand eagle spreading its wings, hovering over beyond the circle, enveloping a huge portion of the park. An incredible downpour was about to unfold, and yet the ominous cloudburst held back and waited until Jim was the last one among 40 persons to smoke the pipe for a prayer offering. *Tatanka Ska* turned the bowl of the pipe upside down on his other hand to show no embers remained. And there were none.

As soon as you could see his hand completely free of any ashes, small drops of rain began to unfold, followed by colossal rumbling sounds and lightning within a short distance from the circle. We exchanged our Hopi rings to honor those who were a part of the circle, and the ceremony concluded with Jim introducing us as a newly wedded couple. The Thunder Beings held off until Rosa Lee and I were officially husband and wife, but then nickel-sized hail began to fall fast and furious on our families and friends. Jim was right. The Thunder Beings didn't undermine the ceremony but waited until the last sacred binding words (*Wakon Kiciyzapi*) were shared to release their respectful energies.

People began to rush for shelter, mostly drenched by the time they entered the nature center. Everybody was completely in awe of what transpired. Most of our friends and families attending had little or no interest in spiritual indigenous connections with nature, and they said they never experienced firsthand anything so mystical. I wish I could say that this ceremony solidified a marriage eternally. It did not. In three-and-a-half years, the marriage fell apart, and we settled for divorce under irreconcilable differences. But that didn't stop me from following the Red Road and this extraordinary spiritual quest that Jim was guiding me toward. Over time, I saw Jim less after my divorce, but he encouraged me to apply as a naturalist-manager at the Trail of Tears Museum in southern Illinois. As a highly honored Cherokee, he had great influence in making this change happen in my life—even though I turned him down and remained in Schaumburg.

In retrospect, that wedding I believe represented the fourth sacred dimension of my journey with him—from the girl with the pink ball guiding me into my first meeting with Jim around the *spring equinox* to meeting that same girl on the *autumnal equinox* ceremony with Jim to having my father cross over on the same day Jim was conducting a *winter solstice* ceremony and to the Thunder Beings attending the *summer* wedding he conducted. Four sacred moments honoring the *four seasons/four directions/four stages of human life/four sacred herbs* in my life that have helped me understand the intuitive powers of paying attention to sacred paths unfolding through Lakota visions. Jim crossed over in June 2002 as a result of a serious car accident several months earlier. He was indeed a *Wocekiye Wicasa* (Man of Prayer).

Chapter Forty-Six
Bear in Mind

When you are where wild bears live you learn to pay attention to the
rhythm of the land and yourself.
– Linda Jo Hunter

Bears have always been a part of my journey, ever since my practical jokester Uncle Russ leaped out of the pines with a mighty Ursus roar and scared the dickens out of me and his son, my cousin Rusty, while we were coming out of a wide-open screened fish house in Lake Namekagon, Wisconsin. The new moon enveloped the mixed coniferous and deciduous forest with a pitch dark and mysterious atmosphere. Crickets were chirping, and the air was still. We were only in our preteens, coming from suburban upbringings and very susceptible to being freaked out by the stark silence of the night.

At Humboldt State University in Arcata, California, during my first year of traveling graduate school with the AEI, we met a medicine man professor named Grizzly Bear Bobby Lake. He was of Seneca and Karuk descent and shared his wisdom about finding purpose in loving Mother Earth. "We do it by acknowledging communication with gratitude and prayer to the plants, animals, rocks, sky, oceans, rivers, mountains, moon, and the creator (sun), with offerings like tobacco, corn meal, sweetgrass, sage, cedar, and osha (bear root). This is our way of making a spiritual contract with them. It is our way of showing reciprocity."

I remember him looking down at his feet on a sunny afternoon while we were all gathered by this incredibly rugged, beautiful, rocky outcropped coastline as the sea swirled and blasted against the shore. "You see those ants all clustered by my feet looking like they're in a frenzy. They're telling you that the barometric pressure will be dropping in the next 24 hours, possibly anticipating a storm in the making." The next day, the ants were right, with heavy showers coming through and the temps dropping by 15 degrees.

I never saw a bear in the wild until the early fall of 1985 after meeting Grizzly Bear Bobby Lake, well into my mid-30s. I had an eerie encounter that kept me up all night, chasing away imaginary bears. Such a self-imposed projection would have produced tears of laughter to my Uncle Russ if he were present around my tent in the windy high Sierras. While on a nine-day backpack with the AEI in Yosemite National Park, our group of 24 students were in a circle meeting. It was pitch black. We could barely see anybody next to us. As a low-impact, experiential environmental education program, we never made outdoor fires and had most of our meetings in the dark, no matter the season. While someone was speaking in our circle discussion, you could hear a paper bag crumpling, with a peanut butter and jelly sandwich being carried off only a couple of people away from where I was sitting on the ground. One of the brawny, feral-minded students, Wes Cunningham, knew exactly who had snatched that bag. It was a black bear. He loudly cursed a slew of nasty words to that bear to put that bag down. The bear promptly responded by dropping the bag on the ground and hightailing it into the forests. We were all aghast to learn that a bear was in our circle, and we didn't know it until we heard the PBJ bag crumpling. We didn't hear the bear's bodily movement or sense its breath.

Later that night, when we were settling into the evening, with the stars glittering beyond belief, Wes asked me to follow him into the woods and bring a flashlight. I agreed, and he steered me to the edge of an open meadow, with a line of trees bordering the other side. He asked me to look across the meadow and point the flashlight straight ahead into the edge of those woods. I did, and what I saw will stay with me forever.

I saw the glowing eyes of a black bear standing about six feet tall, staring straight at me. I nearly pissed in my pants. Wes knew I'd never seen a bear in the wild, as I had alluded to the group during the great attempted PBJ bag theft that night. The next day, our wilderness group hiked to the higher Western ridges of the Sierra Nevada Mountain range. We agreed to solo camp away from the other students to explore the night alone in our tent. That night, the wind was extremely gusty, shaking my tent as if someone was deliberately trying to scare the shit out of me. I was delirious, repeatedly yelling "Go away, bear!"

to the fierce wind in my half-asleep state of mind practically the whole night.

That haunting, sleepless night alone deepened my relationship with bears. Months elapsed, and our grad school bus was passing through Albuquerque, New Mexico, to stock up on food and supplies. I contacted a friend, Jon Schwaber, whose home was directly across the Rio Grande Zoo and whose roof I had the privilege of sleeping on to wake up at dawn, hearing elephants and peacocks calling through the neighborhood. He had spent a few months on St. Lawrence Island, Alaska, trading scrimshaw works with the Inuit and embracing the culture, like paddling in a walrus skin boat *(umiak)* to the shores of Russia. The island was part of Alaska but closer to Russia than to the Alaskan mainland. St. Lawrence Island is thought to be one of the last exposed portions of the land bridge that once joined Asia with North America during the Pleistocene period. Jon talked to our group about living there and said that people still eat 12,000-year-old mastodon meat found in the frozen permafrost. We were blown away. Before he left, Jon gave me two precious items found in the permafrost: a 10,000-year-old wolf tooth and a grizzly bear claw. I held dearly to these gifts for years until I placed them into a medicine bag over my heart.

Knowing that the bear and the wolf are the last true living symbols of the primal, animal world, as a naturalist and environmental educator, I believe that how humans respond and protect their lands and their ecological future will be the most honest depiction of how serious humanity is about preserving our environment, wilderness areas, and the natural resources in balance with *Unci Maka,* Grandmother Earth. After my first divorce and another break-up in a short-term relationship in 2002, I decided to seek counseling from a woman who uses nature to guide people through their inner turmoil. I visited her, and she asked me to lay down on her comfy, therapeutic couch with my eyes closed for a guided imagery exercise. She began by saying, "I want you to imagine living in an ideal world to make your heart happy and strong. What would it look like?"

I said, "I would have beautiful wild gardens of nature and an organic garden to know that my food would be healthy and delicious."

"Who could you trust to be in your garden?" she asked.

"My mom, a fawn, and Rosa Lee, who is my ex-wife."

"Why your ex-wife?"

"Because she knew me more than I knew myself in many ways and realized we should not have been married but just become friends."

"How would you protect your sacred heart space."

"I would have a cave guarded by cascading waterfalls to hide the entrance into the sacred heart garden space."

"Your heart has been hurt. Do you think that's enough to protect you from falling into another collapse of faith in finding love?"

"Probably not."

"Then what do you need to have to shield you from having your heart spirit wounded again?"

I was quiet for a couple minutes and then I told her, with my eyes deeply closed, "I need to have a bear before the waterfalls in the center of the stream, projecting a strong image of guarding my heart from being hurt again."

Shortly after that session, I lost my grizzly bear claw after misplacing it around a campfire at a local forest preserve during one of my storytelling programs. Some lucky person may find this Pleistocene claw and have an insurmountable time trying to figure out how it got there by a firepit. I was now on a quest to replace the lost gift from my medicine bag given to me by my friend Jon, who later passed away in 2008. The bear spirit became dormant, waiting for a vision to reawaken that power of protecting me from any further emotional wounds in my heart. Jump ahead to summer 2012. I'd been steadily seeing Randee Lawrence for about two-and-a-half years. We seemed compatible in so many ways and were weaving our lives together to make our future seem abundantly adventurous, exciting, and deeply purposeful. We decided to go camping in the Smokey Mountains before visiting the countercultural artsy town of Ashville, North Carolina. On one of our lovely wild saunters, we headed up to one of the idyllic little waterfalls called Spruce Flat Falls on the Tennessee side of the mountains with our Native American flutes. When we arrived by the creek, you could feel the mist from the waterfalls and hear the gentle ripples flowing by us. We decided to bring our flutes out and play in this beautiful Appalachian forest sculpted by the ceaseless flow of mountain clear waters.

At first, we looked at each other while we were playing, then I began to turn my body towards this cascading creek with my eyes closed. I remember playing for just a couple minutes, deeply entranced in trusting my heart to feel the energies of this place. When I reopened my eyes, I saw the vision I'd been hoping for. A large rock protruded out of this creek, flowing from these tranquil waterfalls, which was in the natural shape of a large bear's head, facing outward as the rushing waters passed over this visionary rock. It had the imagery of stability, strength, and protection, one who immerses oneself into dreams and visions, guiding me to balance the dream with the practical realities of nurturing everyday life with purpose and true value in what I love to do. And knowing the flute I prayerfully played at this sacred spot in my heart was carved from a company named Thunder Bear solidified my acceptance of the bear as my guardian protector for life.

By the Spruce Flat Waterfalls, Tennessee in the Smokey Mountains, while playing my flute crafted by a company called Thunder Bear accompanied by Randee also on flute, I experienced a vision of seeing a large bear's head projecting over rushing waters. Closing the loop in my quest to find a totem guardian to shield my fragile heart, I am so gratified to find clarity by envisioning an eco-spiritual kinship awakening to strengthen my journey toward balance and harmony in all my relations with the web of life. *2012*

I now, all day and night, wear a bear necklace, which was given to me by my dear soul partner Randee, over my heart to keep me from going astray in my quest to always honor and protect the center of who I am and wish to be. She'll always be first and foremost inside that inner peaceful garden where I can always love and trust her. Living in a town where there are more black bears wandering around the area than the entire Rocky Mountain National Park, I have been able to encounter them through first-hand experience about once a year. And

I know the bear will be my trusting spiritual kin to help me if and when the time is needed.

I have always wanted to have a personal close encounter with a grizzly bear ever since I backpacked through Glacier National Park in the summer of 1991. My only consolation was to sight a towering scat pile of grizzly consumed cow parsnip along the rugged wilderness trail.

Needless to say, I was disheartened not to spot one as terrifying as that moment might be. It wasn't until the summer of 2022 that my wish was granted in the most unforeseen mystical way.

For decades I have been captivated with the breathtaking images looking down at the magnificent Upper Waterton Lakes International Park bordering along the U.S.A. and Canada from atop the Prince of Wales Hotel. The night before arriving in Waterton I dreamt of a grizzly bear showing its face through a glass window in an open garage. In the dream I ran away bellowing to everyone that a grizzly bear was in our presence. A large colorful print of a psychedelic trippy rainbow grizzly bear face hung in the living room in the house where we were staying in Jasper, Alberta. That intense image certainly drew me into the spirit of the bear through my dream that night. When Randee and I spent just a day wandering around this wild and scenic awe-inspiring fresh water gem, we eventually made our way to that overlook only to be stopped in the mid-afternoon by the gatekeeper who said there was a fee for parking.

We decided to wander into the town where we found a local park established by the Rotary Club to honor this grand place as the world's first international peace park. Randee and I had been involved in establishing a Peace Park also sponsored by the Rotary Club in our town and found this visit to be very apropos. We later drove up the road toward Red Rock Canyon where we returned for a photo op with a bear display off the road affectionately embraced by Randee.

After dinner we walked into a souvenir shop where Randee bought a "mama grizzly" bear magnet and headed back to a free parking lot where we could walk up the short trail leading to the spectacular vista at the Prince of Wales hotel. As we began to enter the trail head, a couple of older women approached us trembling, quite alarmed as to what they had just witnessed.

"Do not go up that trail. There is a grizzly and her two cubs hidden in the shrubs. Be careful," one woman warned with both hands on her heart. That is all I needed to hear. I walked downwind slowly up the trail with all my senses on high alert, just to try to get a glimpse of them. I began to see some thick shrubs moving with the upper body of the mother bear in sight about 40 feet from us. I stopped and then it happened. This roughly six and a half foot 400 pound sow with a distinct hump between the shoulders made her presence known exposing her entire brawny body on the trail. She tried sniffing us out but the downwind fortunately kept her from sensing us as a potential threat. Possessing a biting force of over 1200 PSI, enough to crush a bowling ball or an iron skillet with an incredible speed at the same pace as a greyhound, Randee and I slowly backed down the trail as we moved backwards and then realizing how incredibly dangerous this situation appeared we hustled down the hill back to our car. It was my first grizzly sighting.

We drove back to the parking lot of the Prince of Wales Hotel and told another gate keeper on a different shift about this sighting. Ironically, he told us we could have parked as a non-guest visitor for 30 minutes. Had we parked earlier there, we probably would have missed seeing this glorious visionary moment with an *Ursus arctos horribilis*. I may have lost the grizzly bear claw at that Cub Scout campfire program in the forest preserve but have fortunately gained a grateful lifetime memory of actually encountering such a legendary bear up close and personal and lived to tell the story.

The fading blue sky sunset winds were gusting up to 35 mph as I gazed into the Crown of the Continent's majestic lake ecosystem that had only been in my dreams. Walking from the parking lot to the view I felt a surge of energy rising up from my soul. My vision of coming here was reinforced by this timely forceful wind, reminding me that the great invisible mystery moves through all things, always renewing the heart and mind, refreshing the balance and harmony of life, helping us pay attention to what really matters. I felt a peaceful closure that within 24 hours the synchronistic energy and heightened moments guiding me to this sacred spot in my journey had been fulfilled. That was the last experience from our 13 day dearly treasured Northern Rockies venture before leaving this splendid grizzly domain heading back to a place where these wilderness beasts do not roam anymore in the central Rockies of Colorado.

Embracing a look alike outdoor bear exhibit on the way back from Red Rock Canyon in Waterton International Park, Randee feels safe being that close to such a non-living display. Little did she or I know what lied ahead shortly after this photo was taken. 2022

Initially standing in a territorial posture on the trail while we were just 40 feet away from her, a grizzly sow eventually slowly walks away from us as we moved carefully and swiftly away from her and the cubs hidden in the shrubs along the Prince of Wales loop trail in Waterton Lakes National Park in Alberta, Canada. 2022

Overlooking the upper Waterton Lakes amidst one of their infamous winds during a stunning twilight sky, I am at peace knowing that I paid attention to my vision quest and listened to my heart. Designated as an UNESCO World Heritage stie with an exceptionally unique Western Biosphere Reserve to protect the ecological integrity of diverse habitats, it seemed quite fitting to encounter my first grizzly bear in such a majestic wild and scenic place that honors nature with global distinction. 2022

There are ancient Joycean puzzles that require deep time to piece together. My brother Wayne over the years has been on a relentless mission to find the origin of our roots. He decided to take an ancestral DNA test and what he found was profoundly revealing. My family's descent on my father's side comes from a mountain forest people called the Carpatho-Rusyns, a distinct Eastern Slavic people who lived more than a thousand years in remote villages scattered along the foothills and valleys in the Galicia region by the Carpathian Mountains of East Central Europe. The villages were located mostly among those of Western Slavs (Slovaks and Poles) Hungarians (Magyars), Jews, and Vlachs. Three quarters of the Carpatho-Rusyns population live in and around the border of Ukraine. They are considered to be "people from the nowhere land" never having a land of their own to call their country, ruled primarily by dominant countries like Russia and Poland. As a stateless minority, they worked as modest farmers and caretakers of the forest often too poor to live there with many forced to move in more neighboring countries away from their rooted land. But they do have a national flag despite not having a political legitimate country with a symbol of a *standing red bear* serving as the king of the snowy Carpathian Mountains.

The Carpatho-Rusyn national emblem is a shield divided vertically into 2 fields. The left field is divided into 7 horizontal blue and gold alternating stripes representing the seven largest rivers of the land; the Tisa, Teresva,, Tereb'la, Rika, Borzhava, Latoryca and Uzh. In the right field on a silver background, which represents the rich salt mines of the area, a red bear is depicted as a king of the snowy Carpathian Mountains.

 Years before discovering my DNA ancestral roots, I attended an inipi (purification sweat lodge) ceremony where I envisioned a striking benevolent force of nature in the glowing red-hot grandfather rocks (*tunkashilas*) at the center of the lodge during the 4th round of prayers through a teddy bear image. That same image caught my eye after dinner during a Lakota giveaway of items. The purpose of the giveaway is to release possessions and to let go of those belongings for others drawn to them to receive. I gravitated toward a teddy bear mug knowing how the bear had been a personal powerful force of healing in the past. I gained new eyes, like a child gaining a fresh sense of wonder and curiosity. This was not the first-time teddy bears came into my life as an adult. When my Ukrainian-Russian grandmother Grandma Macko crossed over several years before this enlightening experience, she left a fur coat which was inherited by my sister Joyce and converted into a stuffed fur coated teddy bear.

Having not made the connection until 2023, I realize that the teddy bear mug vision in the sweat lodge honored on my Lakota prayer shrine and the stuffed teddy bear from my Grandmother's fur coat links my rooted past with my present heartfelt journey. I have gratefully lived long enough on this sacred earth to see how things come full circle and am so thankful to the bear spirit for the lessons brought to my attention. Furry teddy bear photo taken by Joyce Fillhaber. 2023

Chapter Forty-Seven
A Bird That Hears My Prayers

In many traditions, hawks are sacred: Apollo's messengers for the Greeks, sun symbols for the ancient Egyptians and, in the case of the Lakota Sioux, embodiments of clear vision, speed, and single-minded dedication.
– John Burnside

The hawk is a dear kinship friend of mine. Over the years, I've developed the uncanny ability to see and hear hawks everywhere I go. Whenever I travel, I'm always looking through my windshield, and, off the side of my speeding car, I see them, assisting and guiding me on my journey. To see a hawk hovering above or flying directly across my car gives me a smile that I know it will be a good day. I also have asked the hawk to show that it has heard my prayers by displaying itself to me in an act of listening. The hawk has never disappointed me.

When I was walking home from my nature center, I was feeling a bit lonely and felt it would be a blessing if a hawk were to pay a visit as a passing friend who feels my sadness. At that moment, a red-tailed hawk hovered over me, broad, wide-open wings suspended in the air, looking directly down to let me know someone was hearing my prayer. I came home that day feeling a grateful kinship connection.

One day, while teaching an after-school class to Cub Scouts at the nature center, we saw a hawk in the distance. I told the children I could call to them, and they tended to curiously hover above me. When I gave my asthmatic squeal call *keeer-r-r*, the raptor continued to go its own way, fading from our view. I began to show the children the wild bergamot, or what I call the spicy pizza plant, to get their attention because it smells like oregano. My face was down, kneeling toward the plant, when one of the scouts tapped me on my back and said, "Mister, Mister, look up."

And there, hovering above us, was that same red-tailed that heard the distant call from me. Having an exceptional ability to hear and see, the curious hawk paid an impressive visit to our group, and I knew there was a curious winged *amigo* up there ready to hear my call. Perhaps my most wistful moment with hawks came when I was in a major traffic jam on a Friday night, heading to a storytelling program at the Reed Turner Woods log cabin nature center in Long Grove, Illinois.

I had unconsciously left my barrel of storytelling items in the back entrance to my condo building and drove back about five miles to pick them up. With bottled up traffic, it took me about 45 minutes round trip to take care of this scattered forgetfulness. Getting back on to Interstate 290, cars were bumper to bumper and became outrageously tight when I exited onto Route 53, coming to a complete standstill. While waiting for an opening, I peered to my left and saw a pair of red-tailed hawks perched on a couple of autumnally leafless cottonwood trees only about a hundred feet from me. I didn't call out to them but rolled down my window, looking directly at the distinguished twosome. I delivered silent prayers for them to clear the road and allow me to pass in time to perform my indigenous storytelling program on owls, along with an interpretive nature night walk.

The hawks took off together in the direction I was heading, going north along Route 53 until I could no longer see them. And then it happened. Traffic began to move swiftly in the direction I was heading toward, as if the invisible gates were lifted, and I was able to make it on time to perform a full program before a packed house. As I nurtured my relationship with hawks, I could ask specific messages to them, and I seemed to get answers that gave me peace of mind. Over the years, this has developed into a wonderful and effective vocabulary with hawks that enables me to know road conditions and the presence of danger ahead. For this to work, you must develop a humbling relationship and ask for the signs. Hawks are one of the most intriguing and mystical birds of prey. They are the messengers of deeper understandings with nature, protectors for those with good intentions, and visionaries of the air that help one see the inter-play between life and death.

My encounters with the red-tailed hawks constantly bring me back to indigenous mystical ties with this bird of prey. To the Pueblo, this large raptor, found throughout most of North America, was known as the *red eagle*. Its feathers and energies were used in healing ceremonies and for bringing rains and waters necessary for life. I have watched an Aztec hawk ceremony, sponsored by the Aztec Chicago dancers, specifically intended to draw hawks, and I have witnessed a dozen hovering red-tailed hawks attend this event, flying over these colorful feathered dancers at the Theosophical Society in Wheaton, Illinois. To the Ojibwe, the red-tailed hawk represents leadership, good intention, and foresight. The red-tailed hawk, with a wing span of over 40 inches can teach you to use creative energies with great vision and commitment. As a retired environmental educator living in the raptor friendly tall perching firs and pines of Colorado, the red-tailed hawk continues to be a true visionary neighbor close to home.

Part IV
Milagros

(Miracles guiding me toward a deeper spiritual and more mystical
awakening with the universe.)

Chapter Forty-Eight
For Whom the Tire Tolls

There are only two ways to live your life. One is as though nothing is a miracle. The other is as though everything is a miracle.
– Albert Einstein

When I signed up for my first overseas humanity-bound adventure with the US Peace Corps, I was extremely nervous about entering a new language, new culture, new traditions, a challenging climate, and a high contact with people who looked and acted much different from my lily-white suburban self. But driving a taxi to pick up a passenger from O'Hare International airport catapulted my move to join with exciting, liberating anticipation. As a privately-owned business, the company was owned and operated by a small family. Knowing how maintaining the vehicles was costly, they cut corners like avoiding regular checkups on the cars before the drivers started their day. There were no on-site mechanics to inspect the cars daily.

One mid-March morning, I was dispatched to pick up a businessman from O'Hare and return back to Schaumburg. After picking him up, we began driving down the tollway, when I could feel and hear a rattling sound coming from the right front end of the car.

"Maybe you should pull off and check out what's happening?" said the passenger.

"Good idea." I said while looking for the next exit.

I turned off onto Higgins Road, and the car began to shake more dramatically. Fortunately, a gas station was in sight. Unfortunately, as I pulled into the lot, the right front-end tire detached from the car and rolled about 35 feet through an open garage door. The mechanic stood totally bedazzled, with his hands on his hips, as the tire rolled past him into the shop like the tire was some kind of animated character with a nonverbal message: "If you don't mind, can you please take care of this?"

We felt a heavy thump, and then the car stopped abruptly on the edge of the gas station lot entranceway. No one was hurt. I called the home office and was told to just have it fixed, and they would take care of it, which they did follow through with, as promised. I drove the passenger home and thanked him for his supportive ears in hearing that death-ridden rattling sound. Especially in this case, the customer is always right. I could not help but imagine what could have unfolded if we kept driving down the tollway at 70-plus miles an hour with a detached tire. Losing control, the vehicle could have rolled over a few times, and the loose tire could have flown into the air and bounced into other vehicles at high speed. We could have been DOA, along with possibly other victims.

But instead, we were extremely lucky. The lug nuts hadn't been tightened properly, so they eventually loosened enough to detach the tire. No mechanic had spotted this because the company didn't hire one on a daily basis. Hired drivers and management had to rely on their own daily inspections before operating a car, and, considering the daily demands of such a small, privately owned taxi business, the results were dismal.

If there was ever a catalyst to launch me into a new and adventurous direction, this life-threatening incident did the trick. When buddies of mine were drafted into the Vietnam War, I decided to sign up as a Peace Corps volunteer, assigned to the equatorial tropical country of Liberia, West Africa. I wanted to serve my country as an act of patriotism not to go to war but to test out my humanitarian ideals and the experience of living in a country far removed from my parents' materially rat race driven, toxic, consumer-chosen lifestyle—dipped with a splash of white privilege.

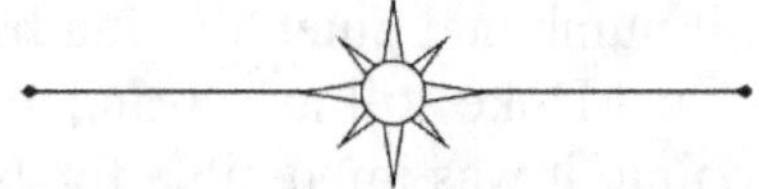

Chapter Forty-Nine
Never Count a Loyal Lucky Dog Out

The bond with a dog is as lasting as the ties of this earth can ever be.
–Konrad Lorenz

Every Wednesday, my little community school of multi-aged children and youth would load up in a Volkswagen micro-bus and embark on consensus-approved field trips around north central New Mexico, bringing a pet dog or two for a recreationally fun time in the endless natural playgrounds surrounding Santa Fe, New Mexico. In particular, one amiable black Schnauzer named Duke, cared by one of the older students, came with us to Villanueva State Park, approximately 65 miles from the school. The park is nestled between high sandstone bluffs dotted by mature junipers that form a challenging canyon for hiking along the Pecos River, with trails surrounded by grand, elderly cottonwood trees. Because it was a long day during the summer, we had plenty of light time to explore the wild and scenic terrain. A full day of play brought all of us together as one big, happily exhausted family. The time had arrived, as the sun was sinking late in the afternoon, to return home. Charlie Bentley, the acting principal, and I began to gather up the kids to head home when we were having a hard time finding Jacque, the owner of Duke. As a teen, she was so emotionally involved, looking for her lost dog, that she completely lost track of time. When she reunited with her Dad, Charlie, she looked scared and totally heartbroken.

"What's going on?" Charlie asked.

"I can't find Duke," Jacque cried, at a loss for words.

"We'll find him," Charlie assured her. With the sun setting over the western foothills, all of the kids and staff started a search party to track down the pet dog. We divided into two groups and hit the trails, calling out Duke's name loudly to no avail.

As the night reached peak darkness, with no moon in sight, we had to call off the search. Jacque was completely devastated, crying her heart out. We were all numb and quiet, driving back to the Santa Fe Community School—and Duke still lost, wandering in the night, far from home. That evening, it was impossible for Jacque to sleep. She worried about the predators attacking Duke at night, like a mountain lion, a great-horned owl, or a coyote. Others like myself had a hard time sleeping too, wondering what could we have done more to find him.

Toward the end of the next school day, a *milagro* appeared. Not to return home but to the school, Duke found Jacque in the backyard and jumped all over her. Unbelievable! Call it luck, a miracle, determination, the power of love, or a mix of all four. Without the benefit of maps, language, or GPS, Duke managed to find his way back to his caring worried master. How could that happen knowing Duke traveled in a vehicle over 60 miles removed from his scented gift of knowing where to go? Did Duke follow the highway south along Interstate 25 and know from there how to get back to the school? Why did Duke choose the school and not his home? Could Duke smell Jacque from many miles away and know she would be at the school?

The general consensus is that a dog's sense of smell is 10,000 to 100,000 times more accurate than a human smell. Canine scientist James Walker once made the analogy of smelling in vision terms, claiming that "what you and I can see at a third of a mile, a dog could see more than 3,000 miles away and still see as well." You read of amazing stories like this but to experience the power of love, luck, an astonishing sense of smell, and an uncanny ability to gauge location visually while in an enclosed vehicle, it leaves a humbling permanent imprint in the mind, even to this day, over 45 years later.

Chapter Fifty
Milagro at My Little House in the War Zone

*Listen cousin, the way things are supposed to work out, one day the
struggles of all you screwed up little underdogs will forge a
permanent rainbow that'll encircle this entire earth, I should live so
long.*
– John Treadwell Nichols, *The Milagro Beanfield War*

The Milagro Beanfield War is a novel by American writer John
Nichols, published in 1974. When I moved to Santa Fe, New
Mexico, in the mid-1970s, that was one of my favorite books,
entailing a whole range of clashing elements to stir a great story about
a developer baron illegally rerouting water from an impoverished
traditional village bean field. Land and water rights go hand in hand
when protecting that which is sacred, especially when generations of
families have been nurturing the earth there to fit their heritage and
customs. The town wrestles with this invasion with humor and
warmth, grappling and stumbling toward its own stubborn salvation.

I was not so lucky as to have such a *simpatico* amiability with my land
rights situation until a *milagro* appeared. After teaching at the Santa Fe
Community School as a Federal Title I reading aide and outdoor rec
teacher for a few years, settling in an abandoned underground pithouse
resembling a pueblo kiva for two years and living in a small, boxed-in
room in the school for another four seasons, I received permission from
the board to build my home on the property. Since I donated most of my
entire income to support the school, I was looking to cut corners in building
my home. The location was distant from the school and in a totally open,
degraded sagebrush landscape surrounded by beautiful, distant mountain
views of the Jemez to the west, Sandias to the south, and Sangre de Cristo
to the east. The main construction material would be adobe, all of which I
made from my own hands—approximately 1,400 adobe bricks, 14 by 10

by 4 inches thick, each eventually cut like a trapezoid to make the building oval like a goose egg, all derived from the earth where I lived. I received help from a Hispanic-Apache neighbor, who not only showed me how to make the proper formula and frames for layering the mud mix but also how to burn grooves with an axe with linseed oil into railroad ties for prepping a frame to install a windshield I salvaged from a 1971 Rambler convertible.

When my parents visited me one summer, I had all those handmade standing bricks stacked up in three rows for the high desert sun to bake them, so proud that I had the determination and fortitude to complete this arduous task. My dad, who was a comptroller, had seldom performed any dirty jobs for any length of time—apart from the work he did as a young man in a stuffy bread factory line. He made a comment that stuck with me on how he felt about where I was heading in my life. "Denny, I don't get it. You got a master's degree from Northwestern University and you're playing in the mud."

With the help of a female Taos Pueblo friend who worked for the Department of New Mexico Human Services, I learned how to make the inside walls, buffing them by rubbing rabbit skin after applying a mixture of sand and clay to the surface. I was now living in my own space made entirely from the local earth, shaped like a goose egg with scrap lumber, collected rocks for the fireplace, donated color-coated wine bottles to border around the ceiling, loose straw from the school's horse stable to make adobe, chicken wire, and a forgotten car windshield. The cost was around $200, and most of the expenses were incurred from the purchase of a chimney flue, Portland cement mix, plywood for laying the foundation, and a Franklin stove for cooking. I never used firewood but rolled up my own newspapers donated from the Santa Fe Public Library in a paper log machine with an added adhesive solution and dried them out in the open sun. I remember reading reputable month-old papers from the United States and around the world like the *Chicago Tribune, Los Angeles Times, Egyptian Gazette, London Times*, and *New York Times* before turning them into fire, which provided a multi-use resource for living and learning.

Few of us live in round houses anymore, where there are no four-sided walls or corners, so I built my home in the shape of a goose egg. Indigenous architecture tends to the small and round, following the model of nests and dens and burrows, eggs and wombs, planetary objects, the sun in our solar system, our galaxy, and future ones beyond, as if there was some universal pattern for a home.

The doorway faced east to honor an ancient design of greeting the dawn. As a round structure, the earth home was wind resistant, and the nature of adobe made it heat efficient. Like a pebble thrown into a calm pond, the journey of building and living in a self-made adobe *casa* had a profound rippling effect in exemplifying teachable, demonstrable lessons for unveiling a wholeness of body, mind, and spirit. I felt like an instant native New Mexican until trouble began to unfold along the border of my little 18-foot diameter by 9 feet in height dream home.

The school administrator's son Wyatt Nagel accompanies me by the door with his companion free ranging shaggy dog Milou during construction. Inside the building an adobe finished wall with a fireplace can be seen. *1978*. Photo taken by Janis Paige Moylan

In early spring of 1978, we were told by the owner of the land Bill Spillers that my home was slightly on his property, and that he was in the process of selling his property to an adobe-making entrepreneur. The school had asked permission to have my home remain during this sales transaction, and he agreed. He was a creditable lawyer, and so our school felt we could trust his word. But we learned different. A fence post bordered along my adobe home, edged ever so slightly along the property line. As a lawyer, he found in a Utah case that, if a fence post was up for over 10 years and not contested, then that border would be considered legal. The legal plait map indicated that the property line moved into my home. Knowing that this adobe company required a power line to feed electricity into the business before a contract could be signed, this shady man pulled up all the posts on this contested property line, except for one, where we caught him in the act. He was attempting to remove all the posts so we would not have any legally contested teeth to build in this matter.

That was the beginning of an intense border dispute that lasted for two years.

When I first met the new owner, Eloy Orgulloso (pseudonym), including his wife and his wheelchair-driven, physically challenged son, I invited them into my goose egg adobe dwelling, and we had a very cordial meeting. He had a very established business in Santa Fe selling adobe bricks made on his commercial land. But our amiable meeting was short lived, for, just a few days after that, a dirt road was being widened in anticipation of a power line going up right along my home. Ed Nagel, the administrator, a solid friend and teacher at my school, immediately organized a meeting to address this pernicious property power grab. We as a community decided to gather all the junkyard cars and minibuses scattered throughout our land and drag them over to the property line through hand pushing and towing them with help from a bunch of supportive residents, kids included.

It was a sight to behold: a line of forgotten, stripped down, cannibalized vehicles serving as a fortress to keep any development from unfolding along my home. Sheriff Archuleta came out with a few back-up police cars and ordered all these broken-down vehicles to pull back from the contested property line. We knew there would be serious tension from that point on, but I had no idea such a confrontation would escalate into an all-out war, New Mexican style, *mano a mano*.

While teaching in the school toward the end of the day, one of the younger students we amiably called Danny Boy ran into the building yelling, "Dennis, Eloy is trying to burn your house down!" I and a few other students ran with buckets of water and saw that nobody was nearby, but there was a pile of wood and a huge pile of tumbleweed stacked along my home, blazing, reaching the top of my wooden roof. We put out the fire, but I knew from then on to be on watch at all times during the day. Thank goodness the kids were my extra eye. A few days later, Eloy brought a bulldozer and dug a ditch line during the rainy season to flood my home. He was partially successful along the foundation to the fireplace, but I repaired it. We had to take Eloy to court to stop his rampage. While the school was in session, Eloy wouldn't stop harassing me. He needed to get my house levelled to put the power line along his property, but New Mexico law required that no power line could be within 20 feet of any building.

As a way of provoking unrest and anger in me, he transported with his tractor huge cement blocks and piled them up along the fence line next to my house a few feet from my front door. Not a pretty sight to see. I decided to play a reverse macho mind game and set up a small pile of rocks opposite where he dumped his pile. That really upset him, especially since I had a compact, inoperable tape recorder, and I pretended I was recording every verbal threat, so, if he ever caught me alone, I'd better be ready. He stopped short of swearing at me when I held that tape recorder in the air to remind him that words could be held accountable in court if something were to happen to me.

Eloy was completely losing his patience. He began to threaten the livestock on the school property, like the burro and horses. He sideswiped our school Volkswagen mini-school bus while we were coming back from a field trip, and he threatened to have his working goons club me at a grocery store if I didn't cooperate with him. Such a warning he issued inside a store, where I was shopping with Jon Kim, a student intern friend, which really scared and angered me. John, who was a tall and gentle yet strong young man, was on board to back me up if I needed protection. I also contacted Lorenzo, who ran the produce department at Albertson's Food Store. He said two of his sons working with him there would back me up. They played Varsity football for Santa Fe High School. I also contacted the manager of the store, who said he would have his hand by the phone if trouble exploded.

With an alerted back-up waiting inside the store ready to join, I headed outside alone, and Eloy was waiting for me in the parking lot, about a hundred feet from his workers, who were sitting on a flatbed truck, possibly anticipating a signal from the boss to beat the shit out of me. "Hey, didn't I tell you what would happen if I saw you alone."

It was then that I signaled to my protectors to come out of the store to show some strength. Once he saw this show of equal strength, Eloy buckled under and said, "All I want to do is talk to you. Can we talk?"

"I don't talk to bullies," I said. With Jon joining me in the car, we drove away.

Several days later, believing that, during this court case, Eloy would pull back, wait for the outcome, and leave me alone, I received a knock at my door at night. I didn't open the door but asked who it was.

"This is the sheriff, and I need to ask you a few questions."

I opened the door and saw Eloy with the sheriff. "What do you need?"

"I understand you're not supposed to be living in this house since you don't have a building permit."

"Sorry, Sheriff, but my understanding is that the case is under litigation, and I'm entitled to live in this house until the situation is resolved in court," I said, completely winging an answer that I didn't know would work.

"Okay, sorry to trouble you. Have a good evening," the sheriff politely replied and left.

That made Eloy livid. A few days later, Eloy brought the State building code inspector over to my house during the day. This time there was no knock on the door but an official voice yelling. "Hello in there. This is Harvey King, the state building code inspector."

I opened the door, and there was Eloy, standing next to the inspector, hoping this time he would get his way and have me permanently evicted from my home.

"Sorry to trouble you, but I received a complaint from Eloy Orgulloso that you don't have any adequate sanitation conditions or water in your home, and therefore it is unfit for living. You can't live here without having a building permit too."

That was the *last straw in the adobe brick.* I couldn't hold back my sense of outrage any longer. "If Eloy claims I have substandard living conditions, then he better explain why he doesn't provide adequate safe water and sanitation conditions for the illegal workers making his adobe bricks."

There were shock waves of silence from both of them, and then Harvey said, "Sorry to trouble you."

It was over. No more confrontations. No more bullying. No more restless nights wondering where or when Eloy's next harassing move would occur.

After two years, with the case dragging on, the judge ruled that the dwelling would remain unless destroyed by nature, but I was to halt any further construction on the building. In other words, I was not allowed to finish an adobe stucco wall to protect the building. Nevertheless, I was to live there for almost six years—though with a third of those years facing mental duress along with legal and physical threats, all just to live simply in my austere, incompletely done, self-made, adobe *casa,* where I would fetch water from the school building a hundred yards from my house, living off a Franklin stove and fireplace while using water run-off from the pueblo designed roof's canals to feed into a small non-edible ornamental garden or for taking a shower. Life was good especially since I had access to an outdoor privy with a nice crescent moon sign on the door entrance only a few yards away.

Then a year or so after all these events subsided, a *milagro* happened. In addition to his administrative and legal duties, Ed Nagel was also the driver's ed teacher for the school and was instructing one of his student drivers, Happy Fisher, to turn from Airport Road onto Agua Fria Road, but he was too heavy on the peddle on the turn and headed down into the heart of Eloy's property, where the car became stuck in the mud. The more Happy tried to escape, the more the tires spun deeper in the flooded clay terrain. Guess who rescued them from calling a towing service? Eloy Orgulloso. He seemed cordial, considerate, and not inclined to hold a grudge against the school. He was able to put a power line on the opposite side of my house about 20 feet away, and, while I taught and lived at the Santa Fe Community School, I was never hassled by him after the court ruled in my favor.

But I must admit that, despite the hard-fought legal battles, confrontations, and mental anguish, building that adobe home from the very earth it rested, living off the grid all those years, was undoubtedly the purest act of simplicity I ever had. And a *milagro* came into my life, hearing my prayers for a peaceful outcome. Even though I never completed this little adobe round house on the outside, I'm forever grateful for the experience, and I'll cherish the years I dwelled there. It's what's inside that counts.

My unfinished self-made adobe home lies along a contested fence line where I lived off the grid for six years. Given a stop work court order by a local judge made my life more austere and starkly challenging, but never regretful. *1978.*

Chapter Fifty-One
Five Minutes of a Miracle Shower

And in this moment, like a swift intake of breath, the rain came.
– Truman Capote

For three consecutive summers, I attended a Sufi-based camp in Bedford, Virginia, called Legacy International. The primary vison was to provide an inspirational place for children and youth from around the world to tap into their practical idealism by exploring a wide range of multicultural arts, cooperative living, conservation projects, recreational challenges, and meals related to a healthier planet, engaging outdoor adventures, a happier self, and attempts to bring everyone together in lively assemblies to embrace the global celebration of music by prominent artists from around the world who have indigenous and ethnic backgrounds.

Several kids came from war-torn situations, and I learned from their own mouths the horrific impacts these events had on their lives. Many friendships from adversarial sides evolved through the course of the three- to eight-week camp sessions, which opened a profound range of possibilities, showing that people do not have to be locked in their cultural-politically prejudiced traps but can become globally minded in body, mind, and spirit. It certainly worked for me as a cabin counselor, environmental educator, adobe brick builder, and vegetarian intern cook. Over time at the camp, I developed the reputation of being a *fakir,* an ascetic celebrant of wisdom and humor.

With that kind of uplifting energy interacting in this little seasonal global village, new and wonderful moments leading toward a greater love for humanity and the earth seemed possible. It was my first year I attended this summer camp that I met up with an outrageous counselor and in-house photographer teacher named Mikel Davis. The camp had been experiencing a record-breaking drought, lasting over

12 years, and so I asked Mikel if we could go inside this huge water tank in a remote area on the land and pound away with our hands to invite the rain spirits to come.

As loud and fun as it was, nothing happened. I proposed offering a half-hour, mid-afternoon workshop focusing on bringing rain back to this sweet little spot of humanity. People could bring drums, pots, pans, wood blocks, and anything percussion that could draw rain clouds over the stage. The activities coordinator thought it would be fun and entertaining, so she approved unhesitatingly. On a partly sunny day, a small crowd of curious observers, mostly staff, attended while children and youth, led by myself, partook in this multidimensional pounding rain chant. We began to play loudly, trying to keep in spontaneous organic rhythm, repeating the word "Rain" as one puffy cloud circled over our stage.

Then it happened. There was a complete cloud burst dousing us, exclusively falling on the stage. We were all deliriously soaked. Our prayers were answered for about five minutes. I never forgot that moment. Jump 12 years later in the summer of 1997, I had returned to Legacy with my first wife Rosa Lee (pseudonym) to revisit friends and walk those wonderful sacred grounds of global consciousness. As we drove across the little creek by the Buddha statue, it began to pour. Laura Ingram, one of the kitchen staff members I knew when I was an intern vegetarian cook at Legacy, was standing by the flowing creek while the rains came down. I rolled my window down to say hi, but we were in total sync in this most memorable moment. She had witnessed that rain chanting workshop moment which miraculously produced the unthinkable downpour. The first glorious word that instantly bellowed out from both of us when we recognized each other was "Rain!"

We had remembered that phenomenal moment when the fortunate souls who were there shared a synchronistic, mystical connection to draw rain during a severe drought as a direct method of appealing to a compassionate higher force. And it worked.

Chapter Fifty-Two
An Unsurpassable Grand Opening

The sight filled the northern sky, the immensity of it was scarcely conceivable. As if from Heaven itself, great curtains of delicate light hung and trembled.
– Phillip Pullman

Working as an interpretive naturalist, I would present on a monthly basis a walk when the moon was full. For many years, people would experience the wonders of the night when the lunar sphere was completely illuminating as a natural light to guide us into the evening through the forest, prairie, and wetlands. We usually met at the nature center to check in and then started from there. On this unusually bitter cold evening in early November 1989, my assistants Cheryl, Teri, and I witnessed what was perhaps the most glorious dark sky spectacle.

The damp temperature was in the upper teens, and it was extremely tough to stand in one place. We waited for the full roster of 20-plus participants to arrive, but only two people showed up. It was that bitter cold. We were about to call it a night when I noticed off in the distance to the north a shimmering, bright, white light, spreading across the backside of a distant main commercial road, perhaps Golf Road. We all believed it was a grand opening light for some car dealership.

The light began to shimmer and shake to an incredible depth, moving swiftly south toward our nature center. We knew the northern lights were coming our way. Pulsating with extended spikes of white light reaching to the stars, the predominant colors began to shift to spectacular shades of green. The intensity of the *aurora borealis* was beyond imagination. With ebbs and flows fluctuating in strength, the swirling lights began to add another color, approaching the backyard of the nature center, where a Lakota tipi rested in the back. All of us were gasping with irrepressible astonishment.

The dimensions of the sky hovering over us took on a magnificent spectrum of kinetic vibrant red, folding like grand, ruffled, eagle-feathered wings directly above the tipi. It was as if the poles pointing to the heavens were like antennas drawing energy above this lone indigenous conical structure. The vision was so inspiring to experience. We all took something with us that night that would stay imprinted in our unique journeys. My spiritual connection with that magnificent nocturnal sky illuminating over the tipi would soon return in the form of Thunder Beings at my first wedding, deepening my transcendental journey with the Lakota way.

Chapter Fifty-Three
Rainbow Peace Warriors Join Pow-Wow

As Native Americans, we believe the Rainbow is a sign from the Spirit in all things. It is a sign of the union of all people, like one big family. The unity of humanity, many tribes and peoples, is essential.
– Thomas Banyacya, respected Hopi elder

In August 2007, my second ex-wife Samantha (pseudonym) and I drove to Matthiessen State Park in LaSalle County, Illinois, to attend the Midwest SOARING Pow-Wow. The foundation's goals are to save ancestral remains and the resources of Midwest indigenous peoples, working toward repatriation, protecting sacred sites, and educating the public while promoting community building among all people regarding indigenous lifeways. MSF began with the Native American medicine wheel and its four sacred directions, represented by the colors black, white, red, and yellow. Three years later, a burial mound and the red-tailed hawk were added to the logo. These elements were included to commemorate the day when the Miami ancestral remains were given back to the Miami Nation and reburied near their longhouse. During their three-year stand at the New Lenox site, Illinois (an ancient Miami village), a red-tailed hawk appeared.

"Since that time, the hawk is always a part of what we do," said Joseph Standing Bear.

The burial mound represents the work done by SOARING to return the ancestors back to Mother Earth. Surrounded by an open, tall grass prairie with patchy clouds and an early afternoon royal blue sky, we arrived in the parking lot by the pow-wow when the ceremony was about to commence. We could hear the singers on the central drum and the heartbeat of Mother Earth, which holds a special place in the arena, while emcee caller Blackfoot Leonard was welcoming everyone to the pow-wow circle. I told Samantha we needed to hustle because the grand entry was about to begin, where veterans carry flags, followed by the elders, younger men and women and then the children. All the dancers were dressed in bright regalia, characteristic of their specific, traditional dance. We arrived at the entrance, opening to the east end of the circle, and moved to the south, then to the west, following the path of the sun. The circle permeates most indigenous traditions because of the belief that the movement of all life operates in cycles. The entrance to the east symbolizes the direction from which the Creator Father Sun sends power to all things on Mother Earth. As we turned the corner on the southwest end of the circled crowd, I felt a momentary strong breeze pass through me.

I spontaneously told Samantha, at that mystical spot in time and space as the veterans were proceeding by us, "Why doesn't the pow-wow honor those who fight for peace and have no weapons?"

I was referring to Native American peace activists like Winona La Duke, Zitkála-Šá, Madonna Thunder Hawk, Sarah Deer, Oren Lyons, Tom Goldtooth, Russell Means, and Dennis Banks. As soon as that thought faded, I heard Leonard bellow out from his mike, "Hoka hey, look up at the sky. It's a rainbow." Rainbows usually arc across the sky after passing rains. No rain transpired that sunny, mostly blue-sky day. Instead, the dancers and crowd began to look up and see a rainbow in the shape of a grand, almost complete halo, coming from the south, hovering over the entire pow-wow circle. Imagine looking at a rainbow ring above you over 1000 feet in circumference, about 1,000 feet above you, moving completely in alliance with the pow-wow circle. With the ends almost touching, the horseshoe-shaped halo completely faded directly across the sky of the grand arena.

People pulled out their smartphones and cameras and began to rapidly record this surreal, beautiful scene in the blue sky. Dancers paused and looked up in awe. I could only stand there, frozen in absolute wonder, with a smile that could only be described as spiritually blissful. To know that the organization sponsoring this event pursues the return of ancestral remains to their homeland made me feel as if the ancient homebound spirits wanted to open up their hearts in an act of gratitude for remembering them. For days, I wondered what had just transpired, and this is what I believe. I believe that the gentle wind, which passed through me, was a spiritual energy that compelled me to say, "there needs to be a place to honor those who carry no weapons but fight for peace through nonviolent, noncooperation, as many of the peaceful spiritual warriors have demonstrated in the past and present." I never felt such a strong benevolent feeling at a pow-wow before, questioning the intent of the event, until now.

Veterans who have bravely fought in wars as well as peace activists standing up for humanity and the planet. This was my vision for widening the circle of global balance and inclusive justice in my journey. Warriors must be honored from both sides of the spectrum.

Chapter Fifty-Four
Who Knows Where the Clouds Go?

It is only with the heart that one can see rightly; what is essential is invisible to the eye.
– Antoine De Saint-Exupery

In the early spring of 2007, I was invited to be the keynote speaker at Prospect High School in Mt. Prospect, Illinois. The topic would be "Choosing a Career." At first, I didn't believe I was the best person for the invite. After all, I had seven jobs with no retirement benefits, all of which were related to what I love to do or have a strong interest in what I believe to be important in my life. I was a part-time interpretive naturalist, habitat restorationist, native plant landscaper/consultant, motivational speaker on earth ethics and eco-gardening, a folk musician-percussionist, earth-friendly storyteller, and outdoor adventure-ecology summer camp coordinator/bus driver.

A few years before, I was an environmental writer for a major newspaper, where I actually convinced the *Daily Herald* the idea for creating a weekly column which I wrote for a few years titled *Green Light: Living with Nature*. In addition to other eco-friendly work, I would ride my bicycle for about 10 miles roundtrip at night twice a week to work at a health food store after working at my nature center. In short, I worked my tail off with unconventional hours at various places of employment for something I believed in.

None of my jobs had retirement benefits.

My speech was short and to the point: Do what you love to do and start early in life. Money will imminently come if you're good at what you do and have the passion to prove it. If anything, you'll be happy and thus have a rippling effect in the greater community. There's nothing worse than waking up every morning and going to work at a job you hate or find boring, only to stay there because the benefits are great. Like folk singer John Prine's verse out of *Angel From Montgomery* declares, "How the hell can a person go to work in the morning, then come home in the evening and have nothing to say." Case in point: I was once hired as an environmental education coordinator at the Chicago Academy of Sciences in Lincoln Park two years after working at the Spring Valley Nature Center. But, after two days riding my bicycle five miles from my suburban residence with my suit in a suitcase, taking a train to transfer to a bus to take me to my workplace in the big city—and then enduring an indoor world of stuffed animals and a static museum setting for educating the kids about nature every day, I pleaded to my manager at my previous place of employment to ask for my job back as a part-time interpretive naturalist. He said, kiddingly, "yes, but there would be no repeat of a farewell party when you do finally leave from Spring Valley Nature Center."

I retired from there 27 years later, with a wonderful farewell party. I loved being outdoors, but it meant taking a serious financial hit, with a benefit package much less than the position offered at the Chicago Academy of Sciences.

When I finished the keynote speech, I had swarms of teenagers and only one adult teacher thanking me for coming. The message seemed to understandably intimidate the establishment and inspire the kids.

But there are angels among us. Those with illuminated eyes, who stand at the crossroads of life and lift us up to heights unknown. We will know them by the unconditional love that radiates from their souls, by the way their truth and ours so nicely intertwine. In the presence of their being, we become alive and more fully engaged in the process of finding our paths. They never ask us to trade our beliefs for theirs, never demand that we become something we are not. For they seem to honor the truth in everyone while at the same time holding their own beliefs deeply within. They encourage us to take a leap of faith, to believe in ourselves and trust the voice that whispers, "You can do it!" I was fortunate and grateful to have a living angel before and after crossing over into this great mystery and that was my mother.

My mom usually sided with the establishment, knowing how frugal and austere my lifestyle was, consistently saying to me when I was well in my 50s, "Son, you aren't getting any younger. You better start thinking about your future." The difference between these high school job career counselors pushing the success-driven message to future student workers and my mom was that she loved me for what I was and what I was becoming: someone who cared about nature and walked the talk.

My mom worried about how my life would eventually unfold when I got older. She passed away on January 6, 2008, and was loved by many, especially yours truly. My sister Janis and I held our hands together, with tears over her lifeless body in the hospital, mourning her loss that evening. The next day, in early January, the temperature rose to a balmy 60 degrees. I made a visit to the Spring Valley Nature Center, just to walk the grounds alone and view, off in the distance, from the tall grass prairie hill called the Mother Prairie, an eerie fog of misty ghostly images enveloping the pond. I took pictures of this dreamy scene, and it appeared haunting but not scary, like a gathering of drifting figurine angels trying to get my attention.

A few days passed, and I was driving down the Elgin-O'Hare expressway, heading off the exit onto Roselle Road, listening to Judy Collins sing *Who Knows Where the Time Goes?*, when I saw in the sky angel-like figures in the clouds, moving slowly from west to east. I began to cry, with a burst of sadness for the loss of my mom. Little did I know that may have been a sign of a mystical intervention about to happen in the next few days.

Within two weeks, my siblings Joyce, Wayne, Janis and I received an inheritance. My wife and I were able to buy a Honda Fit, and we left the remainder in the bank. By late January, that money was put to wise use. Eating lunch with my working colleagues, my friend and manager Dave Brooks at the Spring Valley Nature Center came up to me and said, "Dennis, the park district is being audited, and it looks like, as a part-time employee, you're entitled to a pension. The only thing is, you have to pay back what you owe to make up the difference that you didn't pay all those years since you started."

Dave didn't tell me how much I needed to pay back, but I contacted the Finance Department handling pensions and was told I needed 13,000 dollars to have a decent regular, growing pension for the rest of my life when I retired. Because of my inheritance from my mom, I had the money to rescue me from ever worrying about being old and broke. I believe there was an angel in my life, and her name was Lucille Paige, my mother. As a devout Christian, she still knew over time that she couldn't change me, and eventually she helped me embrace the meaning of being truthful to what really matters. I was good to her, and she knew it, living close to her home, taking her out on nature walks, spending time together on a weekly basis, dining out and catching up on our lives. When we sat in some wild natural area in and around northeastern Illinois, we always felt comfortable with our healthy surroundings, just being ourselves, wearing our hearts a little further down on our sleeves, expressing our truths with honesty and love.

She eventually accepted who I was and never attempted to manipulate me with guilt or some self-proclaimed authority. I freely showed her my emotional scars, and she in turn shared hers. She knew my journey was from the heart and gut. Knowing that the security for retiring was brought to me by such an endearing angel at the right time has helped me acknowledge my place in the circle of life and breathe easier about the incredibly timely gift given from my mother to me. "You always did what you love to do. I just worry about you taking care of yourself when you get old," Mom would say.

Well, thanks to her, not anymore.

With my mother Lucille Paige in 2003 at one of our favorite eateries, Al's Café & Creamery in Elgin, Illinois. A pure grateful moment with a true living angel. Unknown photographer.

Chapter Fifty-Five
Who or What Watches over You in the Dark?

Nature shall be the visible spirit, and spirit, invisible nature.
– Friedrich Wilhelm Joseph Schelling

The pipe keeper Gentle Spider Man Quentin Young had extended an invite for me and others in the *Northern Branch of the Red Spotted Bead People* clan to attend a sacred Lakota ceremony called *Lawampi*, performed by a medicine man to invite the spirit world to help heal seven people with serious personal issues. I had never attended such a heartfelt gathering, held in the dark in the den of a home on the land where we partook in purification lodge sweats (*inipi*). Gentle Spider Man quite clearly said, "The spirits know when you're paying attention. You'll be reminded by them if you don't."

My conservation workday at my nature center that morning was arduous, and I was tired, but I decided to attend *Lawampi* to offer my prayers to those requesting healing offerings. The medicine man *Chief Red Spider Iktomi Sha* Steve McCullough performed a singing ritual, shaking a rattle around the altar to invite the spirits to come. Sparks began to pop around him like it was the 4th of July. Lights flittered through the room, little flashes of lightning coming at you from the darkness. I felt the wings of birds brushing my face and the light touch of a feather on my skin. You could sense the energy in pure darkness, bringing powerful, life-affirming forces of healing to the circle of prayerful participants as a spiritual magnet for healing. But, through the course of this mystical ceremony, I was starting to doze off. My head slumped onto my chest. Without any warning, I felt a strong hand slap hard on my shoulder twice to awaken me. I opened my eyes, and it was completely dark. How did anyone know I was falling asleep? Did someone have special night-vision goggles and see I wasn't *paying attention*? After the ceremony, I asked people who sat around me if they did it. The answer was an emphatic "no." I never forgot that compelling moment, where, afterwards, I listened to the spirit world and prayed deeply for the others who came to have their prayers heard no matter how tired I was.. I knew then, back in the summer of 2009, as I know now, that this beautiful Lakota sacred ceremony invites guiding shared intentions to connect with the spirit world.

"Aho Mitakuye Oyasin" in Lakota means we're all related, all of us, everyone. This includes all human beings upon the earth, all living things grand and tiny. We all came from the earth, we live from the earth, we return to the earth, and we are of the earth—as are all the beings who make up this incredibly complex and beautiful web of life. I continue to walk a mystical path, with an eternal love for nature, and see the interwoven sacredness of life everywhere, spiritually apprehending truths that are beyond my intellectual comprehension.

Chapter Fifty-Six
That's the Spirit

*Darkness cannot drive out darkness; only light can do that. Hate
cannot drive out hate; only love can do that.*
– Martin Luther King, Jr.

For a few late nights in mid-October, when the ancestral spirits are annually reunited with the living world in 2021, I laid in my bed, staring at my skylight window between 4:00 a.m. and 6:00 a.m. On the side of the angled walls of that sky light window box, where I could see our home galaxy, streaming ever lucidly, there appeared shimmering fleeting streaks of white light like a mini *aurora borealis*. But the northern lights were too far north to be seen in Conifer, Colorado; they were mostly sighted along the Canadian–US border. Where did the light come from? My soulmate partner, Randee, and I grappled with this captivating mystery. In the pitch darkness of our location, where the neighborhood sees the abundance of starry wonders, there is this fleeting illumination above us inside our home. We wondered why that light wasn't coming from the outside.

After a couple of nights viewing this highly unusual sighting while Randee was out of town for a few days, I decided to take a photo of what seemed to be a paranormal phenomenon, but the photo didn't capture the fleeting streaming light. I needed a night camera lens to capture this strange imagery. About 10 minutes later, a picture frame of lovely photographed flowers taken by Randee fell off the bedroom bathroom wall, turning on a light switch as it crashed on the floor, destroying the frame and shattering the glass plate into hundreds of fragments, while the picture plunged into a bowl of water for the cat. At approximately 4:30 a.m. a bizarre coincidental incident freaked out my pet cat Roo and me. I spent a good hour cleaning up the debris and mopping the floor. For a few days after this shocking coincidence, I stared up at that skylight window box, anticipating more activity to appear. But the area remained relatively dark and uneventful. Maybe this inexplicable phenomenon didn't want any photos taken or perhaps I should have asked for permission to photo first. Were there ghostly spirits in our home, or was there some other kind of nonhuman paranormal happening visiting that space and why? I decided not to document any photos of these fascinating, milky white flashes of fading light, keeping this sighting between Randee and me somewhat to ourselves.

A week passed, and our water softener installer Todd Hart came by for an annual check-up on the filters. A conversation started up about our strange visitor in the skylight window area. He said he had spirit-hunting dowsing copper rods in his truck and was willing to test out the source of the light energy in our bedroom. Dousing is a way of using the body's own reflexes and cosmic energy to help interpret the world around us. When applying dowsing, the only requirement is a conscious and intentionally receptive "you." Through dousing, one is able to feel the "aura" of a person and almost every aspect of nature. Dowsing rods can also be used to look for lost items, locate pets, discover underground water, locate buried metals and gemstones, and identify paranormal activities.

We walked upstairs in the middle of a bright, sunny, blue-sky day to the skylight bedroom window, and he began to ask questions about that mysterious energy field, firmly holding the copper rods. If the rods spread out in his hands, the answer was affirmative; if the rods crossed over, negative.

"Are you from a human source?" (affirmative)

"Are you from a non-human source?" (negative)

"Do you mean harm to Dennis and Randee?" (negative)

"Did you help knock down the picture in the bathroom?" (affirmative)

"Are you stuck here for some reason?" (affirmative)

"Can Dennis or Randee help you move on?" (negative)

"Are you the previous owner who lived here?" (affirmative)

"Were you happy living here?" (affirmative)

"Dennis and Randee see you in awe and wonder and do not mean any harm. Do you realize that?" (affirmative)

"Is it okay for Roo, our indoor pet cat, to stay on the bed at night?" (affirmative)

We bought the house in July 2016 from a man whose wife had recently died in May 2016. The next-door neighbors claimed they didn't know the woman was ill. She probably died suddenly in her home in our bedroom, reportedly from a brain aneurysm (her obituary requested in lieu of flowers donations could be given to a brain research organization), and didn't make any plans to cross over into the spirit world while alive. She seemed to be temporarily in limbo between the spiritual and physical world, grappling to figure out where to go from here. But we weren't afraid of her, and she seemed to not be afraid of us.

After settling into this unprecedented, mystical situation, Todd and I talked outside about the path I've been following for decades in embracing spiritual energies that we can see and not see. I told him several other personal, worldly instances of connecting with the cosmos. I described my beautiful experience with the rainbow halo over the pow-wow circle, and I told him that the event was sponsored by an organization to bring back the ancestral remains of the Miami indigenous people to their proper burial grounds. He stood back, totally amazed, and said, "My ancestors are from the Miami nation on my mother's side." I knew then that Todd and I had to meet under these mystical circumstances. His great, great, great, grandmother named *Nah-wah-na-cong-ga* was of Miami descent and lived in Indiana. She stayed back, declining to partake in the grueling, forced displacement trek known as the Trail of Tears, enroute to a reservation in Oklahoma. What are the odds of matching with a particular tribe when there are literally hundreds besides having spirit hunter dowser rods? I believe this wasn't a coincidence. Such benevolent feedback on this dazzling aura has certainly brought a fascinating dimension to this skylight window, which displays a glorious stream of Milky Way stars, often considered by many indigenous nations to be a spiritual passage way to the sky.

In the five years we have lived here, we never saw anything like that in our home. While paying attention to this pre-dawn enlightening vision of mystery and awe, my dream world for those few days of initial sightings were incredibly gentle, loving, and filled with happy children playing, my parents harmlessly wandering in and out, festive summer-like picnic settings, pleasant conversations with my fellow colleagues at the Spring Valley Nature Center, and a gravity-free environment where I was serenely floating around in a classroom, sharing my power of blissful flight with the children and teachers. Now that these surreal lights have faded, my dream world seems to not be so consistently euphoric.

By communicating with this spirit with respect from the use of these dowsers, I chose to honor the fleeting, innocuous light that brought mystical enchantment to our bedroom in the wee hours of the morning—and, with sanctioned approval from these divining rods, to video record any signs of this amazing visualization with an advanced approval from that spirit energy.

Weeks afterward during lucid starry pre-dawn mornings, the fleeting illuminating flashes of white streaming light eventually faded away in our skylight window box leaving nothing but a permanent beautiful restless remembrance into wanting to know more. We barely knew this paranormal being and in all probability the spirit barely knew us. Such a profound mystery in our home brings us closer to other worlds we cannot fully fathom but know are there if we just open our hearts and minds to a spiritual realm transitioning beyond our human lives. Perhaps we do not die as followed by the Lakota way but instead "walk on" continuing on a non-stop journey (wanáǧi wičhóthi) that never ends but always transitions toward a greater non-linear mystery. Gazing at the Milky Way through that skylight window I can only wonder in awe of my grateful journey ahead.

Chapter Fifty-Seven
Summary

*All things are inconstant except the faith in the soul, which changes
all things and fills their inconstancy with light.*
– James Joyce

The pandemic that struck the world in 2020 changed everything, causing stress about the unknown cost of such a virus. Add to the accelerating climate crisis, including the devastating loss of nature we and the planet are facing, and one has to ask where are we as a collective force of humanity heading? But that hasn't stopped me from loving my life while pursuing an uncompromising eco-spiritual need to commune with nature. If anything, it has made me more humble, deepening my quest to embrace my retiring years of joyful living, being in the present and adapting to a practical environmental ethic in the beautiful Rocky Mountain state of Colorado. I couldn't be happier at this grateful moment in my time on earth. While harvesting the fond and not so fond memories of my life experience and what I have received materially, I age with a curious smile, looking back at all those unforeseen twists and turns that molded me to where I am today.

John Lennon's famous words that "life is what happens to you while you're busy making other plans" certainly rings true for me. But there's one constant in my life that has always brought me wisdom, balance, and spiritual gratification: connecting deeply with nature and all the mystical awakenings that follow. They have been my ultimate regenerative force of inspiration and vital sustenance. The great human global community does not have much time to come to terms with our ominous future, but we must pursue a global mindful course that actively includes balance and harmony with the third rock from the sun in whatever we decide for future generations. *Enriching our lives without impoverishing the earth* should be the global mantra for all humankind. There is no one way toward a higher self, no one correct spiritual path, no one way to write a memoir. There is no one roadway, no one way bridge, no one kind of flowering plant, no one kind of bee, no one way to knowledge and wisdom. Diversity inextricably permeates the planet, the galaxy and beyond. May each of you courageously follow your dreams with this in mind and have a wonderful rippling effect with your growing circles of influence.

Recommended Readings

Adams, Frank. 1983. *Wurlitzer Juke Boxes, 1934–1974*. Arlington, WA: AMR.

Andrews, Ted. 2015. *Animal Speak: The Spiritual & Magical Powers of Creatures Great and Small*. Woodbury, MN: Llewellyn.

Baker, J. A. 2004. *The Peregrine*. New York: New York Review Books.

Blum, Edward J. 2014. *The Color of Christ: The Son of God and the Saga of Race in America*. Chapel Hill: University of North Carolina Press.

Brown, Joseph and Epes Brown. 1983. *The Sacred Pipe: Black Elk's Account of the Seven Rites of the Oglala Sioux*. Norman, OK: University of Oklahoma Press.

Bull, Richard. 1970. *Summerhill, U.S.A.* London: Penguin Books.

Campbell, Joseph. 1988. *The Power of Myth*. New York: Doubleday.

Caduto, Michael J. and Joseph Bruchac. 1989. *Keepers of the Earth: Native American Stories and Environmental Activities for Children*. Golden, CO: Fulcrum.

Cohen, Michael J. 1988. *How Nature Works: Regenerating Kinship with Planet Earth*. Portland, OR: Stillpoint.

Cousins, Norman. 2005. *Anatomy of an Illness*. New York: Norton, W.W. & Company.

Fire, John, Richard Erdoes, and Lame Deer. 1972. *Lame Deer: Seeker of Visions*. New York: Simon and Schuster.

Gardner, Mark Lee Gardner. 2022. *The Earth is All That Lasts*. Boston: Mariner Books.

Gaudreau, Tick. 2006. *Spirit Rescue: A Dowser's Ghostly Encounters*. Bloomington, IN, iUniverse.

Hart, Mickey and Stevens, Jay. 1990. *Drumming at the Edge of Magic*. San Francisco, Harper San Francisco.

Haas, Jeffrey. 2009. *The Assassination of Fred Hampton: How the F.B.I. and the Chicago Police Murdered a Black Panther.* Chicago: Chicago Review Press.

Hanna, Warren L. *The Grizzlies of Glacier.* Missoula, Montana: Mountain Press Publishing Company.

Hatch, Stephen K. 2012. *The Contemplative John Muir.* Raleigh, NC: Lulu.com.

Hynek, J. Allen. 1977. *The Hynek UFO Report* (1st ed.). New York: Dell.

Jung, Carl Gustav. 1969. *Man and His Symbols.* Doubleday.

Jung, Carl Gustav. 1978. *Flying Saucers.* Princeton University Press.

Klein, Tom. 1989. *Loon Magic.* Minocqua, WI: North Word Press.

Lake-Thom, (Grizzly Bear) Bobby. 2000. *Call of the Great Spirit: The Shamanic Life and Teachings of Medicine Grizzly Bear.* Rochester, VT: Bear and Company.

Lukianoff, Greg and Haidt, Jonathon Haidt. 2018. *The Coddling of the American Mind.* NY: Penguin Press.

Liebenow, Gus. 1969. *Liberia: The Evolution of Privilege.* Ithaca, NY: Cornell University Press.

Loeffler, Jack. 2002. *Adventures with Ed: A Portrait of Abbey.* Albuquerque: University of New Mexico Press.

Lopez, Barry Holstun. 1978. *Of Wolves and Men.* New York: Charles Scribner's Sons.

MacDonald, Mike. 2015. *My Journey into the Wilds of Chicago.* Downers Grove, IL: Morning Dew Press.

Macy, Joanna. 1991. *World as Lover, World as Self.* Berkeley, CA: Parallax Press.

Mails, Thomas. 1996. *The Hopi Survival Kit: The Prophecies, Instructions and Warnings Revealed by the Last Elders.* New York: Penguin.

Mails, Thomas E. 2001. *Fools Crow: Wisdom and Power.* San Francisco: Council Oaks Books.

Marshall, Joseph M. III. 2001. *The Lakota Way: Stories and lessons for living.* New York: Penguin.

Mays, Willie and John Shea. 2020. *Life Stories and Lessons from the Say Hey Kid.* New York: St. Martin's Press.

McCrohan, Donna. 1987. *The Second City: A Backstage History of Comedy's Hottest Troupe.* New York: Perigee Books.

Meacham, Jon. 2015. *Destiny and Power: The American Odyssey of George Herbert Walker Bush*. New York: Random House.

Micklos Jr., John. 2017. *Muhammad Ali: Fighting as a Conscientious Objector*. New York: Enslow.

Montagu, Ashley. 1981. *Growing Young*. NY, NY. McGraw-Hill.

Nabhan, Gary Paul. 1982. *The Desert Smells Like Rain: A Naturalist in O'odham Country*. Tucson: University of Arizona Press.

Nagel, Ed. 1978. *CHEEZ! Uncle Sam*. Santa Fe, NM: SFCS Publications.

Neihardt, John G. 1972. *Black Elk Speaks*. New York: Simon and Schuster.

Neill, Alexander Southerland. 1960. *Summerhill: A Radical Approach to Child Rearing*. New York: Hart.

Neill, Alexander Southerland. 1970. *Summerhill: For and Against*. New York: Hart.

Nichols, John. 1974. *The Milagro Beanfield War*. New York: Random House.

Olson, Sigurd F. 1956. *The Singing Wilderness*. New York: Alfred A. Knopf.

Orloff, Judy, M.D. 2017. *The Empath's Survival Guide*. Louisville, Colorado: Sounds True, Incorporated.

Paige, Dennis Swiftdeer. 2021. *Community Eco-Gardens: Landscaping with Native Plants*. Jefferson, NC: Toplight Books.

Patinkin, Sheldon. 2000. *The Second City: Backstage at the World's Greatest Comedy Theater*. Naperville, IL: Sourcebooks.

Plotkin, Bill. 2003. *Soulcraft: Crossing into the Mysteries of Nature and Psyche*. Novato, CA: New World Library.

Radner, Gilda. 1989. *It's Always Something*. New York: Simon and Shuster.

Yeager, Chuck. 1986. *Yeager: An Autobiography*. London: Arrow Books.

Young, Quentin H. 2017. *Mystic Visons: Black Elk's Great Vision Clarified*. Marble, NC: Word Branch.

The End

About the Author

Dennis Swiftdeer Paige is an environmental educator, conservation practitioner, naturalist, author on Midwestern ecological gardening (winner of several prestigious awards in native landscaping and habitat preservation), professional earth caring indigenous storyteller/eclectic percussionist. Living for many decades in the Chicagoland area, he now lives in the coniferous montane community of Conifer, Colorado.

www.ingramcontent.com/pod-product-compliance
Lightning Source LLC
Chambersburg PA
CBHW050325160726

48002CB00001B/182